01 14

THE
LAND
TRAP

THE
LAND
TRAP

A New History of the
World's Oldest Asset

Mike Bird

PORTFOLIO | PENGUIN

Portfolio / Penguin
An imprint of Penguin Random House LLC
1745 Broadway, New York, NY 10019
penguinrandomhouse.com

PORTFOLIO and PORTFOLIO with javelin thrower design are registered trademarks of Penguin Random House LLC.

Most Portfolio books are available at a discount when purchased in quantity for sales promotions or corporate use. Special editions, which include personalized covers, excerpts, and corporate imprints, can be created when purchased in large quantities. For more information, please call (212) 572-2232 or e-mail specialmarkets@penguinrandomhouse.com. Your local bookstore can also assist with discounted bulk purchases using the Penguin Random House corporate Business-to-Business program. For assistance in locating a participating retailer, e-mail B2B@penguinrandomhouse.com.

Book design by Alissa Rose Theodor

LIBRARY OF CONGRESS CONTROL NUMBER: 2025012641

ISBN 9780593719718 (hardcover)
ISBN 9780593719725 (ebook)
ISBN 9798217178926 (international edition)

Printed in the United States of America
1st Printing

The authorized representative in the EU for product safety and compliance is Penguin Random House Ireland, Morrison Chambers, 32 Nassau Street, Dublin D02 YH68, Ireland, https://eu-contact.penguin.ie.

For my parents, to whom I owe everything

Contents

THE
LAND
TRAP

ONE

The Lie of the Land

A bout 3,200 years ago, more than a millennium before Caesar's crossing of the Rubicon and the beginnings of the Roman Empire, more than six centuries before the birth of either Plato or Confucius, a lucky servant named Munnabittu received a gift of land from Meli-Šipak II, one of the Kassite kings who reigned in ancient Babylon.

We know quite a few things about Munnabittu and his patch of earth. We know that he owned several hundred acres, a little more than a square mile. The parcel would have made him moderately rich, but not immensely so. We know that the land was on the banks of a canal in a place called Hudadu, possibly an ancient name for Baghdad. We know the name of some of Munnabittu's neighbors too, because he faced a legal challenge over the ownership of his plot, and we know that the decision eventually fell in Munnabittu's favor. We know the names of the officials who adjudicated the disagreement, and we know the names of the bureaucrats who trekked from the royal palace of Marduk-apla-iddina I, the son of Meli-Šipak II, to confirm the size of the estate.

We know more with some degree of certainty about Munnabittu—a

Babylonian servant who lived in the dying days of the Bronze Age, who was otherwise a historical nobody—than we do about many of the kings, warriors, scholars and prophets who were born during the centuries and millennia that followed. We know about Munnabittu specifically and solely because of the land he possessed, the ownership and saga of which is carved into a piece of smooth black limestone around half a meter long. The stone was recovered from Susa, in Iran, by archaeologists in the early twentieth century. Known as a *kudurru*, the stone was the centrally held record of the servant's landownership. Munnabittu likely would have had a replica of his own to prove possession to any subsequent doubters.

The fact that Munnabittu's story was recorded in such a permanent manner, and survived for thousands of years even as so much other knowledge was lost, is not some fluke of history. Munnabittu's wealth was carved indelibly into solid stone for a good reason. For many early civilizations, land was power. Governments collected taxes in the form of grain, for which records of ownership were of the utmost importance. Without knowing who owned each segment of earth, it was impossible to know who owed what to the tax collectors. For the very earliest agricultural economies, the way in which land was owned, organized and used was one of the foremost priorities of state-building, which made the difference between economic survival and total collapse.

Across a range of ancient languages, among different civilizations spread thousands of miles around the world, some of the very earliest surviving records are those that delineate landownership. In India, flat copper plates recorded grants of land from local rulers, often to religious establishments, from as early as the third and fourth centuries BC. In Egypt, tombs that were built and sealed more than four thousand years ago are inscribed with the details of the lives of the men buried within—

including descriptions of the land they owned. Before the existence of investment funds, pensions, stocks, bonds or international currency markets, even before human history was recorded in any meaningful way, land was the original asset. The ability to own and control territory was the first means of turning power into wealth.

Munnabittu would presumably find a lot of things about the modern world very confusing, but there are elements that might seem familiar to him. After centuries of gargantuan social and economic change, land is still at the center of our world. Owning it still confers social status and financial security. It is still the asset that governs the course of our lives, our successes and failures, more than any other form of wealth. Today, land remains the world's largest single asset by some margin and a prized possession to its owners. One estimate, by the McKinsey Global Institute, pins the total value of land at about 35 percent of the $520 trillion in real wealth on earth, a category that includes all of the physical and intangible assets in the world, from buildings to intellectual property.[1] The total sum of the machinery, infrastructure and equipment across the planet makes up another 17 percent, while commercial property and residential housing—the actual structures on top of the land—are worth another 11 percent and 21 percent apiece.

That makes the market in land about twice as valuable as all of the listed companies on every stock exchange in the world. While those publicly traded securities are monitored, second by second, by a global army of investors and a breathless financial media, land is relegated to a second-order asset, hidden within the categories of housing and real estate. When we talk about commercial and residential property, the terms we use tend to give the impression that it is the buildings rather than the earth below them that hold most of the real value. But in the bustling cities where housing and property are most expensive, that is overwhelmingly because of the high price of land. Most of the variations in the price of properties, street by street, town by town and indeed country by country, are variations in the cost of land, not the structures on top. In places where real estate is most expensive, land makes up a far larger share of the total value of properties.

In an increasingly intangible and digital world, the centrality of land poses a puzzle. Since the turn of the twenty-first century, the share of land in private assets in the countries across the rich world (those for which data is available) has risen from 18 to 26 percent on average.[2] Relative to all the other forms of wealth taken together—both financial assets like stocks and bonds, and real wealth like buildings, machinery and intellectual property—the importance of land has only increased, even as the world seems to have become more incorporeal. In the booming economies of East Asia, the source of so much of the world's economic growth over the last three decades, the value of land has exploded. In China alone, a tremendous real estate boom has created tens of trillions of dollars of land wealth. No asset is more powerful in global finance than land, which serves as a form of vital security to lenders in rich and poor countries alike, enabling tremendous volumes of borrowing for households, small companies and entire governments.

The immense power of land is also what can make it enormously dangerous. Many of the biggest economic and social challenges that we believe are disparate and unrelated problems—financial booms and busts, sluggish economic growth, the persistence of inequality and the bitter zero-sum politics of today and throughout history—are rooted in land and the unique ways it functions as an asset. The explanation of why the world is still so hooked on our most ancient form of wealth, how we reached this state of affairs and the dangers it poses to us all are the focus of this book. The nature of land, who owns it and its vital position in the financial system matter enormously for every one of us, even when we don't know it. It is not just the most important asset to the billions of ordinary people for whom it is their greatest store of wealth, but one that can make and break families, businesses and even entire nations.

For the vast majority of recorded human history, through the Babylonian Empire and for millennia afterwards, well into the twentieth century for most of the world, life was simple, local and rural. People were overwhelmingly poor. What wealth they had, if any, stemmed mostly from their land: what could be grown from it, raised on it and mined from it.

For those who owned a great deal of land, their holdings often conferred power over and responsibility for the people who lived on it too. The very highest positions of status in preindustrial Europe and Asia often went hand in hand with huge quantities of arable land. The inhabitants of the land owed a chunk of their labor, crops, income or all three to the class of elites who possessed the vast agricultural estates on which peasants lived and died. When the men who tilled the soil were called on to fight and die in wars in Europe, it was the landed gentry—earls and barons, seigneurs and Lehnsherren—who pressed the unfortunate conscripts into service. These landed aristocrats played a vital role in governing their countries, acting as the sometimes-brutal intermediaries between the rural population and the feeble central government, a hierarchy that emerged all over the premodern world.

This book aims to answer the question of why land is so important today, and why it will continue to shape—and threaten—our future. But understanding how the world's most important asset was once used is more than just a matter of distant social history. It is a vital part of understanding the grip that land holds over society today, and why people are so attached to the idea of owning it. Beyond every other common source of wealth, land is symbolic and stirs powerful emotions. Throughout history, the ownership of land has conferred liberation from serfdom and feudalism, a totem of freedom from the yoke of the landlord. In much of the world, it still symbolizes something similar. Becoming an owner of land and the real estate on top of it secures membership in the stable and independent middle classes. It is a symbol of adulthood and financial security. People believe not just that land belongs to them, but that they belong to it too. It is deeply wrapped up with conceptions of belonging and identity—the very core of how people define who they are.

But the last three hundred and fifty years of human history, which will be the focus of this book, have been profoundly different from the centuries, even millennia, that preceded them. That chunk of time has been a transformative but brief sliver of our history, like a sudden handbrake turn after thousands of miles of familiar, steady driving. As the era of industrialization began, the world shifted from one in which the production and distribution of food was the dominant form of commercial activity to one in which agriculture accounts for not even a twentieth of global economic output. In the richest nations of the world today, farming usually accounts for less than a percentage point of a country's GDP, and fewer than one in fifty jobs. Taxes are paid not in grain or military service, but in money.

During the eighteenth and nineteenth centuries, the last of Europe's tens of millions of serfs, who had previously been tied directly to the land on which they lived, were emancipated from attachments to their land-lords. The previously rural populations of Europe and North America flooded into new and burgeoning cities. Places that barely registered on the map were quickly populated by hundreds of thousands of residents. New and vastly more productive forms of manufacturing, transport, trade and communication emerged. The ancient role of land began to ebb away. The enormous estates where tenants farmed the land, which had previously been the most valuable assets of all, declined in both value and esteem. The world we know today was being born.

Almost everything about the way we live has been transformed since Munnabittu's era, and even since the first Europeans began to arrive in North America. But land is still crucially important to the global economy and the everyday lives of people all over the world. Its significance stems from three crucial features, which explain why its value has only risen, even as its original role as a source of food and raw commodities has become so much less important. These features help to explain why it remains the most important asset in the financial system and the store of such enormous wealth today. They are also what makes it the source of a great deal of global inequality. Land defies some of the usual laws of capitalism that apply to other assets and goods. Its special features are also what make land so profoundly dangerous, and such a crucial component in catastrophic financial crises.

The first of these special features is that it is incredibly difficult—usually impossible—to create more land. In the terminology of economists, its supply is fixed. A few modest slivers of earth have been created in a process known as "reclamation." It has been possible on the coasts of the Netherlands and the city-state of Singapore and in Tokyo Bay. Where that is possible, it is an enormously worthwhile pursuit, which can create hundreds of billions of dollars in valuable earth. But in the aggregate, there is barely any more land in the world today than there was before the Industrial Revolution began. That makes land unlike any of the other goods or assets we produce for one another, which have exploded in scale in response to ever-growing demand. When people want more of something, it rises in price, and new producers rush to make similar items. In stark contrast, acquiring more land, especially in popular areas, means buying or taking it from someone else. Most forms of wealth are what economists call "positive-sum," meaning that one person gaining more of it does not mean another person is losing out. But land is very often a zero-sum asset.

During the period of rapid economic growth since the beginning of the Industrial Revolution, the supply and nature of all the other things we value has changed continuously. Inventive new ways of doing things have rapidly eclipsed old methods. Among the five largest American companies today, collectively worth more than $15 trillion at the end of 2024, just one (Microsoft) has been around for as long as fifty years. Several of the mighty corporate giants of the recent past—former technological leaders like Kodak, Polaroid, Nokia and Motorola among them—once seemed immovable but have plunged into irrelevance. Businesses are continually pressed to create new goods and services by relentless competition, and those that stand still are quickly crushed. If much of the machinery, technology and intellectual property that was enormously valuable as recently as twenty years ago was transported to the modern era, it would be almost completely worthless, designed for markets that no longer exist and with methods that now seem archaic. Land is fundamentally different. In the old real estate investor's platitude, they're not making any more of it.

The second crucial factor that makes land so different from every other asset is its immobility: it can't be picked up and moved somewhere it might be more useful. When the land in a buzzing urban area becomes enormously valuable, more land cannot be brought in from a place where it is still dirt cheap. The other parts of an economy are far more fluid and movable. People migrate between neighborhoods, to new cities and across borders in search of fresh opportunities. Equipment and machinery can be transported by road, rail, sea and air. Ideas flow so very freely that governments institute laws to prevent the theft of new concepts and inventions. Even the buildings on top of land can be moved in extreme circumstances, and the parts from which they were built can be recycled and reused. Not so with land.

The fact that new land is both rarely created and cannot be moved around explains why a patch of otherwise unremarkable earth in the center of New York City is worth tens of thousands of times more than one of identical size in North Dakota. The two are not interchangeable. As economies around the world have become more industrial and more urban in the last three centuries, the value of land has been increasingly determined not by what can be grown from it or dug out of it, but by what sort of activity is going on all around it. That is the reason previously cheap land surges in value when new transport connections open nearby. Land in a bustling city has many uses. It can host housing, commercial property, transport infrastructure or vital green space. But when it is in use, it cannot be used for something else. As industry boomed in the nineteenth century, land in the center of cities became far more important. Areas surrounding new canals, docks and railways, the arteries of burgeoning trade, were increasingly sought-after. Space was needed for any manner of factories, mills, transportation and housing for the new urbanites.

The third special characteristic of land is perhaps the least well understood, but one of the most important in explaining its role in the modern economy. Unlike almost everything else we value, land does not really decay. In accounting terms, it does not depreciate. If a plot is located in an area with a large population and bustling economic activity, there is no reason to expect it to lose any value over decades or even centuries. As a result, some of the oldest fortunes in the world are held by ancient families who have done little more than hang on to land in the city centers that have stood the test of time. Britain's Dukes of Westminster and the Earls Cadogan survived the financial collapse of the British aristocracy through their huge landholdings in London, which have made the current holders of those titles the third and fourteenth richest people in the country today.[3] Those storied families are only the tip of the iceberg when it comes to dynastic wealth in land: there are many thousands of miniature monopolies in the most productive, dynamic and land-constrained cities.

No other asset of any significant value is so long-lived. The buildings on top of the land, however well constructed, will eventually collapse, or at least require extensive and costly renovation. A new car plunges in value the moment it is driven off the salesman's lot. Machines made with the best new technologies will eventually (and sometimes quickly) become obsolete. Human beings age and die. As technological progress marches on, entire categories of things that were once crucial assets for businesses everywhere, like horses, wagons and canal boats, are now irrelevant across much of the world, retained for entertainment but worthless for their original purpose. Even the most valuable ideas and innovations collapse in value as they are overtaken by improvements and alternatives.

Unlike the value of a company, the price of land is not based on the innovation, leadership skills or hard work of its owners. Its value is based overwhelmingly on the actions of people living and working near it. Indeed, the very people who make land increasingly valuable are often those most disadvantaged by increases in its value. The thousands of workers that flow into bustling cities each morning on buses, cars and trains are what give the properties in those places their eye-watering rents and exorbitant prices. The same people pay steep rents to live nearby, often scrimping and saving for decades to acquire some modest share of land wealth for themselves. The windfall from rising land values is reaped by those who had the good fortune to buy it in a particular place, at a particular time, before prices began to rise. It is, for the most part, a game of luck.

These three crucial factors—the fixed amount of land available, its immobility, and the fact that it does not naturally decay—are what mark it out from every other asset in the world. They explain most of why land assets are still such a store of enormous wealth today, even as its earliest functions—as the basis of agriculture and the organizing node of state power—are so much less relevant in modern economies and political systems. And they are also why land can be so profoundly dangerous to our collective prosperity today.

As the importance of agriculture began to decline, the social structures and ways of thinking that had governed Europe were on the way out too. The Age of Reason and the Enlightenment ushered in the new ideas that would reshape the Western world. Political ideologies like liberalism, socialism and nationalism as we know them today were beginning to come into focus. In English coffeehouses, at universities dotted from Edinburgh to Naples and among intellectual networks stretched across the Atlantic

Ocean and into the Americas, the Western world was abuzz with new discussions and fiery debates about philosophy and science.

The ideas about money, finance and wealth that emerged from these new intellectual circles would come to transform the world as much as any of the new political ideologies coming to life at the same time. The discipline of political economy, which would eventually become the formal study of economics, was emerging. Thinkers were preoccupied with how markets and commerce functioned, as new routes of trade emerged all around them. Some, like the alchemists who had obsessively aimed to turn lead into gold, were mostly concerned with how they could make their own fortune.

At the turn of the seventeenth century, money was still overwhelmingly backed by gold and silver, assets which were both valuable and portable. But the limited supply of precious metals—the factor that made them valuable in the first place—was also becoming a barrier to trade. In places where carrying a lot of valuable currency was difficult or dangerous, especially in the budding settlements in the New World, alternative methods of exchange were emerging. Money was sometimes backed by paper IOUs, which could be converted into precious metals by their issuers. The delicate system of trust was the beginning of what would eventually become far more widely accepted banknotes. Some financial innovators began to think more boldly. If gold could be the backstop of paper money, why couldn't any other form of wealth? Perhaps land, a far more valuable asset than gold, could be deployed as the security against huge volumes of credit, boosting the supply of paper money. Ideas about the relationship between land and money bubbled through networks of discussion and debate across Europe. Could land, the most adventurous thinkers wondered, even become the backing of an entire currency?

Borrowing money against the value of land was hardly a new invention. The word "mortgage" entered the English language with the Norman conquerors who arrived in the eleventh century. The *gage* was a pledge— a promise to the borrower to repay. Further back, the Roman Empire had markets in land, and mortgage lending to go alongside them. But lending money against land was controversial and difficult in large parts of the preindustrial world. Restrictions on usury in Christian and Muslim countries were often huge barriers to lenders and borrowers alike. The legal and record-keeping institutions that explained who owned what, and who owed what, were often lacking. Deploying land as the backing for loans violated some of the principles of an agricultural aristocracy too. Landholdings conveyed enormous power over the tenants of the land and across the country at large. Those responsibilities and rights could not simply be exchanged at the whims of the current owner. Using land as collateral required that the lender be able to claim the asset if he wasn't repaid. In some nations, a powerful landlord's sons, grandsons and descendants not yet born had a moral right to their inheritance, and cash-strapped members of the gentry could not simply risk the family's all-important assets on some unscrupulous moneylender.

But the old rules of aristocratic society were falling to the wayside, along with a range of prohibitions and limitations on financial activity. The necessary record-keeping and rules that would allow for a far more extensive financial system were emerging, and the role of land in finance was being unleashed. For the first time in history, the asset was beginning to rise to its current position as a banker's best friend. The unique attributes of land—that it is impossible to hide and doesn't decay—make it the perfect collateral to guarantee a loan. A crafty borrower cannot run away with it, and it is unlikely (or so it seemed) to suddenly collapse in value before the loan is repaid. For borrowers, using land to borrow money was ideal too. They did not have to pawn their assets to a creditor, as they would with any precious metals or other trinkets. They could keep using the land which they had borrowed against—for farming, housing or the operation of a business—while also accessing a loan of greater size and at lower interest rates than would otherwise ever be available to them.

The insight that land could be transformed into liquid financial power, and at enormous scale, is still one which is molding the world today. The asset is still ultimately the biggest single source of security against credit globally. Loans extended against the value of real estate, in the form of residential and commercial mortgages, are the most common forms of borrowing. The very smallest enterprises usually borrow by offering their modest holdings of land (often in the form of an entrepreneur's home) as collateral against the loan. In the poorest and worst-governed economies, companies and individuals with the ability to prove that they own a particular plot have precious financial heft that those without it lack.

Today, around the world, bank lending is overwhelmingly made up of mortgage loans. In America and Britain, 61 percent and 68 percent of bank loans are mortgages, up from 32 percent and 9 percent respectively at the beginning of the twentieth century.[4] But even those numbers downplay the huge role of land. It is not just loans to buy property that matter, but the huge share of business lending globally that is backed with land. Some countries have discovered the ability to use land sales and leases as a replacement for taxation, giving the government enormous fiscal firepower, a feature that gives rise to its own dire problems. The world's oldest form of wealth is the beating heart of the modern system of credit in the global economy, and it is just as important—perhaps even more important—to this vital role than it ever has been.

In the early days of industrialization in Europe and America, the role of land in finance was beginning to grow, but so too were the tremendous financial risks surrounding it. The asset's deployment as a safeguard for lenders has made it an unfortunate, crucial player in most of the wounding financial crises over the last three centuries. Because banks are so intimately exposed to land markets, almost every crash, slump and downturn of any importance relates to some land-related turmoil. As asset prices go up, banks can comfortably extend more and more credit to borrowers, based on the new and higher value of their landholdings. When prices fall, creditors are suddenly deprived of their valuable security against default and become far more reluctant to lend. The decline in investment that follows can turn an economic boom into a bust. Investors, financiers and central bankers have gone through endless cycles of arrogance, implosion and regret, realizing only after the fact that they were riding a wave of surging land prices, rather than profiting from some new form of financial genius.

The fact that land does not decay makes its price enormously sensitive to expectations of the distant future. When outlooks for the future are optimistic, when growth is buoyant or when the population of an area is expected to keep rising, land can be a popular object for speculation. Much of the time, the speculation about the future proves to be correct. But it can also tip into outright financial mania. In places where land has risen rapidly in price, an ever-growing group of investors pile in for further rapid gains. First movers in any frenzy will mop up the lion's share of any gains, and latecomers—often with less financial expertise than those early birds—will be left holding the bag in the event of a downturn.

The cycle of booms, financial busts and lingering recessions is an American tradition, running from the speculation on rural land in colonial

Virginia, through a series of land booms in the nineteenth century—often based around the development of railroads—and leading all the way to the mortgage-backed cataclysm of 2008. But it is certainly not a phenomenon unique to the United States. Slumps in land markets plunged Ireland and Southern Europe into brutal financial crises after 2008 too. The financial convulsion of Japan's economy in the early 1990s, the beginning of the lost decades from which the country has never truly recovered, are intimately tied to the country's postwar land boom. Today, China is beginning to confront the immense financial consequences of perhaps the biggest land bubble in human history.

The unique attributes of land as an asset—its scarcity, immovability and essentially indefinite shelf life—are also what make it a tremendous source of conflict. Disputes over land, who should own it and how it should be used have been the fuel of wars between nations, the inspiration of guerilla movements for national liberation and the obsessive object of political radicals. The word "land" appears in the title of more than a dozen national anthems and the lyrics of dozens more. It is not just blood that nationalists agitate over, but soil too. Land is an object of envy on the part of people who own none of it and a keen focus of anxiety for its fortunate owners, who are desperate to protect their greatest source of wealth.

But even where it is not the cause of armed violence, as it has been over and over again throughout the course of history, land is the hidden core of political disputes the world over. For several decades, during the twilight of the nineteenth century and the years leading up to the First World War, it looked as if the issue of land, and the way in which enormous landlords benefited from the booming industrial economy, would be the defining political battle of the twentieth century. The most well-read political thinker of the nineteenth century was not Karl Marx, Friedrich Nietzsche or Georg Hegel, whose legacies have stretched on long since their deaths, but Henry George, a San Francisco journalist who mounted a tireless political crusade over the injustices of land. In New York and London, across Europe, and as far away as Australia, New Zealand, Cuba, Spain and China, radical political movements homed in on landownership as the single crucial issue that explained the increasingly visible injustices associated with the newly urban world, and why so much grinding poverty seemed to run alongside enormous new wealth.

To an observer at the end of the nineteenth century, it might have looked as if land would be one of the defining battle lines of twentieth-century politics. Reality proved to be very different. Land became all but irrelevant, driven to the margins of debate by huge shifts in politics around the world and the emergence of a large and prosperous middle class. In Britain, America and much of the rest of the rich world, widespread homeownership transformed a landed elite into a landed majority. The political left, which had once joined the uproar over the iniquity of landownership, began to lose interest in the asset. To the socialists and communists who were growing in influence, land was simply one form of capital among many others that had to be undermined, or even seized and appropriated. But even as land disappeared from the discussion in politics, its role was ever more vital in business, quietly becoming the linchpin of the global financial system.

The political conflict caused by land was hidden away, but it was never eliminated. It is likely to pop up again and again. If there are huge winners from land wealth, there will be losers too. When prices rise, as they have been doing (often rapidly) in large and important parts of the world over much of the past half century, the unmeritocratic nature of landownership becomes increasingly obvious. The winners who were lucky enough to buy land at the right time, and in the right spot, have been able to reap huge rewards. Dramatic shifts in the economic geography of the developed world over the last four decades and the growing dominance of highly productive and desirable cities have only magnified the importance of land as an asset. Buyers who didn't get into the hottest markets at the earliest opportunity, or who had the misfortune to buy in a declining region, have lost not only the opportunities that come with a thriving area but also their greatest source of personal wealth and a crucial guarantee of their children's prosperity.

The reality of how land works leaves governments all around the world torn between irreconcilable goals. They are anxious to promote homeownership—which remains the aspiration of billions of families, just as it has been since the demise of feudalism. At the same time, political leaders are desperate not to lose the support of the existing crop of owners, who are keen for the value of their real estate to rise. Unlike a century ago, homeowners now make up a majority of most developed countries and an even larger share of the voting population. It is impossible to achieve both mass homeownership and constant rapid increases in the value of land. The defense of land wealth is what props up huge and pernicious advantages in the tax and financial systems, which have helped to make land a highly profitable asset to own throughout modern history. Combined with its zero-sum nature, those advantages also magnify the inequality in wealth driven by landownership.

The unique attributes of the world's oldest asset, and the credit, crises and conflict that it generates are a thread that runs through the last three centuries of history and into the modern day. Because of land's crucial position, the prospect of either a sustained rise or a sharp fall in land prices each pose immense threats, whether from the erosion of economic dynamism or a poisonous climb in unmerited wealth inequality. Surges in land prices are the cause of credit booms and busts among both home-buyers and businesses. They are a magnifier of the growing inequality between lucky landowners and nonowners, between places that are successful and those that are on the decline, and the bitter political battles that come with it. The distribution of land determines which businesses can borrow, shifting investment towards the already land-rich. When prices fall, our perilously landlocked financial systems are put at serious financial risk, leading to collapses that have sometimes proved unrecoverable. Making sense of land doesn't just fill a missing part of the puzzle of how the world works. It reveals the immense trap that countries around the world find themselves snared in today.

TWO

The Making of Nations

The dangerous journey from England to its new and tiny colonies on the east coast of North America took as long as three months in the second decade of the seventeenth century. Handfuls of men and women made the arduous crossing, disembarked from the merchant ships that had transported them across the Atlantic and arrived on a new continent that they knew almost nothing about. Most of the earliest coastal settlements would founder as a result of the settlers' limited understanding of the local environment and its existing inhabitants. The colonists had no real conception of how far the land ahead of them might spread. Spanish explorers had discovered the west coast of the continent via the Pacific a century earlier. In 1579, English explorer and privateer Sir Francis Drake had—a little unconvincingly—claimed the coast of California for the English crown during his own circumnavigation of the world. But the understanding of what would be found between the two oceans, in either scale or content, was close to zero. The Rocky Mountains, which mark the division of North America, would not be seen by a European explorer for more than a century after the earliest colonies began popping up.

"Of this 2000 miles, more than halfe is yet unknowne to any purpose," wrote Captain John Smith in 1616, describing the east coast of what is now the United States. Smith understood the uncertainty and danger of England's new American territories as well as anyone. He had been one of the pioneers of the original Jamestown Colony, which was temporarily abandoned in 1610 after a wave of deaths from disease and hunger among the settlers. His descriptions of the lands he had explored were published and consumed voraciously by readers at home who were eager to know the details of a new continent in the process of being discovered. Smith did not mislead his readers as to how little was yet known of the new continent. "Not so much as the borders of the Sea are yet certainly discovered," Smith wrote. "As for the goodness and true substances of the Land, wee are for most part yet altogether ignorant of them."[1]

But one thing about the country was very clear to Smith, and to all of the English colonists from the very earliest years of permanent settlement: the societies being established on North America's eastern coast would be defined by an enormous wealth in land. The seemingly endless continent stretching out for thousands of miles ahead of the new arrivals would become a symbol of freedom, an object of cultural fascination and obsession, as well as the source of the country's early prosperity. It would be an enormous object of financial speculation too.

What Smith could not know was that over the subsequent two hundred years, the colonists and their governments would pioneer new ways of using land in finance. Monetary innovators would write and experiment, both in Europe and increasingly in the Americas, learning how useful land could be as an asset in the nascent world of modern banking. The new Americans even established how land could be used to create money itself and provide the lubrication for a new and flourishing economy.

Those lessons learned by the colonists, and by the citizens of the new United States of America that followed them, would ripple across the globe over the centuries that followed—for good and for ill.

Land would also play a crucial role in the clash between the societies on either side of the Atlantic, pitting the old English establishment against a new and emerging American one. A fresh class of political and business elites was rising in the Americas, but without the same aristocratic pedigree as their forebears in Europe and with vastly different interests. The increasingly differing views of the financial leaders on either side of the Atlantic when it came to the accumulation of wealth in land, and the ability to use it to lend and borrow money, have been an overlooked catalyst in the growing frictions that eventually set the British Crown and the American colonists on the path towards outright war.

The pioneers arriving on the American coast at the beginning of the seventeenth century quickly realized that the ground was fertile, even bountiful, when given the right attention. It was well suited to cultivating not just native foodstuffs like maize, but also many of the English crops they brought with them. It was fecund ground too for new cash crops of tobacco and cotton. Inhabitants who had previously worked the lands owned by others were liberated in the new colonies. "Here are no hard Landlords to racke us with high rents," Smith explained. "Here every man may be master and owner of his owne labour and land."[2]

The land may not have had landlords, but it was certainly not empty. Relations between the new colonists and the Native Americans who lived, hunted, fished and cultivated crops in and around their settlements were sometimes friendly. In the earliest days of colonization, trade with the Native Americans—and occasionally their charity—would be the difference between life and death for the new arrivals. But the gradual expansion of settlements farther and farther inland was a predictable recipe for conflict. The constant growth of colonies in search of more and more fertile farming land sparked skirmishes and violence from the very earliest days of English settlement. It would come to define the next three centuries of relations between the colonists, their descendants and the native inhabitants of what would eventually become the United States.

The hundreds of settlers in colonial America became tens of thousands in the decades that followed, but the numbers were piddling in the context of the vast North American coast and its endless interior. The outposts the new arrivals established were constantly short of labor relative to their enormous wealth in land to cultivate. In 1700, the American colonies had a population of around 250,000, no more than a modest city today.[3] Even on the eve of the American Revolution, just two and a half million people lived in the Thirteen Colonies across the roughly three hundred thousand square miles of official territory. It was an overwhelmingly empty and uninhabited place, with a population density not much higher than sparsely populated modern nations like Australia or Libya.

The leaders of early settlements groused constantly about the shortage of skilled labor and the enormous expense of acquiring more of it. Lord Baltimore, who founded the colony of Maryland, offered dozens of acres of land to new settlers in the hope of inducing men and women in England to make the uncertain trek across the Atlantic. The House of Burgesses in Virginia, North America's first elected legislature, did the same. Travelers who brought families and laborers with them were granted even larger plots; the wealthiest residents of the colonies would happily pay for their passage in exchange for the promise of several years of indentured labor.

But those who survived the treacherous journey and populated successful settlements quite quickly surpassed the neighbors they had left behind in health and wealth. By the end of the seventeenth century, and likely much earlier in many places, American colonists lived decidedly better lives than their peers in England. The persistent shortage of labor guaranteed high wages and meant that men who had been tenants and farm laborers in England could become landowners themselves in America. When measured by their ability to afford basic foodstuffs, meat, simple textiles and fuels, Americans were roughly 50 percent better off than Brits during the prerevolutionary eighteenth century.[4] By the early years of American independence, American men were about two and a half inches taller than their English contemporaries.[5]

By European standards, the new settlements were also profoundly egalitarian in both income and politics, just as John Smith had suggested they would be in 1616. Income inequality across the colonies was dramatically lower than in Europe at the time, or in modern America. By the estimates of economic historians Jeffrey Williamson and Peter Lindert, the top 1 percent of earners in America made just 7.6 percent of the country's total income immediately before the American Revolution in 1776, compared to around 20 percent today.[6] Circumstances were likely even more equal a century earlier. In England, agricultural laborers without their own land were denied the right to vote. But in America, landownership was so common that political participation, which was then contingent on property ownership, was widespread across the male population.

If the new settlements were an egalitarian wonder compared to a deeply unequal England, the parallel society steadily being established on plantations across the American colonies was its ghastly antithesis. The shortage of laborers to engage in agricultural work helped to turn some of the wealthiest settlers of the colonies into the world's largest traders in human flesh, eventually eclipsing the already-booming slave trade in the British Caribbean. Slave traders, especially in the sparsely populated South, brought tens of thousands of West Africans to the east coast of America before the 1600s were over. It was just a tiny fraction of the more than twelve million men, women and children that were eventually taken into bondage and shipped across the Middle Passage.

Labor was not the only thing in short supply. The colonists were rich in fertile land, but they lacked all the other trappings that made commerce function. Unlike in South America, where gold and silver supplies were plentiful, the new settlers in the English colonies found few sources of precious metals. In the seventeenth century, monetary transactions almost everywhere on earth were still mostly conducted with specie—coins made of silver and gold. The new colonists were prosperous, but they faced a persistent dearth of actual physical money. Alongside English sterling, a scarce supply of Spanish dollars circulated from trade with the older settlements in Mexico, the Caribbean and farther into Central and South America. The shortage of money made economic life in the colonies strange: Prices may have been quoted in pounds, shillings and pence, as they were in England, but they were actually paid for with a variety of alternative means. The exchange of various IOUs was common, leading to frustrating legal disputes when debts went unpaid. Cash was so scarce that settlers sometimes resorted to barter. They exchanged goods for animal pelts, tobacco, corn or even wampum—beads made from seashells and stitched into ornate belts.

That absence of coins, like the shortage of labor, was a constant complaint from settlers trying to conduct business. Merchants found themselves unable to trade as much as they otherwise might have been able to, especially with their new countrymen. Using commodities in place of cash was a frustrating improvisation, which only worked as long as a vendor wanted to take possession of whatever the buyer had to offer. Swapping materials that the other party might not need, and in some cases ones that rotted or degraded over time, was a deeply inefficient way to manage the commerce of the new colonies.

The shortage of money also kept the new settlements in a tightly constrained economic and social role. To elites in England, the function of the colonies was to send raw agricultural goods and commodities back across the Atlantic to the mother country, where they could be turned into finished goods. In exchange, settlers imported almost all of their more complex products from English merchants. Tobacco, lumber, iron and foodstuffs headed eastward across the North Atlantic, and manufactured metal goods, textiles, firearms and even coal were transported back west.[7] The lack of coins made life difficult for entrepreneurs who wanted to invest or produce anything more complicated and valuable in the Americas and stymied the efforts of any businessmen who intended to produce goods for the domestic American market, rather than the English one.

In the very earliest days of the colonies, that division of roles made sense on both sides of the Atlantic. In fact, it was a vital necessity for the colonists, who would not have survived without more specialized English goods. The absence of money may have been a perennial annoyance to the new Americans, but such a tiny population such a long way from the hubs of commerce in Europe could hardly have been anything much more than a source of raw materials. But as the decades passed, with a growing population and an increasingly clear American identity emerging, the unequal economic relationship became more and more difficult to maintain. Time and again, the British government would try to smother

attempts by America's new colonists to follow their own economic interests. Policy was set in London mostly in defense of English elites, to protect
the monopolies over colonial commerce and finance that country's merchants and bankers prized. But of all the limits placed on their new world,
the inability to fully exploit the value of the seemingly endless land in
front of them would become one of the most egregious sources of rancor.

The seventeenth century was a time of profound intellectual upheaval. In
Europe, the Scientific Revolution was underway. As the American colonies were founded and expanded, Galileo Galilei, René Descartes and
Isaac Newton were publishing their trailblazing works. The groundwork
for that profound change was being laid in the intellectual and academic
hubs of Europe, rather than in the largely agricultural Americas. The tiny
population of American settlers in the seventeenth century was more focused on survival than science. But the effects of the shifts in thinking
underway in London, Paris, Florence and Amsterdam would come to rev-
olutionize the American colonies, both figuratively and literally.

The inquiry of the intellectuals across Europe spread across the disci-
plines of philosophy, ethics and the physical sciences. Writers were also
becoming increasingly interested in what we would now call "economics,"
searching for a theory that might explain the relationships between commerce and wealth—why they sometimes boomed and sometimes floundered. In London, an English land administrator named William Potter
was in the process of writing two tracts on his theories of trade, money
and land. He made the case that a scarcity of money was the cause of a

lack of economic activity, and an increase in the amount of money circulating through the economy would boost trade and prosperity more generally. Since money was backed by and usually made of precious metals, the limited stock of gold and silver in the world was a painful bottleneck preventing what we now call "economic growth."

Like thousands of scholars before him, Potter was preoccupied with the study of alchemy, how easily available base metals like lead might be transformed into rare and valuable gold. But in land, he believed he had found something as good as gold—or even better. Another, even more valuable asset could replace the critical role of the precious metal, Potter argued, as the asset that provided the value of money. If gold could support a currency, he wondered, why couldn't the value of land? To relieve the shortage of money, Potter argued that banks could lend newly printed paper money to wealthy estate owners who needed cash. In exchange, the borrowers would pledge their wealth in land to the bank, which they owned but could not otherwise really use without selling. The landowners could then use the new paper money they received to invest in improvements, to pay the salaries of their employees or to buy goods and services from any merchants who would accept it.

Once Potter's new money had been extended to needy borrowers, he believed it would circulate, allowing employment, production and trade to grow at a far more rapid pace. Land could eventually replace the role of gold entirely, Potter ventured, providing the inherent value behind an entire currency. His vision was published in 1650 in a book titled *The Key of Wealth*.[8] He argued that money backed by the value of precious metals was throttling the economy and that it would eventually be replaced by paper money. Potter was early and prophetic in his diagnosis. Gold and silver standards would persist for centuries after the book was published, before the world finally caught up with the little-known English land administrator.

In *The Key of Wealth*, he offered a forerunner of economic concepts that would eventually become commonplace around the world. His understanding that money and its circulation were crucial to the functioning of a growing economy was the vein of thinking that would gain popularity with researchers like Milton Friedman three hundred years later—without the diversions into mystical metallurgy more common to the seventeenth century. What Potter called "the revolution of money," a modern economist would call the "velocity" of money. Potter also grasped how a large and extensive banking system, where loans were made against the value of land, could raise what economists would eventually call the "supply" of money. Today, commercial banks create the vast majority of money in the economy. Most of their lending is extended in the form of mortgages, against land and the buildings on top of it. Potter's model was extraordinarily farsighted.

His writing was disseminated enthusiastically through the new intellectual circles popping up across Europe. One of its keenest promoters was Samuel Hartlib, a polymath who had assembled a cabal of similarly minded thinkers throughout Europe known as "intelligencers," with whom he communicated and collaborated by letter. The members included Henry Oldenburg and Robert Boyle, two of the founding fathers of modern science as we know it today. At the time, the direct and public expression of political and intellectual ideas was not always easy or wise: a year before Potter's book was published, Charles I of England had been tried and executed. It was an era of political and religious strife, which both threw open the door for forms of intellectual debate and sometimes made it more dangerous. Hartlib's shadowy gang, known as the Hartlib Circle or "invisible college," would eventually become the foundation of the Royal Society, the scholarly institution given a royal charter by King Charles II on his return to the English throne in 1660.

Neither Hartlib nor Potter ever crossed the Atlantic, which was still a dangerous and typically one-way undertaking for travelers in the middle of the seventeenth century. Britain's American possessions would remain an intellectual backwater for almost another century, and its colonists would continue to be mostly the recipients of ideas from Europe, rather than the authors of transformative new ones. But if the idea that land wealth could be turned into real money was compelling in England, it had a far greater appeal in the American colonies, which suffered from the shortage of money to an enormous degree and had far more land with which to remedy the situation. It wasn't long before the early American elites grasped the potential that the idea held for the young colonies to alleviate their shortage of cash. Potter's theories were about to be launched off the pages of his thesis and into the growing political conflict over land in the American colonies. The colonists would be the first to unlock a secret that many countries would discover over the centuries that followed, both to their advantage and to their detriment: land can be leveraged and turned into enormous sums of money.

Among the first to see the potential of the idea was John Winthrop Jr., the newly elected governor of Connecticut. He had discovered Potter's work through correspondence with Samuel Hartlib in 1660.[9] Winthrop's father had been a wealthy Suffolk landowner and subsequently one of the founders of the Massachusetts Bay Colony. The new colony had at one time suffered from a shortage of coins so severe that Winthrop Sr. attempted to institute bushels of corn as a replacement for silver. Indeed, Massachusetts was the first colony to try to produce its own currency in 1652, melting down the specie of foreign nations at the Massachusetts Mint to make the "pine tree shilling," a new series of silver coins. Strict laws were instituted to keep the new currency within the colony, in an attempt to prevent what little money Massachusetts could muster from being frittered away among its neighbors and sent overseas. But with the extremely limited resources available, the scheme did little to relieve the colony's lack of cash.

Despite Winthrop's interest, it was a false start for Potter's revolutionary concept. The new governor failed to find a political means to advance the idea, and it went no further in Connecticut or Massachusetts at the time. But the commercial limits faced by the American colonists made the idea of accessing the country's land to relieve its shortage of money irresistible. Similar proposals and experiments popped up again and again in the years that followed, pursued in different ways by a coterie of radical idealists and financial entrepreneurs. Reverend John Woodbridge, a nonconformist minister who had befriended William Potter in England, was one of the early promoters of the idea of land-backed money, and he tried to launch a private land bank in Massachusetts in 1671. Another nonconformist, Captain John Blackwell, settled in Boston in 1684 after his own land in England was confiscated as punishment for his deep involvement in Oliver Cromwell's Commonwealth regime. Blackwell proposed the establishment of a public institution—essentially, a central bank—that would issue paper currency in exchange for collateral, in the form of land.[10] All of these efforts, impeded by a lack of political autonomy in the new colonies, hit brick walls.

By the end of the seventeenth century, ideas about land and money in the American colonies were no longer just of interest to the emerging cohort of monetary theorists. The debates were beginning to take on a discordant and hostile political character that would only grow over time, helping to fuel the eventual American Revolution. The dividing lines that would tear American society into armed camps in 1776 were already becoming visible. Questions over the ownership of land, and the way American colonists wanted to use it to foster trade and credit, were rubbing up against English interests.

When they arrived in America, the colonists had brought with them six hundred years of English law, stretching back to the Norman Conquest, some of which was deeply unsuited to the new American economy. English feudalism had subsided centuries earlier, but the country's most valuable land was still overwhelmingly owned by a class of agricultural aristocrats rather than the emerging merchants and industrialists who would become far more important in the eighteenth and nineteenth centuries. The idea of land-backed money of the sort which Potter and Blackwell had proposed required a vital element that the English system lacked—the easy ability to repossess land from any borrowers who pledged it as security against a loan. In the seventeenth century, English law divided property into land and chattel.[11] The latter was movable, personal property, which could be borrowed against and repossessed. Without the ability for a lender to take hold of the borrower's land, the value of the loans would always be suspect, and there would certainly be no hope of any land-backed currency.

To England's landed elite, the idea of the country's storied estates being lost to moneylenders and the emerging merchant class was outrageous. It would have been a violation of the rights of the owner's heirs, even if they had not yet been born. England's governance was still driven for the most part by the interests of its aristocracy, and the power of its aristocracy stemmed from its ownership of immense swathes of farmland.

To a creditor who was chasing a borrower for repayment, the options available were far more limited than they are today. In some cases, lenders might be allowed to take control of their wayward debtor's land, but on the strict understanding that he only held the asset until the debt was repaid in what could be made from it, at which point the land would be returned to the original owner.

If a new system of land-backed credit or land-backed currency was going to work, the lenders issuing banknotes also needed to know that their claims on a borrower's property wouldn't be bogged down in court proceedings for decades, as was often the case in England. The possibility that the land that had been promised to a lender to secure a loan would instead be handed over to a son of the debtor, as his ancient legal right, was a risk that hovered over all of the proposals for land banks. To make the new forms of lending function, the American colonists required an orderly system for default and repossession. By the 1670s and 1680s, new laws began to crop up in assemblies across the colonies, allowing land to be used to satisfy a variety of debts.[12] By the end of the seventeenth century, this uniquely American approach to land, alien to the English elite, was already embedded in the colonial economy.

The Americans had no intention of giving up on their attempts to turn land into money, despite the political difficulties faced by the earliest financial pioneers. By the early eighteenth century, the advocates had their breakthrough: a wave of public land banks like the one Blackwell had imagined were finally being instituted. Between 1712 and 1717, South Carolina, Massachusetts, Rhode Island and New Hampshire founded new public institutions that would lend owners a proportion of the assessed value of their property, with the land itself pledged as collateral.[13] Some of the schemes were more successful than others, but all were pursued at a relatively small scale: the painful shortage of currency continued to frustrate America's merchant class.

The ability of creditors to foreclose on American land was formalized across the colonies in 1732, when the Debt Recovery Act was passed in London, enabling lenders to pursue unsecured creditors for all of their assets—movable property, slaves and land alike.[14] The law only applied in the colonies; similar rules would not be instituted in Britain itself for another century. The legislation was enacted in the interests of British merchants, who were tired of chasing colonists for their debts. It was nevertheless an important landmark: even the British government was now accepting the reality of the divergent needs of the American settlements when it came to land and finance. The act represented a fork in the road, separating England's legal system from its colonial offshoots.

But the limits on the use of land as a source of borrowing led colonists to new and warped ways of securing their credit too. Land was the largest source of wealth for the new colonies, but the next largest was the enslaved men and women arriving in chains at the American coast. From the middle of the seventeenth century, moneylenders began extending credit against slaves—hence the description of the practice as "chattel" slavery, named after the category of movable property. The Anglo-Saxon practice of slavery had been suppressed in Norman England five hundred years earlier, and so English law had limited precedent for the practice of lending against the value of slaves, allowing the colonists far more room to experiment with their own system. The combination of credit and bondage was the "invisible engine" of slavery, according to historian Bonnie Martin. Slaves had value not just for their labor, but for their ability to be used as collateral. Two thirds of all the secured lending recorded in Virginia during the colonial era was recorded not against land, housing or other property, but against slaves.[15]

By the early decades of the eighteenth century, America was no longer just a recipient of European ideas. The eldest of the men who would eventually become Founding Fathers of the United States were entering political life and beginning to play their own roles in the discussions about American wealth, autonomy and governance. At the age of just twenty-one, after returning from a trip to London, a young Benjamin Franklin founded his own intellectual circle in Philadelphia, known as the Junto. The group would be the forerunner of what became the American Philosophical Society, just as the Hartlib Circle had been the kernel of the Royal Society before it. Franklin was agitated about the damage the persistent shortage of currency was doing to the American colonies, and he saw a way in which land could be used to empower them. In 1729, at the age of twenty-three, he published *A Modest Enquiry into the Nature and Necessity of a Paper-Currency*. Franklin had seen that banks in the larger European financial centers were already issuing bills of credit—early paper banknotes that were redeemable for gold and silver. An American bank could do the same, Franklin believed, by issuing bills against the value of land. Just as the paper notes that were issued against the value of gold and silver became money, so would bills issued against the value of land: they could, in Franklin's words, become "coined land."[16]

When the General Court of Massachusetts commissioned suggestions for expanding the supply of money in 1740, the proponents of land banking leapt on a new political opening. Hundreds of men signed a petition in favor of a new private bank that would issue new money against land, and against commodities like iron, flax and rope in far larger volumes. Without approval from the Massachusetts assembly, the bank issued almost £50,000 in bills, an enormous sum at the time.[17] The new notes immediately sparked another political crisis. Governor Jonathan Belcher attempted to suppress the use of the new money and dismissed local judicial officials who accepted it. Despite Belcher's efforts, some parts of the colony began to accept the banknotes in the payment of taxes. The new land bank's domestic opponents eventually alerted the British government to the bank's activities. Suppression came swiftly. The bank's opponents relied on legislation that had been passed to prevent a repeat of the devastating South Sea Bubble, in which thousands of investors had seen their speculative bets on Britain's South Sea Company wiped out in 1720. The law was extended to the colonies in 1741, with an expanded remit that would explicitly kill off any new land banks.

The bank's founders were left with a collapsed financial institution, with many large debts to be repaid. One of its architects, Deacon Samuel Adams, died in debt in 1748, with the fallout of the bank's blowup unresolved. His son and heir was pursued for the debts of the bank well into the 1750s, several years after his father's death.[18] The ordeal provided Sam Adams Jr. a personal experience of how it felt to be on the sharp end of British imperial interests, providing the fuel for a lifelong opposition to the rule of the Crown. He would become one of the most fervent and early revolutionaries in America. He led the Boston Tea Party in 1773 and was a signatory to the Declaration of Independence in 1776.

Most of the preoccupation with land among the new Americans was based on even simpler grounds. Land was by far the most common asset in the colonies. Opportunities for greater and greater affluence were constantly expanding, as growers of grain and tobacco and slave-driving cotton farmers pushed westward into a territory that seemed to stretch as far as they could imagine. In New England, the part of the country least exposed to the noxious trade in chattel slavery, land made up over 80 percent of the local wealth.[19]

Speculation on land was a favored habit of early American elites, who sought out any expanse of earth that was unoccupied and without an owner—at least, any European owners—to acquire. The practice covered a wide range of activity: Some speculators were hucksters, who would flip the plots to another buyer almost as soon as it was acquired. Sometimes, the acquisition of new land involved violence not just against the land's previous native inhabitants, but also against white Americans who had already settled there without legal title. For other speculators, the process of acquiring and profiting from land was a longer one that was seen as more respectable in polite society: the original buyer would help to clear, prepare and parcel out the land for future owners and tenants before selling it on.

By the middle of the eighteenth century, speculation had gone far beyond the small-scale efforts that were common from the very earliest days of American colonization. In 1747, a group of Virginia speculators began to pool their resources together to establish a venture they named the Ohio Company, which would explore the lands west of the colony.[20] Among the men involved were two of the sons of a wealthy landowning family, Lawrence and Augustine Washington. Their younger half brother George would be shaped by the family's land wealth too. Another venture, known as the Loyal Company, was founded a year later. The groups appealed to the government of Virginia for grants covering hundreds of thousands of acres. Speculation had become big business.

The extensive exploration for land at the western fringes of the Thirteen Colonies helped to spark the French and Indian War in 1754, pitting Britain's American colonists against the Kingdom of France, with each side supported by their own Native American allies. The government of Virginia had extended land grants to speculators beyond the inhabited borders of the state, encouraging expansion farther and farther northwest, threatening French control of territories around and beyond the Ohio River. The rapacious demand for land was not just a cause of the war, but also the means of financing it. The troops who joined the new regiments marching out against the French gained a personal stake in the campaign: they were collectively promised hundreds of thousands of acres of land as a prize for their service. What began as a border conflict far from the imperial cores of the British and French empires did not end there. In 1756, Britain formally declared war on France. Prussia sided with Britain, and Austria joined the French coalition to settle old scores with Prussia. Russia and Sweden joined the fray on the Austrian side. The broader conflict lasted until 1763 and was the first major European war to be fought not just at home, but across Asia and the Americas too. It became known as the Seven Years' War.

At the age of twenty-two, a young George Washington was one of the men who set out on the campaign against the French. The young Virginian was already an up-and-coming land speculator, enamored with the potential wealth that further expansion could provide. Later in life, he would write confidently that "land is the most Permanent Estate we can hold, & most likely to increase in its value."[21] Washington accumulated land grants as a reward for his early military service for Virginia and for Britain, and he acquired tens of thousands of acres across the country in other speculative schemes too, adding to the wealth of his father and brothers. Most of his investments were a success over the decades that followed the Seven Years' War; on the eve of the eventual revolution, Washington was one of the richest men in colonial America.

The future president was by no means the only Founding Father whose interests were deeply tied to land speculation. James Wilson and George Mason, two other prominent American revolutionary leaders, were knee-deep in bets on lands in the West. Thomas Fitzsimons, Jonathan Dayton and William Blount, three of the signatories of the American Constitution, were large-scale speculators too. Robert Morris, who became known as the "financier of the revolution" for his role as the revolutionary government's superintendent of finance, would eventually become one of the largest landowners in the newly independent United States. Of the fifty-five men who sat in the Constitutional Convention, at least fourteen were land speculators, compared to just eleven with interests in manufacturing and trade.[22] Even those estimates are a narrow interpretation that excludes the founders who had smaller personal interests locked up in land.

After a series of embarrassing losses in the early part of the Seven Years' War, Britain and its allies eventually triumphed on the American front, cementing enormous territorial gains. At the end of the conflict in Europe, France was forced to cede all its claims east of the Mississippi River, hundreds of thousands of square miles of additional land; the Crown's dominion over a huge swathe of North America seemed to have been assured. But for the land-hungry colonists, it was a disastrous form of victory. In October of 1763, a royal proclamation was announced in London, drawing a new border across the western edge of the colonies. The partition ran along the Appalachian mountain range, cutting through chunks of what is now Georgia, North Carolina, Virginia, Pennsylvania, New York and all the way to New Hampshire. Rivers east of the line flowed into the Atlantic, and rivers west of it flowed into the Mississippi. The line marked a new limit beyond which westward settlement by colonists was prohibited. The government was tired of the conflict that the endless push westward was generating with the Native American tribes and aimed to make the entire area west of the Appalachian Mountains a buffer state, which was to be policed by ten thousand British troops.

The Proclamation Line was not just a political border, but a new economic regime. The British government also declared that merchants would have to obtain licenses to trade with native tribes for the first time. The proclamation condemned the "great frauds and abuses that have been committed in the purchasing of lands of the Indians."[23] The colonists' interests when it came to the relentless appetite for land wealth were under threat, just as their efforts to establish land-backed money had been decades earlier. The decision would eventually prove to be one of the most fatal to the British government's own interests in the Thirteen Colonies.

The line was not intended to be a permanent barrier to settlement, but it soured the already-tense relationship between the British government and its American colonists even further. It also meant that the expansion into the West was now an imperial project, not a matter of local discretion on the part of the colonists. The further accumulation of land wealth by the families that had taken and purchased greater and greater space in North America for over a century and a half would now be subject, in one way or another, to approval from London. The land speculation ventures launched by colonial elites like George Washington and his brothers were in jeopardy. The areas that the Ohio Company had aimed to explore lay on the wrong side of the British government's line. The Mississippi Land Company, a club of speculators that Washington was involved in directly, was incorporated in June of 1763, just a few months before the proclamation was announced.[24] The period of benign neglect, wherein the colonies had managed to make their own way in the world because the government in London left them to manage their own affairs, was coming to an end.

Some colonists had no intention of abiding by either the spirit or the letter of the new law. Frontiersmen continued to explore the future state of Kentucky. In 1775, settlements popped up across the territory, established by a mixture of purchases and violence. The new outposts were flagrant and brazen violations of the Proclamation Line. Even established elites like George Washington, a colonel and the head of a respectable family, did not really plan to abide by the new restriction. In a letter to his land agent in 1767, Washington confided that he expected the proclamation to be a temporary measure. The current restriction, he argued in private, was designed to placate native tribes and would not last forever.[25] Anyone who neglected the opportunity to mark out land for future settlement, Washington said, would never get it back.

Land speculation was much more than a moneymaking scheme. The egalitarian and prosperous world that the colonists had pioneered, and by extension the American concepts of freedom that had emerged, only really worked if the residents had high levels of landownership. With the land in the east now owned and populated, Americans had two options. They could either push west, or accept a more European economic and political model, with tenants and landless laborers slowly growing to become the majority. Writing as early as 1751, Benjamin Franklin had laid out the difference between the reality of a country with land to expand into and one without. In Europe, Franklin noted, "all lands being occupied and improved to the height, those who cannot get land must labor for others that have it." In America, by contrast, "a laboring man, that understands husbandry, can in a short time save money enough to purchase a piece of new land sufficient for a plantation, whereon he may subsist a family."[26]

It was not the first time that Britain had curtailed the Americans' rights to own, expand and borrow against their land. But the colonies had changed dramatically since the first land banks were crushed by the Crown in the late seventeenth century. The Thirteen Colonies were not just ten times larger by population, but far more distinct from the mother country. When early arrivals like Captain John Blackwell and Reverend John Woodbridge set foot on the new continent, the idea of a separate American nation was faintly ridiculous. But by 1776, only eight of the fifty-six signatories to the Declaration of Independence had been born in Europe.[27] Several came from families with increasingly deep American roots: Washington was a fourth-generation American whose grandfather was born in Virginia over one hundred years before the revolution. The sons of the American gentry studied at the University of Pennsylvania, Columbia, Yale, Harvard, Princeton and Rutgers, among their fellow countrymen. Insults from the government in London didn't just result in upset colonists who could quickly be quelled. British slights were now dangerous, providing the fuel for an increasingly widespread American identity.

A decade before the American Revolution, Franklin, who was serving in London as Pennsylvania's agent to the Crown, attempted one last throw of the dice to bridge the gap between the increasingly discontented colonists and the British government. The Stamp Act, instituted in 1765, had imposed the first direct taxes on the American colonists, giving rise to the complaints of "taxation without representation." Franklin proposed that instead, Britain should allow the creation of a General Loan Office—the name of the small public land bank established in Pennsylvania in the 1720s—to raise revenues itself.[28] Franklin offered a characteristically detailed proposal on the potential bank's operations and governance to the British authorities.[29] The bank would lend money against land, Franklin suggested, and use the interest earned to fund state expenditures in the Thirteen Colonies, having the valuable side effect of allowing more money to circulate in the colonies. It was a version of the idea that Franklin had been proposing since before many of America's Founding Fathers were born. The Stamp Act was repealed in 1766, but the relief from the pitiless rules instituted by the British government was brief. The punitive laws kept coming, and the reach of the British state was felt further and further in the once–lightly governed colonies. Franklin's proposal went unheeded.

The argument that the curtailment of land speculation and the restrictions on the use of land led to the revolt in 1776 was once popular among historians. Charles A. Beard, a Columbia history professor in the early twentieth century, published an extensive history of the economic interests of the founders, arguing that their personal financial affairs were a major driving force behind the American Revolution. Writing immediately before the war itself, the future American president John Adams (second cousin to Samuel Adams Jr.) certainly believed that the restrictions on using land in finance had been a major contributor to the schism between Britain and the colonists. "The act to destroy the Land Bank

Scheme," he wrote, referring to the 1741 smothering of the Massachusetts bank, "raised a greater ferment in this province, than the stamp-act did."[30] There is no denying that Britain's constraints on the use of American land was seen as a major injustice: preventing westward expansion and the continued population of the colonies was the seventh grievance listed in the Declaration of Independence.

Exactly how much the founders were acting to protect their own narrow commercial interests will never be known for sure. But by 1775, it was increasingly difficult to tease apart America's material and philosophical dreams. Land and liberty, the economic backbone of America and its new secular doctrine of freedom, were irrevocably bound together. When Thomas Jefferson enumerated the inalienable rights to "life, liberty, and the pursuit of happiness," he was amending the sanctity of "life, liberty and estate" described by philosopher John Locke, one of the greatest influences on Enlightenment liberals in England and America. When the rebel colonies triumphed against their former British rulers in 1783, their speculative energies were unleashed again. They had hardly even paused during the conflict itself: some states confiscated the land belonging to American Royalists before the war had finished. Settlers and investors flooded across the defunct Proclamation Line. In the subsequent twenty years, the Thirteen Colonies would become seventeen states, as Vermont, Kentucky, Tennessee and Ohio all joined. Even then, the westernmost settlements were not even at the midpoint of what is now the United States. The settlers had thousands of miles to expand into, with a government that would no longer hold them back from doing so.

When the United States was founded, the incredibly widespread ownership of land among the new country's citizens marked it out as an oddity in the world, a new kind of society. Much of Europe was still in a state of relative peonage to powerful landlords and would remain so for genera-tions. The keenness of the American colonists in turning their assets into credit and money with which to power their new economy was just as unusual in the world as their new form of government. But in the centu-ries that followed, they proved to be the forerunners of what would even-tually become normal not just across the Atlantic, but almost everywhere around the world.

Ironically, the ancient rules that governed Britain's approach to land, and its use in finance, were already being loosened at home in the decades before the American Revolution, though not in time to bridge the politi-cal gulf between the colonists and their rulers in London. The number of parliamentary acts that permitted land to be used as collateral began to climb from 1750 onwards, with liberalization reaching a peak in the early nineteenth century.[31] The residual vestiges of feudal rights associated with land were swept away over less than a century, allowing British merchants and landowners to borrow against the value of their holdings with ease and making moneylenders far more able to lend against land as collat-eral. The growth in the ability to borrow against the most valuable and widespread asset in the country helped to power the budding Industrial Revolution already underway in Britain's cities. Change was on the way in Europe too. Lenders that extended credit using land as collateral began to emerge in Prussia in the late eighteenth century.[32] As emperor of France, Napoleon would institute an enormous cadastral survey in 1807 to map and catalogue the country's land, its fertility and its ownership in a cen-tralized database, providing the groundwork for its greater use as collateral. The American way was becoming the way of the world.

But the proponents of land banking in the American colonies, Benja-min Franklin among them, made certain assumptions about land and its use in finance that would not hold true indefinitely. To Franklin, the persistent shortage of currency meant that the higher land prices went, the more the colonies would be relieved of their economic straitjacket. There was very little discussion of whether land values might ever rise to levels that posed a new set of problems. In Massachusetts in 1684, or Philadelphia in 1729, or anywhere in the newly independent United States in 1783, such a future must have been very difficult to imagine. The country was still populated incredibly sparsely, and with lands of unknown scale still to be explored to the west; the reality that the seemingly endless plenty would eventually be exhausted seemed a truly remote prospect.

But the new Americans who had asserted their rights to life, liberty and land speculation were living in the twilight of a world that was mostly agricultural in nature, as it had been for thousands of years, in which the value of land mostly came from what could be grown on it. Even London and Paris, then Europe's two largest and most powerful cities, still had fewer than a million residents apiece when the United States was born. A transformation was looming—one that would permanently alter the use and abuse of land as an asset. And the politics of land, even in the abundant new American republic, were about to change dramatically.

THREE

Land Wars

On a cool summer's evening on Friday, the 30th of July, 1909, four thousand people assembled in a packed hall in East London, awaiting a distinguished political speaker. The venue was the Edinburgh Castle, which had once been a rowdy gin palace and was now a meeting place owned by local temperance campaigners. The building loomed over the Limehouse Cut, a canal that linked the teeming docklands on the River Thames to London and the country beyond. The endless goods from the British Empire and farther afield flowed through this grubby, poor and industrial corner of the city, past its impoverished slum houses, and onwards to the rest of the country.

The audience was gathered to hear David Lloyd George, chancellor of the exchequer and rising superstar of the British Liberal Party. Three months earlier, Lloyd George had unveiled the Budget of 1909, a proposal that included a barrage of new taxes on income and inherited wealth, as well as new duties on alcohol and tobacco. Taxes were being raised to fund new programs of unemployment and health assistance, pensions for the very elderly and increased military spending to counter the rising German Empire. The Budget was a landmark shift from the old small-government model pursued by the British Liberals to a new, more interventionist approach pursued by the young progressives of the early twentieth century.

But the Budget's most politically incendiary proposal was not the taxes on income or the government spending. The Budget's new taxes on land, and the threat they posed to the men who owned it, were the most intensely controversial in Britain's parliament. The chancellor wanted owners to face a small capital gains tax on any land they sold—a 20 percent levy on any increase in the value of the land since its owners had purchased it.[1] In addition, the government planned to set about valuing the country's estates, with the aim of applying a modest tax to the total value. Owners would face a bill for about 0.2 percent of the value of their undeveloped urban land each year. In terms of its absolute size, the land tax proposal was one of the Budget's more modest elements. The revenues it raised would have been worth less than half a percent of the following year's revenue.[2] But the reaction—from the Budget's supporters and its opponents alike—was explosive.

Lloyd George took the stage in Limehouse and delivered one of the most inflammatory public addresses any British politician who held one of the greatest offices of state had ever made. "The landlord is a gentleman who does not earn his wealth," he said, speaking through frequent interruptions of cheers and applause. "His sole function, his chief pride, is stately consumption of wealth produced by others." The country's wealthiest men, he said, wanted a colossal expansion of the Royal Navy to pursue an arms race with the increasingly belligerent German Empire. But they did not want to pay for the new, modern dreadnoughts themselves. The owners of the land, Lloyd George said, wanted to live off the toil of the miners, farmers and industrial workers who were their tenants and employees. "This system is not business," he roared. "It is blackmail."[3]

In a letter written a little less than a month after his own speech, David Lloyd George told his brother that 1.25 million pamphlet copies of the speech had already been sold.[4] Demand outstripped supply: street hawkers were buying and reselling copies. In the decades that followed, "Limehousing" became a term in its own right in British politics, synonymous with rabble-rousing and fiery provocation. Britain was on the edge of a constitutional crisis that would trigger two elections in 1910 and eventually force an intervention by the new king, George V, to break the impasse between the Liberal government and the landowner-dominated House of Lords.

The cheering crowd in Limehouse and the horrified gentry at Westminster were embroiled in the greatest political contest of their era. Land, and the way in which its owners seemed to mop up the gains of the new industrial prosperity, was the obsession of progressive thinking on both sides of the Atlantic. By the time of the Limehouse speech, the advocates of taxes on the values of land could be found in statehouses around the United States and parliaments across Europe. Revolutionaries around the world had come to believe that expropriating the wealth of landlords, the aristocrats who hoarded the fruits of the labor of ordinary people, would be crucial to the development of their nations. Aristocratic elites around the world felt the ground shifting beneath their feet: the land agitators represented one of the most serious threats the monied class had ever faced.

The ownership of land had risen to prominence as a major political issue internationally at astonishing speed. Thirty years before Lloyd George's speech at Limehouse, a novice author in California sparked the beginning of this new political era. In 1879, Henry George, an unknown San Francisco journalist (of no relation to the future British chancellor) published his first book, *Progress and Poverty*. George would come to shape politics both at home and abroad to a greater degree than anyone else in the world during the decades after the book was published. Though it is hard to believe today, given George's relative anonymity, and his lack of a significant political legacy, the book was almost certainly the single most influential piece of writing of the era.

Henry George was born in Pennsylvania in 1839, at the beginning of a deep and protracted economic recession in the United States. Two financial panics, one in 1837 and another in the year of George's birth, had rippled through the nascent international commodity market, sending fragile American banks to the wall. The crises sparked a downturn that lasted until 1843 and threw millions of men out of work. It was an apt beginning for George, given the questions with which he would be preoccupied for the rest of his life. At the time, fewer than two million Americans lived in cities, and almost 90 percent of the country lived in rural areas.[5] The number of Americans living in urban areas almost quadrupled during the first twenty years of George's life and reached more than eight million by the end of the nineteenth century, making up almost 40 percent of the population.

His upbringing was modest, devoutly religious and without advantages of any significance. As a young man, George took odd jobs, including a stint on a merchant vessel named the *Hindoo*, which traveled to India and Australia. At the age of nineteen, he made a decision that millions of Americans would later follow and headed west. He settled in the booming city of San Francisco, where the defining work of his career would be written. In 1861, George married Annie Corsina Fox, with whom he eventually had four children. Life was punctured by periods of acute immiseration, not just for George and his young family, but for millions of others all across the country. Even as the American economy was surging in size, the repeated bursts of speculation and crisis among the country's new financial firms resulted in brutal economic downturns every few years. George experienced the effects of the slumps himself. "I am starting out afresh, very much crippled and embarrassed, owing over $200," he wrote in his diary in February 1865, shortly after the birth of his second child. "I have been unsuccessful in everything."[6] In the middle of the 1860s, the family was not just struggling, but near starvation. George had been temporarily reduced to begging in the street, where he once accosted a wealthy passerby for money. The man took pity and gave the new father five dollars. Years later, George said that he had been so desperate that he might otherwise have robbed and murdered his benefactor.

As a boy, George had learned how to set type at a printer's office, a trade that helped him find intermittent work with a range of newspapers and publications. He was hired by the San Francisco *Times* as a typesetter in 1866. His big break came a year later when he was elevated to the role of managing editor, a position in which he made $50 per week, and he found some security, if not any great wealth. Journalism was no more lucrative as a business at the time than it is today. His ideas were already germinating: as far back as 1868, he had mused in a short essay about how the arrival of the railroad would drive land prices higher in California, making it harder for poor men to afford space for themselves and their families, promoting squalor and vice.[7] He established his own newspaper, the *Daily Evening Post*, which he ran from 1871 to 1875, but the paper was no financial success either. He became active in the politics of the

Democratic Party, serving from 1876 as California's state inspector of gas meters, a job handed down as a favor from William Irwin, the recently elected governor of the state.

By the time his magnum opus was published in 1879, George had been thinking about land and how it related to the huge economic trends of his era for over a decade. When he looked for a publisher, not everyone could see the potential in *Progress and Poverty*. The book was rejected as an unlikely commercial success by several publishing houses. Its eventual publisher, D. Appleton & Company, told George that the book was "written with great clearness and force, but it is very aggressive."[8] By May of 1879, he had determined to publish it himself, come what may. He paid for his own typesetting plates, printing an author's run of five hundred copies which sold for $3 apiece. It was not until George offered the plates to Appleton that the firm finally agreed to publish it.

The underlying question posed by the book was the same one preoccupying thinkers around the world in the dying decades of the nineteenth century: Why, given the huge material and technological progress through which they were living, did there seem to be so much misery too? The telephone and the electric lightbulb had been invented during the decade before *Progress and Poverty* was released, and the first automobile powered by an internal combustion engine was about to be commercialized for mass production for the first time. The modern world was coming into focus. At the same time, new and horrendous forms of urban destitution were on show in San Francisco, New York, London and across every European capital. It was the pressing moral dilemma of the day.

George had an answer: the value of land was surging in America's burgeoning industrial hubs, and it was placing the fruits of progress into the hands of a small class of landowners. It was the sweat of workers and the innovation of entrepreneurs that made the land increase in value, but they received a much more modest share of the wealth than their idle landlords. Only land, since it was both fixed and immobile, could explain the disparities between such new and tremendous wealth and the crushing poverty with which George was personally acquainted. When any piece of technology or innovation or effort boosted production, landlords simply raised the rents. They needed to do nothing more than collect the income, which was ballooning in the face of the growing urban population. When new infrastructure was built—the roads, bridges, railways and utilities that were being blanketed over urban America—land prices went up, and landlords vacuumed up the benefits, at the expense of the people who built, used and funded those same developments.

The immiserating financial crises that seemed to occur over and over again were likewise the product of speculation in land, according to George. During periods in which prices are booming, George saw that investors seeking rapid gains scrambled to buy more and more land in increasingly marginal areas: when plots in the center of a city, snapped up by an initial wave of speculators, became too expensive, land in the sprawling outlying areas would do for the next wave. Such speculators generally didn't bother putting the land to any productive use, George observed, since that could tie it up for years and prevent them from flipping it for a profit.[9] Companies paid so much in rent that many otherwise productive activities were ruled out—instead of building a factory, industrialists who could not justify the expense of land would opt to not invest. "Adam Smith's invisible hand is blocked by George's invisible barrier," explained Fred Foldvary, a Georgist economist, in 1991.[10] As the share of the pie going to landowners grew and grew, entrepreneurs and workers withdrew their efforts and labor, creating the sudden spikes in unemployment that peppered the era. The specifics of George's model when it came to financial crises and recessions have not survived the test of time and been adopted by modern economics. But the cycle he saw—a frenzy for land, followed by a financial bust and an economic downturn—is still with us.

George's solution to both problems was a blunt one. Land, he believed, was nothing like any other asset, and should not be treated like one. He proposed that land should be taxed at 100 percent of its rental value. Anything the owner did to make the land more worthwhile—building homes, industrial buildings, commercial premises or any kind of structure—would not face the tax. Such a levy would smash speculation, since the tax would climb in response to the sudden increase in values but remain flat whenever the owners improved its use. It would encourage efficiency too, as landlords would lose the ability to simply sit on vacant land as it climbed in value, or put it to very little use. George believed that, done right, a tax on the value of land would be the only necessary levy of any kind—incomes, sales and other economic activity could be entirely tax-free. As a result, George's proposal became known as the Single Tax.

Liberal philosophers and political economists had been making similar arguments for more than a century. A group of economic thinkers in France known as the Physiocrats, particularly François Quesnay and Anne Robert Jacques Turgot, had advocated the value of land as an ideal source of tax revenue. Free-market icons like Adam Smith and David Ricardo had followed them in Britain in the late eighteenth and early nineteenth centuries. English philosopher and political economist John Stuart Mill—with whom George once exchanged a series of letters—also advocated for a tax on land.[11] In fact, the tax had been a favorite of thinkers at the nexus of politics, economics and philosophy for well over a century by the time George came to his conclusions.

But George was markedly different from the economists that went before him. While his predecessors wrote for a concentrated and elite audience, he spoke to a far broader group, writing with the furious pen of a lay preacher. "If we are all here by the equal permission of the Creator," he wrote, "we are all here with an equal title to the enjoyment of his bounty—with an equal right to the use of all that nature so impartially offers."[12] Land and its ownership was the root not just of inefficiency and inequality, but of a raw moral injustice. George drew direct biblical comparisons throughout his work: liberty was the promise given to the Israelites by God, and liberation from monopolies in land, the asset that belonged to everyone in equal measure, was equally as urgent and just. One Scottish land baron, the Duke of Argyll, later said that "the world has never seen such a Preacher of Unrighteousness as Mr. Henry George," nicknaming him "the prophet of San Francisco."[13] The title was not intended as flattery. But it fit the man perfectly: George's followers adopted the moniker for their herald.

The economic and social trends of the late nineteenth century provided a perfect backdrop for George's argument too. The greatest of all the nineteenth century financial crises arrived in 1873 with a financial panic sparked by the collapse of Jay Cooke & Company, a Philadelphia-based bank, which rippled through the budding international financial system and led to bank runs in America and Europe. Though it is largely forgotten in popular history today, the spasm was the nineteenth century equivalent of the 2008 collapse of Lehman Brothers, with a similarly devastating global aftermath. The turmoil in American financial markets sparked an international crisis. By some measures, the economic slump that followed did not end completely until 1897, nearly a quarter of a century later. Readers around the world were in the market for a solution to the seemingly relentless cycle of boom-and-bust.

At the same time, the massive economic advantage that had benefited new Americans since the very first colony at Jamestown was coming to an end. America had been defined by its vast, open expanses and the relentless, violent advancement of settlers into the territories held by its indigenous occupants. When the country was founded, its society was far more equal in wealth and status than any of the European societies its settlers were arriving from. Alexis de Tocqueville, the French official who became the young republic's most famous early biographer, described not just the astonishing economic equality and mobility that he saw in America and its sharp contrast to Europe, but the equality in spirit. "The families of the great landed proprietors are almost all commingled with the general mass," he wrote on his trip to the East Coast of the country in 1831.[14] "Wealth circulates with inconceivable rapidity, and experience shows that it is rare to find two succeeding generations in the full enjoyment of it."

The frontier that had once seemed to stretch out endlessly, the obsession of millions of colonists, was beginning to close. Railroads that could take a man from the farthest corners of the East Coast to George's home in San Francisco crisscrossed the country. As urbanization and industrialization surged forwards in the last decades of the century, America had never been so unequal, nor had its inequality ever been so obvious. The once-bountiful frontier was finally being closed off after almost three centuries of settlement. "As a general rule, for those who have not, it will make it more difficult to get," George wrote in 1868.[15] The result would be high rents, overcrowding and squalor. During the later part of George's life, the frenetic Oklahoma Land Rush would mark the last surge into an expanse of land yet to be populated by white settlers, and in 1890, the superintendent of the US census announced that, for the first time since European colonists set foot on the continent, there was no longer a real, continuous frontier line. Land supply was becoming fixed again.

George seemed to be right about the consequences. The equality that had once astounded the colonists and visitors arriving from Europe was unraveling rapidly. By the early years of the twentieth century, around 20 percent of the country's income was flowing to the top 1 percent, roughly the same level at which it stands today, three times as much as was the case during the American Revolution.[16] But in George's era and for some time afterwards, there was no welfare system, no national income tax and no unemployment insurance to reduce society's inequities. The nation of yeoman farmers that de Tocqueville had described was gone. The gargantuan fortunes of American tycoons whose names are still synonymous with tremendous wealth—the Carnegies, the Rockefellers, the Vanderbilts—were being assembled and expanded. That wealth stemmed from the new types of industrial businesses that benefited tremendously from scale but were feared to be dangerous monopolies too.

In the first year after its publication, *Progress and Poverty* was not an immediate success. George traveled back east in search of work. "My pleasant little home—that I was so comfortable in—is gone, and I am afloat at 42, poorer than at 21," he wrote to a friend at the end of 1880.[17] But New York City, which would become his adopted home for the rest of his life, offered experiences and opportunities that California could not. The city was heaving with new immigrants disembarking from ships each week. Among the men and women arriving from Ireland, George found immediate common cause. They had land-related grievances at home and abroad. In New York, new arrivals were packed into crowded slums like those in the city's Five Points. In Ireland, enormous rural protests had erupted in 1878, led by farmers opposed to the oppressive level of rents. The Irish National Land League was formed one year later, and years of rent strikes, foreclosure boycotts and low-level agrarian agitation began. George did not spark the movement, but he was influential all the same: He met Michael Davitt, a land activist and advocate of a still-distant Irish Republic, in 1880. The men became friends, and a year later George published *The Irish Land Question*, a diatribe against British management of Ireland and the smothering of its tenant farmers.

It was in Ireland that George first became known not just for his writing, but for his radical political activism. He traveled across the Atlantic as a freelance journalist in 1881, when his book was still steadily gathering readers in America, and stayed there for over a year. During his tour of the country, he was briefly arrested twice by the Royal Irish Constabulary, in Loughrea and Athenry, on the west coast of the country. The detainments, which lasted all of a few hours, were quickly ended by a magistrate, but still managed to spark a minor international incident. George wrote to the president of the United States, Chester A. Arthur, to complain about his extremely brief incarceration; a copy of the letter was published in *The New York Times*. By way of an explanation, the British foreign secretary, the Earl Granville, wrote to US Secretary of State Frederick T. Frelinghuysen that "his movements and the persons with whom he associated raised a suspicion in the minds of the local officers that he was there for an unlawful purpose."[18]

Despite his touristic radicalism in Ireland, George was seen as unthreatening enough for a time, even to the class of elites he would have happily expropriated. When he first arrived in Britain in 1882 after his trip to Ireland, he was an object of perplexed interest, seen mostly as a man of interesting if somewhat eccentric ideas. It was the first of several visits to Britain, a country where George would arguably have more influence than any other. The British establishment paper of record, *The Times*, gave *Progress and Poverty* a positive review: "George's reading has evidently been wide; he has reflected deeply; he is an acute reasoner, and he is the master of an excellent style," the newspaper judged in September 1882, while George made a speaking tour across the country. "The readers of this book may dissent from his statements and conclusions without regretting the time they have spent over it . . . They will find in its pages much to ponder with care and much that is highly suggestive."[19]

It didn't take long until the establishment's initial curiosity was replaced by condemnation. Sales of *Progress and Poverty* surged in Britain, taking off far more rapidly than they had in America. Eighteen months later, when *The Times* reviewed George's *Social Problems*, a book of short essays published in 1883, the conclusion was markedly more critical. George's writing was still regarded as lucid and powerful, but with a dark underbelly. "Many persons will regret, perhaps, that these remarkable qualities have not been enlisted in the discussion of some subject less susceptible of inflammatory treatment," the reviewers fretted. "We shall be all the more ready to listen seriously to Mr. George when he desists from proposing that in order to re-establish peace and good will on earth we shall begin by appropriating the property of others."[20]

It was becoming clear just how threatening George's crusade could prove to the landowners of any nation. At City of London College, a technical training school, the mere presence of *Progress and Poverty* as a textbook in the political economy department caused an outrage, forcing the school's administrators to withdraw the book entirely.[21] "Georgism" was spreading rapidly into politics too. The snappily named English League for the Taxation of Land Values was established in 1883. In America, hundreds of Single Tax clubs and Henry George clubs were founded. One estimate in 1887 suggested that thirty such organizations were started each week and that every US state was home to them. Dozens of Georgist newspapers were founded across the country.[22]

Back in America, Henry George made a crucial friendship that would push him into the front line of American politics. In 1883, he met Terence Powderly, who was then the mayor of Scranton, Pennsylvania. More crucially, Powderly was the head of the Knights of Labor, the boisterous and uncontrollable confederation of unions that became the most serious organized workers' movement to emerge in American politics at the time. Labor politics was becoming increasingly high-profile and radical. In 1877, shortly before the publication of *Progress and Poverty*, a railroad strike that began in Maryland had spread to multiple states. The unrest became known as the Great Upheaval. The strikes were eventually put down by federal troops, setting the scene for a more militant era of economic conflict. Work stoppages, industrial violence and class conflict surged across the newly industrialized parts of America.

Powderly had become committed to George's ideas after reading and corresponding with him, and he was not alone. Many of the members of the Knights of Labor were immigrants from Ireland who were positively disposed to George after his advocacy for Irish tenants. In 1886, George was nominated as the candidate of the United Labor Party (ULP) to contest New York City's mayoral election. The pact with the Knights was an enormous boon to George in terms of his electoral reach, bolting his ideas onto a thriving—if rowdy and potentially unmanageable—political movement.

To modern readers, George's moral crusade to liberate the world from the scourge of private land monopolies may well make the Prophet of San Francisco sound like a budding socialist or a proto-communist thinker. But while George was a radical, and even a populist, the core of his views separated him from the growing political left in late nineteenth-century America. George argued that workers were impoverished by the landlords extracting ever-growing quantities of rent from both labor and productive investment, but he did not really believe that trade unionism was the means by which that could be remedied. Indeed, his bestselling book had gone into some detail about why strikes were one of the most ineffective remedies against poverty, concluding that striking was "necessarily destructive of the very things which workmen seek to gain through them—wealth and freedom."[23]

George also diverged from the burgeoning left in his relentless advocacy for free trade. Protectionism, George believed, was a violation of fundamental human freedoms, just as land monopolies were. "Protective tariffs are as much applications of force as are blockading squadrons," wrote George in 1886 in his next enormously successful book, *Protection or Free Trade*.[24] "What protection teaches us, is to do to ourselves in time of peace what enemies seek to do to us in time of war." Unions and their members were, at best, torn over the issues of trade. Many union members and leaders, Powderly among them, were in favor of high tariffs to protect American workers from the ravages of foreign competition.

But for the time, both George and the Knights of Labor shared a vision. They hoped to lift the boot from the necks of working people in the industrialized world—whose boot it was exactly could be worked out later. The mayor of New York would have no control over trade policy, so disagreements over tariffs could be quietly sidelined. In the view of George and his supporters, the struggle against the landed classes could attract supporters from places that organized labor and socialist campaigners would never be able to reach. The arguments in *Progress and Poverty* made clear that industrial workers, the growing middle classes, small businessmen and even many successful capitalists should not be on different sides of the great political battle of their era: their productive activity was being leeched by the same cabal of lazy landowners. George's quasi-religious proselytizing made him attractive to middle-class social reformers and liberals who were far more wary of organized labor. The cause of land taxation even attracted a coterie of progressive industrialists like Tom L. Johnson, who turned from his own successful streetcar business to politics after reading George's work, and Joseph Fels, a millionaire soap manufacturer who funded a variety of Georgist causes.

From the outset, the ramshackle electoral coalition that George headed was straining under its breadth. Six months before his attempt to be elected as mayor of New York City, a demonstration in favor of an eight-hour working day in Chicago's Haymarket Square turned into one of the most violent episodes in the history of the American labor movement. On May 4, a member of the crowd hurled a homemade bomb into the ranks of the police. An exchange of gunfire followed, leaving a dozen attendees and policemen dead and hundreds injured. Four men were eventually executed for planning the bombing. More radical members of the United Labor Party—which was nominating George for mayor—wanted to hear its leaders mount a full-throated defense of the accused, while moderates feared that the violence would drive middle-class ULP supporters into the hands of the establishment.

It was easy for George's critics to portray him as a Trojan horse for anarchy and upheaval. *Puck*, an enormously popular illustrated periodical, lambasted him: the cartoon on the cover of the magazine's preelection issue in 1886, published less than a week before New Yorkers went to the polls, depicted a gigantic vagrant pushing a family away from its dinner table, an enormous copy of *Progress and Poverty* tucked into his pocket.[25] George's opponent, Abram Hewitt, suggested that voting for the ULP would bring the violence of the French Revolution to American shores. Thomas Scott Preston, the Catholic vicar-general of the Archdiocese of New York, issued a public address that George's views were "unsound, unsafe and contrary to the teachings of the Church."[26] The full weight of the establishment—religious, political and journalistic—was stacked against George. But voters could be forgiven if they were not always entirely familiar with the precise differences between a Georgist platform and a more radical left-wing one in which land was just part of the social order to be upturned—indeed, holding the ULP together as a political movement had required the considerable differences between those objectives to be blurred.

On November 2, 1886, Henry George and the United Labor Party received 31 percent of the vote. George lost to Hewitt but managed to beat a young Theodore Roosevelt, the Republican Party candidate, who came in third place. In the context of the two-party political system, the entrenched interests of the New York Democratic Party and its Tammany Hall machine, the short time frame of the campaign and the lack of electoral experience on the part of the ULP, the result was a remarkable achievement for George. It had been just seven years since he leapt from obscurity into the global limelight. Two decades before running for mayor, he had been begging in the streets of San Francisco. But it was a loss nevertheless. It would also prove to be the high-water mark of George's personal political career. He never held elected office. His allies whispered about the corruption they had been pitted against, but no concrete proof of fraud was forthcoming. George was defeated again a year later, in 1887, in the race to become New York's secretary of state, and by a landslide.

In the years that followed, George wrote and spoke internationally, leaving the representation of his ideas in elected politics to his many followers. The National Single Tax League was established in 1890, with representatives from every American state. In the same year, George traveled to Australia, conducting a frenetic lecture tour on free trade and the taxation of land. He spoke in Sydney, Melbourne, Brisbane and Adelaide, cities where his already-large following in the British colony was growing.[27] But the most radical period of his political life was over. In 1892, he endorsed Grover Cleveland, the Democratic Party candidate for president, upsetting many of his previous comrades in the labor movement. But the economic trends that had fueled his rise in the first place were more alive than ever. Yet another debilitating banking panic struck in 1893, triggering a wave of corporate failures; American unemployment surged, tripling to over 10 percent for five years.

George returned to electoral politics one final time, to contest the mayoral election of New York City again in the autumn of 1897. This time he ran as an independent candidate. After a long day of campaign speeches in the city, he returned late one night to the Union Square Hotel. Early the next morning, on October 29, George suffered a massive stroke and died. He was fifty-eight. His wife, Annie, and his son, Henry George Jr., one of the infants for whom he had begged in the street three decades prior, were by his side. It was less than a week before the vote. A shocked crowd assembled outside the Union Square Hotel as the news of his death rippled through the city.

Two days later, at Grand Central Palace, the cavernous exhibition hall that stood on Lexington Avenue in Manhattan, George's body lay in state. Thousands of men and women streamed into the building. As they arrived at George's coffin, New York's *The Sun* described the scene. "Sobbing women lifted their children to look upon the face of the 'martyr.' Tears became contagious, and rough men sobbed without shame."[28] According to *The New York Times*, "no demonstration of popular feeling on the death of a public man since Lincoln's body lay in the City Hall has been so imposing in extent and character as that of yesterday. Call it, if you will, hero worship; but its object was really a hero."[29] Despite the widespread news of his death, George received more than twenty-one thousand votes in the mayoral election.

George's influence as a writer and a firebrand would far outstrip and outlast his electoral record. *Progress and Poverty* was not just a popular book, but quite possibly the most influential piece of political writing of an entire century. There were no bestseller lists in 1879, but by the estimate of George's son Henry George Jr., it sold two million copies in its twenty-five years in print.[30] Given the many translated and abridged editions and the anthologies of George's wider works, the figure may well be a conservative estimate. Over one hundred thousand copies were sold in Britain in the 1880s alone by just one of the book's two publishers.[31] It has been suggested that during the final decade of the nineteenth century, George's book came second only to the Bible in the number of copies sold in the United States. Given its enormous popularity and George's huge influence at the time, that argument is easy to believe.

The small Georgist clubs that sprouted across America in the final decades of the nineteenth century had a huge influence on the country's political life through the Democratic Party, promoting and organizing the election of Georgists into office. By the end of the nineteenth century, America had Georgists at every level of municipal and state government, and many congressmen cited George as an influence. Between 1907 and 1910, Edward Robeson Taylor was the mayor of San Francisco, bringing George's principles back to the city where *Progress and Poverty* was written. The movement was popular in the industrial Midwest: George's friend Tom L. Johnson became the mayor of the bustling industrial hub of Cleveland, Ohio, in 1901, and served in that position until 1909. Hazen Stuart Pingree, another businessman turned social reformer, was not only mayor of Detroit from 1889 to 1897 but also governor of Michigan for four years after that. Joseph Jay Pastoriza, another fan of George's, was briefly mayor of Houston, Texas, before dying in office in 1917. Pastoriza had used a log cabin in a growing area of the city as both the headquarters of the local Single Tax movement and a visual demonstration of the inequities of land.[32] He had bought the plot beneath the cabin in 1903 for $350 and said he wouldn't sell it until it was worth $5,000. He had to wait just eight years.

Around the world, experiments in applying land value taxes were beginning in earnest too. For the most fanatically committed Georgists in America, promoting the cause of land value taxation at the ballot box was not enough. The true believers went as far as to found their own colonies, following in the footsteps of the Puritans who landed at Plymouth Rock. In 1894, Fairhope, Alabama, became the first settlement explicitly founded on Georgist lines, by a group of true believers from Iowa. One thousand miles from Fairhope, members of the Des Moines Single Tax Club were searching for a way to opt out from the mainstream of American politics. Ernest Berry Gaston, another journalist, spearheaded the migration. "The present social and economic order is doomed," Gaston wrote, spelling out the plans for his model community.[33]

The would-be colonists assembled the Fairhope Industrial Association (later the Fairhope Single Tax Corporation) and bought 132 waterfront acres in Alabama's Mobile Bay.[34] Before the handful of initial residents of Fairhope arrived, they had already established their own form of government, with voting rights for men and women. They had also instituted their own scrip (a form of local money). The society was rudimentary at best in the beginning: they lacked any connection by road to the rest of the state. By 1910, the town had 590 residents, and by 1920, it had 853.[35] The town's governance, though based on George's principles, had some flaws in practice. The town did not have any government as such, with decisions made by the shareholders of the company that owned the land, leaving the tenants who arrived without $250 to contribute essentially disenfranchised. The initially freewheeling model was slowly absorbed into a more ordinary American municipal government system. But the Fairhope Single Tax Corporation still exists today as a not-for-profit corporation, reporting $12 million in assets and 4,400 acres of land.[36] Other colonies were established: Arden, Delaware, and Free Acres, New Jersey, were founded in 1900 and 1910 respectively. All the towns still exist, though none are run as the utopian colonies they were established to be.

Today, hundreds of millions of families around the world have a monument to Georgist thinking in their homes. In 1903, designer Lizzie Magie, a resident of Arden, Delaware, created a board game that aimed to demonstrate the Single Tax views on land monopolies. In The Landlord's Game, players traverse the board, snapping up as large an amount of property as rapidly as possible. The more concentrated the holdings are, the more lucrative they can be to the buyer. Unfortunate opponents who land on another player's land are forced to scrape together the rent, until all but one is bankrupted. In 1935, American game and toy manufacturer Parker Brothers purchased the rights to the game. Today, it is better known as Monopoly.

The Prophet of San Francisco's nickname had been adopted in jest, but for the budding left-wing political movements of the late nineteenth and early twentieth centuries, Henry George was as close as it got to a religious leader. "I cannot fully express my gratitude to you for the light your writings have thrown on problems which have filled my mind since ever I could think," Keir Hardie, the founder of the British Labour Party and its first leader in Parliament, wrote in a letter to George in 1884.[37] In 1906, in a survey of forty-five Labour-affiliated representatives in the House of Commons, Karl Marx, the father of modern socialism, received just two mentions. Henry George's works received twelve, only two fewer than the Bible.[38]

In 1896, a young man who would change the face of history picked up a copy of *Progress and Poverty* in London. The reader was not another British liberal, or an American trade unionist, but a young Chinese doctor living in exile from his home country. Thirty-year-old Sun Yat-sen had been closely involved with a failed uprising against China's faltering Qing dynasty the previous year, and he was on the run. Sun was a democrat and a nationalist, but beyond overthrowing China's monarchy and installing a republic, his ideas for what the country should do afterwards were still limited. George had a profound impact on Sun's coalescing aims for China's modernization and development. The "equalization of land rights" became one of Sun's central principles. He eventually—if only briefly—became the first president of the Republic of China, ending four thousand years of royal dynasties. His encounter with the book guaranteed that George's political influence, already cemented in America and Europe, would shape the future of Asia too.

Henry George spent most of his life focused on American politics, but it was perhaps not a surprise that his ideas gained traction in the parts of the world where ownership of land was far more concentrated in the hands of a wealthy elite. Even with the ballooning inequality in America during George's life, land was still far more evenly distributed across America than anywhere else, and landownership was far more common among people with otherwise modest means. Sun Yat-sen was not alone among foreign revolutionaries who took George's ideas for their own platforms. Mexican revolutionary and eventual president Francisco Madero, Cuban nationalist José Martí and Alexander Kerensky, the Russian reformer and leader of the short-lived Russian Republic, were among the proponents of George's ideas.

As the young Sun Yat-sen was assembling his ideas on how to govern China, a small part of the country was already conducting one of the very few experiments in the institution of the Single Tax. In 1898, Wilhelm Schrameier, a thirty-eight-year-old colonial administrator for the German Empire, took over the governance of Tsingtao (modern-day Qingdao) on China's northeast coast.[39] Schrameier had been a member of the Deutscher Bund für Bodenreform (German Land Reform Association), formed in 1898 from a group of smaller Georgist organizations. Land-owners faced a tax of 6 percent of the value of their properties each year, about half of the rental value, and a tax on any increases in its value when sold—a far more aggressive version of the system David Lloyd George would later propose in Limehouse. The colony had no other sources of revenue at all. The bold experiment was cut short by the outbreak of the First World War in 1914 and Germany's loss of its handful of Asian outposts.

Today, it seems difficult to believe that a little more than a hundred years ago, land was such an overwhelming issue in public life. At the turn of the twentieth century the issue animated progressives and revolution-aries, and sparked a movement that was almost religious in nature, one of the first genuinely international political and social causes of the modern world. Politics in much of the world was being shaped by debates we still find fairly recognizable now, but the issue of landownership and its eco-nomic consequences has almost entirely disappeared from political life and public debate. The Monopoly boards in living rooms around the world may be the greatest vestige of Georgism left today. The wave of popular-ity for land-based explanations for the ills of the industrial world was cresting—it was headed for a crash.

FOUR

Shaky Ground

n June of 1881, Henry George had not yet left New York for his very earliest political journeys overseas to Britain and Ireland. He was still a relatively minor figure in transatlantic politics, unknown to most of his future fans or critics and far from the titan he would become over the decade that followed. But in London, one of George's early readers felt that he already had the measure of the man and his ideas. He did not think much of them. George exhibited "the repulsive presumption and arrogance which is displayed by all panacea-mongers," the critic groused in a letter to a friend.[1]

The condemnation did not come from one of the dukes and barons that George had outraged, speaking in fear for the future of their prized land assets. Nor was it written by some reactionary thinker upset by the radicalism of George's proposals. The author was a sixty-three-year-old Karl Marx, then living in a tenement flat in Belsize Park, in the north of London. Marx would die two years later, only briefly overlapping with George's period of real international fame. But his objection to George and his ideas would grow in importance long after his death. "The whole thing is therefore simply an attempt, decked out with socialism, to save capitalist domination and indeed to establish it afresh on an even wider basis than its present one," Marx complained.

George lived on for another fourteen years after Marx's death and never had much to say about the German philosopher in public. There is no evidence that the two men ever corresponded in private either. When the father of modern socialism died, George contributed a short letter to a memorial publication. "No difference of opinion can lessen the esteem which I feel for the man who so steadfastly, so patiently, and so self-sacrificingly labored for the freedom of the oppressed and the elevation of the downtrodden," he wrote. But in private, George did not hold back his real opinions, which were less effusive. In his letters, George called Marx the "prince of muddleheads," judging him to be a superficial thinker who lacked analytical and logical prowess.[2] The Prophet of San Francisco thought it was a shame that some of his friends and associates held the author of *The Communist Manifesto* in such high regard.

A large part of Henry George's working life had been dedicated to the effort to bridge a growing political gap between the burgeoning left-wing movements on either side of the Atlantic and the classes of middle-class progressives and small farmers, which he believed had a better chance of actually carrying his ideas to electoral success. During his life and for some time afterwards, it seemed as if he had more or less won the battle, cobbling together a fragile alliance with considerable success. Even Friedrich Engels, Marx's lifelong friend and financial benefactor, saw the upside to George's strong showing in New York politics in the 1880s, noting that he had done a better job of harnessing the labor movement in America than the early communists had managed.[3] In the first decade of the twentieth century, George's influence on the American Democratic Party, the British Labour movement and most of the progressive parties in Europe surpassed Marx's by a country mile. At the time, the German was held in high esteem on the more radical international left, but as just one of several socialist intellectuals of a similarly high stature—unlike George, he was not yet anyone's messiah.

Though George's followers could hardly have known it at the time, his movement was reaching its historical peak immediately before the First World War. The Single Taxers would never again assemble such widespread support or have so many influential backers. Within the space of just two decades, the movement had been fatally weakened as a political force. By the middle of the twentieth century, it would be a practical irrelevance. New economic and political forces were about to smother George's ideas and their political influence. The Single Tax lost its natural working-class supporters to trade union movements and socialist politics that lacked a special role for land, and lost its middle-class support to a rising conservative, antiradical sentiment in Western politics that was assembling in opposition to the growing power and influence of the international left. The Georgists found themselves at the center of an ideological pincer movement from which they did not survive.

Back in 1881, the grumblings of the author of *Das Kapital* could be waved away as an academic disagreement of little importance—perhaps tinged with a little professional jealousy, given George's growing acclaim. But in the decades to come, the political chaos of the early twentieth century in Europe brought Marx's dismissive views of George to center stage. Socialists and communists, who unlike George saw no specific and crucial role for land in their explanation of the world's ills, would assert themselves as the greatest influence on left-wing movements around the world. George believed in a big tent where radicals of every stripe could club together, even where they did not agree on the specifics. The Marxists who rose to prominence had far less appreciation for ideological variety. They, not the followers of Henry George, would become the aristocracy of the global left, leaving no room for junior partners.

At the same time, the backlash to political radicalism was growing in strength. During the 1886 New York mayoral election, the Democratic Party candidate and eventual winner Abram Hewitt had summoned the long-dead ghosts of the French Revolution to malign George's fragile coalition of trade unionists and land-focused reformers. Hewitt's tactic was mocked as an appeal to a long-gone era: a New York voter would have had to be almost eighty years old to even remember the end of the Napoleonic Wars in 1815 and almost a century old to have lived during the most intense violence of the 1790s.

But at the end of the First World War, appealing to the specter of historical revolutions was no longer necessary. The war had killed twenty million people and left the global political order in tatters. More than six centuries of Ottoman and Habsburg rule in Europe came to an abrupt end. The German kaiser was overthrown after a Naval mutiny at Kiel, and local workers' councils were established across the country in the aftermath. Europe was in flux. But more than any other event, the transformation of Russian politics struck fear into the establishment around the world. The Romanov dynasty that had ruled Russia for three centuries was deposed in February 1917. A flimsy coalition of liberals, moderates and socialists replaced the tsar, and was itself overthrown only nine months later. The Bolshevik government under Vladimir Ilyich Lenin took power by force and the Russian Civil War began. Hundreds of thousands of Russians who were loyal in some way or another to the previous regime fled the country, including its businessmen, merchants and aristocrats. The Russian royal family was executed in a basement in the Urals in July 1918. The change struck fear into the establishment almost everywhere. Prewar worries about Georgism and other social reform movements looked quaint by contrast. Lenin wasn't advocating gradual tax increases on the landholdings of Russia's aristocrats; he was having them lined up and shot.

Lenin and Henry George never crossed paths. When George died, the Russian revolutionary was twenty-seven years old and had just begun a three-year period of exile in Siberia after a conviction by the tsarist courts for sedition. But the future Soviet leader did rub shoulders with Georgists on at least one occasion during his time outside of Russia, when he was already committed full-time to the cause of revolution. In 1907, the Russian Social Democratic Labour Party, the forerunner of the Communist Party, held a conference in London. The gathering, in a church hall in Islington, was attended by not just Lenin but Leon Trotsky and Joseph Stalin too. In one of the more unusual crossover moments in intellectual history, the future political giants of the Soviet Union found themselves shaking hands with the Georgist soap magnate Joseph Fels. Fels had moved to England to expand his business and had continued his political philanthropy there too. He extended a loan of £1,700, around $200,000 in today's money, to the Russian dissidents.[4] He pressed a Single Tax leaflet into Lenin's hand, making the loan one of the most expensive (and unsuccessful) marketing opportunities in political history.

Fels's generosity towards the Russian Marxists, like George's gushing memorial note after Marx's death, was an example of a profound political naivety and a clear demonstration of how the Single Taxers would struggle with the new and more violent era. Fels was one of the most important financial backers of Single Tax causes, giving money to a movement that not only had no interest in George's work, but that would prove willing to deploy violent means to crush its perceived enemies. Attempting to seek out friends and alliances across the political spectrum may have been a noble goal in itself during a more placid era, but it made the sometimes-softhearted Georgists an easy mark for more ruthless parts of the political left in the turbulent years of the early twentieth century.

In truth, Marx had been right about George and many of his followers, who really did want a more effective and just version of capitalism, and did not aim to overthrow it entirely. George was an instinctive individualist, despite his cautious efforts to balance his public persona and maintain his alliances with a variety of socialists and labor organizers. Where Fels saw another gang of reformers in the conference hall in Islington, with a shared foe in Russia's landowners, the men to whom he was opening his wallet recognized him as a member of a hostile class. To them, he had far more in common with the aristocrats they aimed to overthrow at home than he did with their revolutionary movement. Fels did not make much of an impression on Lenin; in later correspondence, explaining to friends in London why the loan's repayment was delayed, he referred to the Virginia-born son of German-Jewish immigrants as "the Englishman." The loan's repayment, due in 1908, never arrived.[5]

The Single Taxers hadn't just unwittingly assisted the Marxists, who were hostile to their proposals. The movement had also proved to be an unintentional launchpad for many socialists and communists in the first place. The Irish-American playwright George Bernard Shaw, who had seen Henry George speak in 1882 during the American's first trip to Britain, credited George with opening his eyes to the economic problems of the world. But he also said that *Progress and Poverty* had taken him to the threshold of socialism.[6] Like many of George's young disciples, Shaw piled on through, drifting further to the political left. For the next seven decades, the Soviet Union provided financial, logistical and diplomatic support to the regimes and groups with which it was aligned. Georgism had no equivalent base of power.

Perhaps the greatest example of the massive ideological shift that fatally hamstrung Henry George's supporters occurred in China. In 1912 Sun Yat-sen briefly became the country's first president, putting an end to four millennia of dynastic rule. The overthrow of the Qing dynasty ushered in four chaotic decades in Chinese politics, and though Sun was highly regarded across the country, he possessed far less military strength than his rivals. By the 1920s, China had descended into a period of internecine strife, as powerful warlords scrapped with one another for territory and political influence. In the years after his short time in office, Sun's personal commitment to taxing the value of land had only grown, as he determined that the approach could help China to develop much more rapidly. His suggestion was thoroughly Georgist: He proposed that landowners pay a 1 percent tax on the value of their land.[7] Landowners would declare the value of their assets for tax purposes, and the government would be able to purchase their land for the same price. The method was a clever suggestion to prevent landlords from deliberately underestimating the extent of their wealth.

In 1920, Sun had published *The International Development of China*, the policy road map of how his party, the Kuomintang, intended to modernize the country. While illustrating his proposal for a huge new port in Shanghai, he explained how such an enormous endeavor could be funded by such a poor nation: the urbanization and industrialization of the area could be paid for by the uplift in the value of the land around it. "If within forty years we could develop a city as large as Philadelphia, not to say New York, the land value alone will be sufficient to pay off the capital invested in its development."[8] Sun had even hired Wilhelm Schrameier, the former German colonial official who had implemented the influential regime of land taxation in Tsingtao, as an adviser.

With a growing movement behind him in the 1920s, Sun might well have risen to prominence once again in the fast-moving political flux of the new republic. But his dreams of rapid economic modernization for China were not realized. In 1924, Sun's health began to deteriorate rapidly, and he was diagnosed with cancer of the liver. In Beijing on March 12, 1925, Sun Yat-sen died at the age of fifty-eight, the same age that Henry George had reached. Like George, he died with much left to do. Schrameier died in the same year, hit by a car in Canton (modern-day Guangzhou).

There was little time for much in the way of domestic economic policy after Sun's death. His successor, Chiang Kai-shek, consolidated the Kuomintang's power and became the de facto leader of the splintered country in 1928 but spent most of the following quarter of a century in a series of brutal civil and international conflicts. Three years after Sun's death, the first stage of the Chinese Civil War began, pitting the Kuomintang against the Communist Party. The conflict was only interrupted by the country's horrendous experiences at the hands of Imperial Japan in the Second World War, after which it immediately resumed. Chiang was eventually defeated in 1949 by the Communists fighting under Mao Zedong. Some of Sun's successors in the left-wing faction of the Kuomintang folded themselves into the new People's Republic, where they still occupy a token position in the Chinese legislature. Chiang and most of the party fled to Taiwan, where the Republic of China soldiered on. The country ended up as the only nation on earth in which the principle of land value taxation is enshrined in the constitution.

The political shifts of the early twentieth century proved to be enormously disadvantageous for Georgists around the world. But it was not the only source of strife for the Single Taxers. In the increasingly industrialized world, aristocrats who had feared for their positions of power and wealth in the 1880s were being smothered, not just by politics, but by new economic realities. In 1921, the *Estates Gazette*, a British periodical that covered the land and property markets, noted that about a quarter of land in England and Wales had been sold during the previous four years.[9] When George published *Progress and Poverty*, the wealth of Europe's dukes, viscounts and barons was already beginning to wane. But the effects of a long agricultural depression and the transformation of the industrial economy were turning a slow bleed into a hemorrhage for the agrarian elite. The politics of land was being transformed, but not to the advantage of the Georgists. The twentieth century would not be the era of land monopoly, but of widespread landownership.

In Britain, where Henry George's ideas had taken hold more than anywhere else, the move away from Georgism was particularly important and rapid. America's municipal governments were peppered with Georgists, but Britain's government had made the implementation of a land value tax one of its signature policies at the national level and threatened to undermine a millennium of aristocratic privilege. Even after land taxes were cemented in law, the procedure of implementation proved to be extremely difficult. Economic historian Sam Watling notes that the process was a nightmare for the small central government of Edwardian Britain, which distributed millions of forms for self-valuation of properties to landowners up and down the country. The Valuation Office, set up in 1910 to carry out the enormous exercise, believed that it might finish the tax by 1917. In its early years, the bureaucratic task cost far more than the revenue raised by the taxes.

The endeavor was already proving difficult before August 1914, when the ambitions of David Lloyd George and the other new liberals unraveled. The outbreak of the First World War punctured hopes for a land value tax in more ways than one. In practical terms, it delayed the vital process of actually valuing Britain's land until the war ended. The conflagration in Europe upturned British politics too. The Liberal Party, the main vehicle for land tax advocacy in Britain, was torn into two competing factions during the process. Lloyd George became prime minister of a coalition government, a pact he continued—in no small part out of personal vanity—into the 1918 election that followed the end of the conflict. The Liberals lost seventy-three seats—and with them, a huge chunk of legislative support for any kind of land tax.

Britain's electoral politics was in a process of rapid transformation. The Representation of the People Act was passed in 1918, less than three months after the revolution in Russia and before the war had even ended. It ushered in near-universal suffrage, and the number of votes cast in the first postwar election rose by more than 100 percent from the prewar level. It was the largest single extension of voting rights in the country's history. Just a few years earlier, the political debate over a wider franchise, particularly for women, had been bitterly contentious. But the act sailed through the House of Commons with overwhelming support. As five years of total war inched towards an end, support for the wider voting rights—in recognition of the contribution to the war effort by both working-class men without property and female workers at home—had become overwhelming. The advent of universal democracy would turn politics upside down in the countries where landownership was most concentrated among a narrow elite.

That change put the former opponents of a wider franchise in a tough spot. The mass electorate, which was far poorer and less educated than the more limited group of voters that preceded it, was expected to be hostile to the Conservative Party and vulnerable to the forked tongues of socialist demagogues. The December 1910 election, the last before the war began, had ended in a dead heat between the Liberals and Conservatives, with 5.2 million votes cast. By the time of the general election in 1922, that figure had risen to almost 14 million. The grand realignment of British politics was becoming clear: the Labour Party took 142 seats, surpassing the Liberals for the first time. Even as the Conservative Party maintained its position as the preeminent force in British politics, the fear that old methods were failing was widespread. Conservative politicians knew that the party needed to establish a new appeal to voters in the lower middle classes and industrial working classes, or else run the risk of being swept away like the Liberals.

Among the thinkers and politicians wondering how to retain the political preeminence of the Tory party was Noel Skelton, a freshly minted MP who had been elected in 1922. His political career was a limited one: he died in 1935 having never held ministerial office. Like Henry George, the influence of his writing would far outlast his presence in frontline politics. Writing in *The Spectator* in 1923, Skelton coined a now-common phrase: "What will that avail," Skelton asked, "unless Conservatism breaks its silence and makes clear to the nation that it, too, has a vision of the future—of a property-owning democracy, master of its own life, made four-square and secure and able therefore to withstand the shrill and angry gales which, in the new era's uneasy dawn, sweep across the world of men?"[10]

Skelton, with his idea of a "property-owning democracy," was proposing something both radical and ancient. It was an inversion of centuries of English political logic. For hundreds of years after the very earliest appointments to the House of Commons in the thirteenth century, the franchise had been limited to property holders. The thinking went that a property qualification would make sure both that electors had some element of personal responsibility themselves and that they had something at stake to lose if things went wrong. The link between landholding and voting had only been gradually weakened by a series of bitterly contested reform acts throughout the nineteenth century, most of which were opposed by the Tories at the time. It was time for the argument to be flipped on its head: if the right to vote would never again be limited to people who had property to conserve, then Conservatives—if they hoped to win elections—would have to make sure that most of the newly enfranchised people possessed some property.

The Conservatives had a new reason for urgency too. After the 1923 election, the Labour Party took office for the first time, making Ramsay MacDonald prime minister, with the support of the much-reduced Liberal Party. Stanley Baldwin, who led the Conservative Party for most of the 1920s and 1930s, had not mentioned housing in either of his election addresses in 1922 or 1923. But local governments in cities run by Labour councils around the country had been building accommodations for grateful voters, and the new Labour government was increasing the subsidies to build them.[11] By the time of the 1924 election, the massive shift in the Conservative Party strategy was clear: Baldwin named housing the second-gravest domestic challenge next to unemployment, promising to massively increase the rate of building and improve the slums across industrial urban Britain. Political competition over housing was underway. By the 1930s, house-building reached its historical zenith. More than 250,000 private homes were completed each year between 1934 and 1938 in England and Wales.[12] More houses were built by the private sector than ever before—or, indeed, ever since. Over the past thirty years, fewer than 140,000 homes have been built by private enterprise on average each year in England and Wales.

Even today, the suburbs that defined the era of rapid house-building are peppered with the same popular, modest semidetached housing. The suburban rings that surround parts of Britain's industrial cities—Roundhay in Leeds, Hall Green in Birmingham or West Derby in Liverpool—are a physical monument to the social and economic change that was afoot. On the outskirts of London, the shift is visible at even greater scale: housing snakes out of the northwest of the city into Middlesex, following the path of the Metropolitan line, the capital's first commuter railway. The expansion of mass transit and automobile transportation made huge swathes of formerly agricultural land habitable for workers in British cities. A century later, the areas are largely unchanged and continue to be sought after by young families, quite unlike the socialized housing that followed later in the century. The private construction boom in the 1930s was undoubtedly the country's most successful period of house-building, marking the beginning of the era of mass homeownership in Britain.

At first glance, the political philosophies of Skelton and George might not look so wildly different. The emergence of a large and newly well-housed middle class, and the decline of slum landlords in the cities, paired with the steady decline of the power of agricultural land barons were all things that both men would have cheered. But the visions of the two men diverged, crucially, when it came to land. Skelton's vision had no particular role for the world's oldest asset. It aimed for a more equitable distribution of property, not the effective abolition of private landownership that Georgists favored. While the two ideas bore a passing resemblance to one another in their short-term goals, the eventual consequences of Skelton's project were wildly out of step with George's dream—and would eventually make land more, not less, important to economic and political life in Britain.

From a partisan perspective, the policies did exactly what Skelton and others had hoped they would do. Suburban England's semidetached homes are a standing reminder of the social and economic revolution that devastated Georgism as a political movement. The massive program of private house-building was creating a new class of owners with something to defend and a far greater affinity with the Conservative Party. Siding with radicals of any stripe, Georgists included, raised the risk of losing their precious new assets. Property-owning democracy was still in its early days at the end of the 1930s, but the proportion of families who owned their own homes had risen to something like a third of the population.[13] By the end of the twentieth century, homeownership climbed to become the dominant form of housing across the country, with almost three in every four British households living in owner-occupied properties. The new middle classes were a natural bulwark against any proposals that the land should be heavily taxed. What had once been the landed gentry was now the landed majority.

As the years went on, Georgism picked up something of an unhelpful reputation too. The semi-revolutionary spirit that animated the Single Tax movement in the 1890s had passed. By the interwar period, it was sometimes associated with a streak of tiresome middle-class do-gooding. Sinclair Lewis, a leading satirist who had once worked as a janitor at Helicon Home Colony, a utopian commune, occasionally took aim at Single Taxers with his wounding pen. In Lewis's *Ann Vickers*, published in 1933, the dullness of the titular main character's husband is illuminated by his decision to attend a Single Tax Advancement Program dinner on the evening of his own wedding.[14] While socialists and communists were taking up the banner of dangerous and sometimes sexy radicalism, George's followers acquired a reputation for hectoring, or even crankery, which they have never entirely shaken off.

The study of economics was changing as well, similarly to the disadvantage of the Single Taxers. While the great classical economists of the eighteenth and early nineteenth centuries had seen the inequities of landownership in very similar ways to Henry George, the economists of his own era, part of an increasingly formal and model-based discipline, were much more critical. Alfred Marshall, the author of *Principles of Economics*, was the founding father of the modern discipline and an emphatic critic of Georgism.[15] He argued both that land was by no means the only source of rents in the economy and that George had offered no unified view of saving or productivity, two of the overwhelming focuses of the newly influential academic economists of the era. The leading lights of the young neoclassical movement in economics saw George as more of a political proselytizer than a student of their own subject. Mark Blaug, an economic historian, suggests that Henry George's work "was thirty years out of date the day it was published."[16] The dismal science was moving on, and largely without the vital role for land that had animated political economists a century earlier.

There were still smaller victories to be had for Georgists in some parts of the world. An early-twentieth-century battle for a land value tax in Denmark didn't flounder as it had elsewhere. The Retsforbundet, Denmark's Georgist party, managed to maintain its place in the Danish parliament and held the balance of power in it as late as the 1950s. The country still has a modest land value tax (of sorts) today. Australia's infatuation with George led to lasting taxes on the value of some land at the state level. But relative to the influence and heft that might have been expected by an observer in the years before the First World War, George's followers were reduced to a rump in almost all of the places where they had once seemed to be on an unstoppable ascent.

In America, the Single Taxers were diluted into the pottage of the American progressive movement. Some of the activists who had been the most ardent Georgists in the very late nineteenth century began to pursue a variety of other goals—whether for direct democracy, the regulation of public utilities or the political rights of women. The once-monomaniacal focus on land was ebbing. Many prominent progressives influenced by George cheered the establishment of the national income tax in 1913, even though the decision shifted the tax base away from the land.

The change in the American political landscape went far beyond the intellectual focus of progressives. The United States was entering a new era of land and housing policy too. The Federal Farm Loan Act was passed in 1916 with the aim of boosting credit for America's small agricultural landowners. It instituted the Federal Farm Loan Board, the first of the government-sponsored enterprises that would eventually pop up across the American land and housing market. Small farmers could now borrow up to $10,000 in low-interest loans, backed by the value of their land.[17] The impulse to support small landholders didn't stop with agriculture. A year later, a campaign by the National Association of Real Estate Boards encouraging Americans to own their own home was taken over by the Department of Labor. Herbert Hoover, who became commerce secretary in 1921, was an enthusiastic supporter of homeownership and its promotion by the government.

Hoover was convinced not only that homeownership was good in itself, but that the economic health of the nation revolved around the capital-intensive real estate industry. As with Noel Skelton's plan for a property-owning democracy in Britain, it was easy to see why the new forms of government intervention to support small farms and would-be homeowners appealed to people who might previously have been enamored with Henry George's ideas. The shift was framed as a part of a broader trust-busting and monopoly-breaking crusade. The tenant who simply wanted his own modest slice of the pie was being pitted against agricultural monopolies and slum landlords. But instead of undermining the idea of private property in land, the changes entrenched the principle. The new regime of support for small landowners created a broader group of supporters that would be disadvantaged by any radical changes to the status quo.

By the standards of anywhere in Europe, America had always been something of property-owning democracy, with widespread homeownership, especially in the countryside. At the turn of the twentieth century, about 47 percent of Americans owned their own home, a figure that rose to 60 percent and higher in several Western and Midwestern states.[18] But the shifting sands of global politics gave a fresh impetus to the government to directly encourage even higher levels of ownership, especially in the cities that had boomed from the mid-nineteenth century onwards. In urban America, the combination of high levels of immigration, uncertain tenancies and febrile industrial relations was a breeding ground for left-wing politics that politicians—not just Republicans but many Democrats too—were keen to guard against.

"Sell a man a piece of land or a house and you have removed a great factor in radicalism or Bolshevism," said Joseph Paul Day, a real estate magnate of the era, in 1920.[19] Day had every reason to fear radicalism. In a puff piece in *Life* magazine in 1937, he was described as "the greatest real-estate salesman of all time" who had netted many millions of dollars for himself selling thousands and thousands of lots of land in New York and elsewhere. "He has founded a great American fortune, which, because it is tied up in real estate, will keep on growing long after he dies," the piece noted, illuminating some of the damaging dynamics of landownership.[20] The plots that Day sold, for himself and others, had surged in value as new transport links popped up in the outer boroughs of New York City—links which the agents, auctioneers and developers had of course done little to pay for.

Another of America's periodic land booms was beginning too. This was the original era of selling sunshine: In Florida, the investment frenzy for land reached a fever pitch, causing a surge in prices and speculation. The population of the state had roughly tripled in the space of thirty years. The frenzy was so wild by its peak in the mid-1920s that buyers could flip land purchased in the morning later that same afternoon for enormous profit. Ads promoting small-scale real estate investment in the tropical paradise of the Everglades popped up everywhere during the peak of the mania. Even the infamous Charles Ponzi set up a land sales company in Florida.[21] While he was already on bail for the original scheme with which his name is now eponymous, he swindled buyers out of their money in exchange for worthless swampland.

The construction of American homes surged in the 1920s, and in

1928, Hoover was elected as president, bringing his ownership project into the highest national office. His time in office would be overshadowed by the almighty crash on Wall Street less than a year into his presidency and the crippling depression that followed it. But he, perhaps more than anyone else, planted the seeds of the modern American system of land, housing and the political intervention that surrounds it. Speaking in 1931, the president stated his views emphatically, linking his efforts to raise the homeownership rate to the country's most fundamental principles—its very reason for existing. "That our people should live in their own homes is a sentiment deep in the heart of our race and of American life," he said. Hoover's appeal stretched even further back, to the ancient connection to land and property that was thousands of years in the making: "They never sing songs about a pile of rent receipts. To own one's own home is a physical expression of individualism, of enterprise, of independence, and of the freedom of spirit."[22]

But even as land was disappearing as an issue of major political importance and being relegated to a second-order issue in economics, its importance remained. In some ways, behind the scenes, it was even increasing. In particular, land was becoming dramatically more important as an asset in the practice of moneylending. At the turn of the twentieth century, the availability of mortgage credit was patchy and varied. Down payments were large, and interest rates were high. The lending was often done by insurers, rather than commercial banks, which focused most heavily on business lending. But in the new era, the existing system would not suffice. Greater credit was needed to accomplish the political dream of turning urban

Britons and Americans into homeowners. On both sides of the Atlantic, politicians set out to reinvent the process of lending for land and housing. The business of financing property purchases for ordinary people has boomed ever since. The change has been largest in countries like Britain, where ownership was once the preserve of a wealthy elite. When David Lloyd George stood up to excoriate the British landed gentry in Limehouse in 1909, just around a tenth of British bank lending went to mortgages; today, they account for two thirds of total loans.[23]

By the interwar years, Britain had long since abandoned its ancient aversion to land-based finance that had so incensed the colonists in the run-up to the American Revolution. The number of estate acts, pieces of legislation that changed the property rights associated with a given piece of land, had ballooned through the late eighteenth century and into the early nineteenth.[24] The acts gave the holder of a piece of land greater rights to sell or borrow against it, creating a much more active market for lending. The American attitude that land was a transferable piece of property, which could be freely pledged as collateral to back loans and be foreclosed upon by a creditor, had spread around the world as the last vestiges of feudalism fell away in Europe. British financiers had rediscovered the simple truths that Benjamin Franklin had explained in 1729: land can be turned easily into money, if the law allows it.

The building societies that financed the land and house purchases by Britain's new cohort of property owners grew rapidly in size through the 1920s, particularly after the government's decision to end the gold standard in 1931. Britain's political leaders pursued a policy of cheap money to counteract the slump that had followed in the wake of America's Great Depression. The length of mortgages offered to buyers grew to as long as thirty years, reducing the burden of repayments and raising the number of potential buyers. The size of the deposits required shrank from 20 to 25 percent of the price of the property to as little as 5 percent, and sometimes even less.[25] It was not just the first era of expanding homeownership, but the first mortgage boom. The confluence of cheap money, mass house-building and eager government support was a powerful mix.

In America, the beginning of the Great Depression lit a fire under existing efforts to incentivize homeownership, out of a desire to spark the moribund construction and real estate industries back into life. Unemployment climbed to above 20 percent in 1932 and again in 1934. It would not fall back below 10 percent again until the beginning of the Second World War and the mass mobilization of the country's industrial base. It appeared at the time as if the survival of capitalism was at stake. The risk of offering too many incentives for households to overinvest in land was a long way from the minds of the policymakers attempting to rescue the American economy from total collapse. Foreclosure rates across the country rocketed as landowners struggled to repay their onerous mortgages. By one estimate, prices in Manhattan didn't entirely recover to their mid-1920s peak until 1960, more than three decades after the Wall Street crash.[26]

A barrage of new programs hurried along the modernization of homeownership and mortgage lending. Though Hoover has a reputation today as a laissez-faire ideologue who failed to recognize the severity of the Depression and respond to it in time, he was a far more interventionist politician than popular history would suggest, especially when it came to housing. In 1932, Hoover instituted the Federal Home Loan Bank Act, which he had proposed even before the slump began and which extended the same sort of government support to urban homeowners that the 1916 Federal Farm Loan Act had to farmers. The act created a network of Federal Home Loan Banks that would lend at low rates to some kinds of banks, insurance companies and other financial institutions in exchange for mortgage loans as collateral. This federal backstop was the first part of the new government support framework for the housing market, most of which still exists today. The Federal Home Loan Banks remain a crucial part of American housing policy, with assets of around $1.3 trillion.[27]

In the depths of the greatest recession in American history, Hoover was ejected from office by a landslide in 1932, and Franklin Delano Roosevelt, the Democrat promising to end the slump, was swept into office. The last real chance in American history that a Georgist might slip into the country's highest office came and went in the same year. Newton D. Baker, a widely respected Democrat, was a well-known admirer of Henry George's principles. He had served as mayor of Cleveland (following another Georgist, Tom L. Johnson), and then as secretary of war under Woodrow Wilson. But as support behind Roosevelt's candidacy swelled, Baker opted not to throw his hat into the ring. He received 0.7 percent of the vote in the first round of the Democratic National Convention as a write-in candidate. His decision not to run was a final nail in the coffin of the Single Tax movement.

With Roosevelt as president, government support for the increasingly large and formalized mortgage industry only grew. A range of institutions, most of which still exist today, sprang up from the reams of New Deal legislation passed in the efforts to rescue the American economy. The National Housing Act of 1934 created the Federal Housing Administration and the Federal Savings and Loan Insurance Corporation, which established deposit insurance for the savings and loans associations that provided much of the credit for mortgages at the time. The Federal National Mortgage Association, known as Fannie Mae, was founded in 1938 to provide even more support to lenders. The organization was charged with buying more mortgage loans from banks and other creditors and selling them on, making mortgages more liquid. It would act to guarantee the debt, and implicitly, so would the federal government. The government-sponsored enterprise would return to the limelight seven decades later, playing a huge role in a catastrophic financial crisis yet again. The Veterans Administration began guaranteeing mortgages in 1944, a boon for some of the millions of servicemen heading home from Europe and the Pacific. The VA still guarantees hundreds of thousands of loans each year.

The emergency responses of the Depression and the mortgage market institutions conceived by Hoover and Roosevelt did not prove temporary. They became the foundation for a new era of massive financial support for land and real estate investments that would not be available to any other assets. In 1936, just 1 percent of home mortgages were supported by the new government programs. By 1950, the figure had climbed to 42 percent.[28] The expansion of support for borrowers helped to foster a huge boom in homeownership, which surged from 44 percent of Americans in 1940 to 62 percent by 1960, making America a majority landowning nation again. It was the bedrock of the special treatment for investments in land that still exists today.

Another huge subsidy to homeownership grew up almost entirely by accident. When federal income taxes were introduced with the Revenue Act of 1913, taxpayers were able to deduct any interest payments from their reported income. The exemption made some intuitive sense, especially for business owners: If a company brought in $10,000 in revenue but spent $8,000 on inventories, wages and other expenses, it was the $2,000 of profit that should be taxed, not the entire revenue. The logic followed that any interest paid on loans should be considered an expense in the same way.[29] Initially, the deduction hardly mattered enough to change the shape of household investment in a serious way. The 1913 threshold for income tax was set at such a high level, $3,000 per year, that it applied to vanishingly few Americans. The idea that the deduction might soon be an enormous advantage to tens of millions of mortgage holders was not on anyone's mind.

But the spending on defense during the Second World War necessitated a huge expansion in the American income tax base. In 1939, just four million Americans had paid income tax; by 1945, forty-three million people were sending checks to the IRS.[30] And the taxes themselves were far higher: the steepest marginal income taxes in the postwar period reached over 90 percent. Suddenly, the interest deductibility on mortgage loans, which had come into existence with little consideration, mattered enormously. Other benefits for homeowners continued to roll in. The Revenue Act of 1951 made owner-occupied properties exempt from capital gains taxes for the first time. The incentives to own housing were stacking up—with so much preferential treatment, so many programs of assistance and so many effective subsidies, it was enormously advantageous to own housing from a purely financial perspective.

America was not alone. After the Second World War, homeownership boomed in Britain, and by the end of the 1960s, over half the population lived in houses they owned themselves. The ownership rate rose to as high as 70 percent in the very early years of the twenty-first century. In France, the Netherlands and northern Europe, homeownership surged too. Even in West Germany, where renting remained a normal and heavily regulated form of tenure for middle-class families, ownership was still far more popular by the late twentieth century than it had been anywhere in Europe fifty years earlier.

New and powerful political forces—a rising and militant Marxist left and the active promotion of homeownership by governments on either side of the Atlantic—fatally crushed the movement that had launched Henry George to international stardom. The financial architecture and web of special treatment needed to underpin a new era of mass home-ownership was in place, one that would outlast the threat from communist revolutionaries. The attacks that Georgists had made on land monopolies had resonated in a world in which a minority of the population owned a growing share of the valuable land. In the urban and industrialized world, the politics of land ebbed away through the early decades of the twentieth century. But farther afield, in the global countryside outside of the Western world, it was only beginning to stir.

FIVE

To the Tiller

During Henry George's rise to global prominence, the new and teeming megalopolises of the world were the focal point for the new inequities of landownership. Cities across the Anglosphere, from Sydney, to London, to New York and Vancouver, hosted the political movements that brought land to the center of political debate. But at the end of the nineteenth century, those booming cities were oddities on the global stage. Most of the world was neither industrial nor urban, and in most of it, the very old models of landownership persisted. When the guns finally fell silent at the end of the Second World War, less than a third of the world's population lived in cities at all.[1] As late as 2006, the population of the world as a whole was still more rural than it was urban.[2] Until very recently, the lives of most people across the world would have been relatively recognizable to their ancestors from a thousand years earlier.

But what is now known as the "developing world" was about to enter a tumultuous period of political strife, centered on land and its ownership. In 1945, war economies across the globe were being dismantled. The process of rebuilding began in the cities of Europe and Asia that had been reduced to rubble and ash by aerial bombardment or bitter urban warfare. The nations of Britain, France, Belgium and Japan, the largest remaining imperial powers, emerged from the conflict financially and materially devastated. Their ability to hold on to their prized colonial possessions was permanently undermined. Over the two decades that followed the collapse of the Axis powers, more than fifty new nation-states would gain independence from their former masters, home to hundreds of millions of people—many billions today.

Across these newly self-governing countries, anti-colonial movements that had resisted imperial control were taking the reins of power. Among them were many leftists, who hoped to wage their own campaigns of appropriation and nationalization over land, industry and other assets. Just as the politics of housing and land in Britain and America in the early twentieth century had been framed by the battle between capitalism and socialism, so it would be in the largely rural rest of the world. The Cold War between the victorious powers in the Second World War was about to begin, a tussle that would last for four decades. Land would be at the center of a battle not just between ideologies, but increasingly between superpowers too. Communists with a power base among urban workers promised peasant farmers in the countryside that only they could offer liberation from landlords.

This was the era of land reform, a series of ambitious attempts to reshape the ownership, distribution and use of agricultural land in the newly independent nations of the world. Some were transformational, upturning the organization of rural economies that had otherwise been little changed for centuries. Others were fruitless, stumbling in the face of intractable opposition. A small handful were worse still, resulting in political disaster, conflict and hunger. To the policymakers pursuing the change, the mass redistribution of land to the peasants who tilled it was not just a more equitable distribution, helping to bind new nations together. As former tenants took control of the land, the profit from any improvements would flow to them, rather than to their often-distant landlords. That, its proponents believed, would make for a far more economically efficient arrangement too. To its greatest proponents, land reform was the first building block for a new and much more prosperous era, the starting gun fired on a period of rapid economic growth.

One American became a particularly central figure in the thinking and implementation of the redistribution programs, and perhaps the most important architect of its greatest successes. Wolf Ladejinsky, an agricultural economist, did not begin his life in America. He was born in 1899 in Katerynopil, in what is now central Ukraine, during the dying decades of the Romanov Empire. Ladejinsky reached adulthood at the outset of the brutal Russian Civil War, and at the age of twenty-two, he arrived in America, having fled his homeland across the wintry Dniester River into the Kingdom of Romania. He never ran for any political office or published anything that was widely read; nowhere in the world is he a household name today. Despite that, he may well have had more of a concrete impact on the way land is owned and distributed than Henry George himself. But Ladejinsky's five-decade career as a researcher, bureaucrat and policymaking gun for hire also makes for a bleak illustration of why so many efforts to build a new rural economy failed.

The young man who arrived in America in 1920 would eventually secure a place at Columbia University, where he studied agricultural economics. But Ladejinsky's views on land did not begin in the classroom. Rather, they stemmed from his early life in the dying days of tsarist Russia and the opening ones of the Soviet Union. His father and grandfather had been landowners—big landlords, in Ladejinsky's own words—who owned several flour mills.[3] The Russia in which the young academic had grown up was in fact the laboratory of an earlier land reform: In a last gasp to preserve the Russian monarchy from revolutionary fervor, Prime Minister Pyotr Stolypin scrambled to introduce his own changes to Russia's rural economy from 1906, which were continued after his assassination in 1911. He wanted to break up the rigid peasant communes that still bound the families who had been emancipated from serfdom half a century earlier, allowing them to opt out of the collective farming system. In Stolypin's vision, the change would turn peasants into independent smallholders, give them a stake in Russian society and make them allies with the government, against Russia's various revolutionary movements.[4] If it were not for the world-changing events that followed, Stolypin's reforms might well have become the model for land reform around the world.

But, as in Britain, the grand ambitions to change an economic system that revolved around land were interrupted by the outbreak of war in 1914. Stolypin's efforts to engineer change simply came too late. The Russian Revolution began in its cities, but Lenin secured the wider countryside with an offer to the agrarian majority of the Russian population. The country was promised bread, peace and land, the last of which would be redistributed from its elite owners to the peasantry. Ladejinsky's family, along with all the other significant landowners across the country, were stripped of their property. But Lenin's promise was not kept for long. In 1929, under the leadership of Joseph Stalin, the Soviet Union began the mass collectivization of agriculture, driving peasants from their own land onto new state-run farms and communes. The campaign of rapid expropriation killed millions, both through direct violence and the starvation that followed.

The end of Ladejinsky's future as a Ukrainian landlord was the beginning of his life as a major influence on land policy around the world. After the election of Franklin D. Roosevelt, Columbia economist Rexford Tugwell—known as "Rex the Red" by his critics—had gone to work for the new administration.[5] He found a role for Ladejinsky, his student, in the foreign affairs section of the Department of Agriculture.[6] It was here that Ladejinsky would become a specialist on Asian rural economies. Tugwell was a resolute advocate of central economic planning, and during his own career, Ladejinsky would be accused of left-wing radicalism. His thirst for redistribution and his foreign birth put him in the sights of political conservatives in Washington. But Ladejinsky was a principled anticommunist. He believed the lesson of his own early life was clear: an efficient, equitable and broad distribution of agricultural land would be a bulwark against violent left-wing revolution; indeed, any attempt to defend democracy would likely fail without it. "The communists would never have attained political power if they had not dealt with the land question resolutely, by turning the land over to the peasants," Ladejinsky wrote later in his life, of his own personal experience. "But for the failure of the anti-Communist parties to settle this issue expeditiously, it is quite probable that I would still be running my father's rather extensive flour-milling and timber interests."[7]

Communists would always eventually pursue the collectivization of agriculture once they had taken power and secured control of the countryside, Ladejinsky argued. But before they took power, he had seen how they could foment turmoil by offering the tantalizing promise of land to impoverished tenant farmers. "The peasants, in sheer despair, believe the promises, not knowing that they will eventually be betrayed, their land nationalized, and they themselves herded into collective farms at the point of a bayonet," he lamented in 1954.[8] Development economist and land reformer Michael Lipton would later call collectivization the "terrible detour" in the politics of land in the developing world.[9] The process Ladejinsky had seen in the early Soviet Union was repeated in Eastern Europe after the Second World War, in China under Chairman Mao Zedong, in the communist halves of both Korea and Vietnam, and in socialist Tanzania. It was always and everywhere a disaster, of varying proportions.

In a less turbulent era, Ladejinsky might have lived the rest of his life as a forgotten pencil pusher in the bowels of the American government. The foreign section of the Department of Agriculture was not the most obvious place to go looking for a world-changing technocrat in the middle of the 1930s. But just as the Russian Revolution had given Ladejinsky the mission that would become his life's work, the reshaping of global politics in 1945 would enable him to bring his ideas to bear far from Washington. Instead of a historical nobody, Ladejinsky became one of the most important figures—if a relatively unknown one—in the early Cold War in Asia and many countries far beyond it. With the world in flux, American policy entrepreneurs with grand ideas had a canvas on which to paint their ideas.

Ladejinsky landed in Tokyo in December 1945, four months after Emperor Hirohito's announcement of surrender. During the war, Japan's economy had been turned into a tool for conflict. Its industry was devoted almost entirely to imperial expansion, at the expense of every other form of production or commerce. In the final year of fighting in the Pacific, that war machine had been functionally obliterated by American bombing as the US military had inched closer and closer to the Japanese mainland. When American bureaucrats arrived to govern and rebuild Japan, they landed in a country that was devastated in every way. Many of its citizens lived in a state of near starvation. Tokyo's population had declined by more than half between 1940 and 1945, and would take another decade to surpass its prewar size.[10] The country's catastrophic rampage across Asia had left it in a position of total dependence on the United States, its wartime enemy. Huge financial and material aid was needed to conduct even the most basic functions of government.

Even before the war, Ladejinsky's research demonstrated his preoccupation with Japan's highly concentrated and unequal landownership. He estimated that about 7.5 percent of rural households owned 50 percent of the country's land, while the most land-poor 50 percent of the country owned only less than a tenth of it.[11] Agriculture and land had already been major issues in Japanese politics: The country's population had more than doubled in the sixty years that led up to the war in the Pacific, causing food shortages. Riots over the price of rice brought down one Japanese government in 1918, and many tenant farmers were heavily indebted as a result of their impoverished conditions. "Rural Japan cannot lay claim either to prosperity or progress," complained Ladejinsky in 1939.[12] Unlike in Britain and America, where the growing population of urban and suburban homeowners caused a major shift in the politics of landownership in the twentieth century, Japan's transformation would have to be first and foremost a revolution in agricultural ownership, transferring the largest tracts of farmland to the tenants who had worked the soil for centuries.

Ladejinsky was by no means the only progressive reformer on the ground in Tokyo in 1945. He found common cause with bureaucrats like Robert Fearey, an officer of the State Department who had been tasked with assembling policies for the eventual occupation of postwar Japan.[13] Arthur Raper, an American sociologist who had written extensively about the agricultural economies and race in the American South, traveled to the country to advise its new occupiers on the policies too. On the Japanese side, Hiroo Wada, a bureaucrat who had been detained for a large portion of the Second World War for suspected left-wing subversion, became minister of agriculture in 1946.

Just two months after Emperor Hirohito's declaration of surrender, before Ladejinsky's arrival, Fearey had authored a memo on Japan's agrarian situation. The document, based on earlier conversations with Ladejinsky, proposed two alternative reforms. The first was a moderate proposal that would have meant the improvement of the conditions of tenancy through limits on farm rents and better legal rights for tenants. The second was far more radical: it proposed the expropriation of Japan's rural landlords and the redistribution of land to the peasants who worked it. The owners could eventually be compensated, Fearey noted, but not until Japan's ruinous financial position was drastically improved. Support was not universal in Washington, and some diplomats feared that upsetting Japan's landlord class would only risk Japan's stability.

The two men found an unusual but crucial ally for their more radical ambition. Dean Acheson, a senior official in the new Truman administration who would become secretary of state in 1949, had passed Fearey's memo to General Douglas MacArthur, the supreme commander for the Allied powers in Tokyo. MacArthur was not thought to be much of a progressive or radical. During the depths of the Great Depression, he had driven a demonstration of World War One veterans campaigning for compensation out of Washington, DC, by force. But the general proved to be an enthusiastic and vital proponent of land reform. Ladejinsky later suggested that MacArthur's interest stemmed in part from his own experience in the Philippines.[14] His father, Arthur MacArthur, had briefly been military governor of the islands. Douglas MacArthur spent extended periods of time in the country, in military and civilian roles, and witnessed the way in which large landlords dominated the Philippines' economy and its politics. Like Ladejinsky, MacArthur had come to believe that the violence and unrest in the countryside was ultimately caused by the monopolies on land and the miserable condition of the peasantry.

As the representative of the victorious Allied powers in the Second World War, MacArthur's authority was as close to that of an absolute monarch as any American has ever wielded anywhere. He was empowered to approve and veto legislation passed by the Japanese legislature and censor the media, and he was the primary force behind the drafting of the country's new pacifist constitution. When it came to land, the change that MacArthur envisioned was not just an economic revolution, but a social one too. In November of 1945, even before Ladejinsky's arrival, American newspapers carried an unsigned statement from the headquarters of the Allied occupation, reportedly dictated by MacArthur, that promised that "Japanese farmers and their families are about to be liberated from a condition approaching slavery."[15]

Less than three months after Japan's formal surrender, the government in Tokyo began to make enormous changes to the way land was owned and used. The country's first land reform bill was approved by the cabinet of Prime Minister Shidehara Kijūrō on November 22, 1945, and went before the country's parliament on December 4. The bill would have dispossessed landlords of anything they owned over much more than five hectares, stripping around one hundred thousand landowners of the very largest of their holdings. But the proposal fell short of the lofty goals set by Ladejinsky and the supreme commander. This time, MacArthur's commentary on the subject was not made anonymously. In an official directive, on December 13, 1945, the supreme commander for the Allied powers ordered the Japanese government to "establish respect for the dignity of man, and destroy the economic bondage which has enslaved the Japanese farmer to centuries of feudal oppression."[16]

In 1946, the Japanese government came back with more aggressive proposals that met the requirements of their occupiers. The amount of land a working owner could hold fell to around three hectares, or just one hectare for absentee landlords. The change increased the number of dispossessed owners tenfold, to around a million.[17] Local administrative committees were established to hand the plots previously belonging to the country's landlords over to their former tenants. The owners were compensated with long-term bonds issued by the Japanese government, though they had little say in the matter. In its original land reform proposals, the Japanese government had initially suggested their own local land commissions should consist of fifteen members apiece, divided equally between landlords, tenants and farmers who cultivated land they owned themselves. After pushback from MacArthur, the rules introduced in 1946 instituted commissions of ten members, made up of five tenants, three landlords and two small farmers.[18] In October of 1946, the new bill was passed without amendment by the Japanese Diet.

The fruits of the change rapidly became clear. The share of farmers who owned their own land went from 37 percent in 1947 to 62 percent in 1950.[19] The perilous politics of redistributing valuable land from one class to another would usually have been a source of enormous conflict, and such change rarely happens anywhere at such a grand scale without an outright revolution. Before the war, the Japanese government had considered redistributing the country's agricultural landownership far more modestly but balked at the likely political fallout of upsetting major landowners. This time, political opposition was steamrolled, since the impetus for the reform came from the victorious American forces overseeing the country's government. Ladejinsky and MacArthur were playing the game of land reform on easy mode. Japan's elites had been thoroughly defeated, and did not have to be courted or convinced as they would otherwise have been.

The incentives of former tenants shifted dramatically: hard work, investment and planning could now boost their earnings, which had previously been soaked up by distant landowners in the form of rising rents. An explosion in agricultural productivity followed, and crop yields swelled. Rising household incomes unlocked new opportunities. "The most vivid impression of a trip in any part of rural Japan," Ladejinsky noted, "is the quest for education."[20] Families were eager to invest in their children's schooling, and they finally had the capacity to do so. With economic recovery came rapid re-urbanization. The influence of American policy was transparent in Japan's cities as well: In 1950, the Government Housing Loan Corporation was set up to provide low-interest loans for the building and purchase of houses, and to foster liquidity in mortgage markets. In the second half of the twentieth century, the institution financed over a third of house-building in Japan.[21]

American land reformers could not simply ram their program through elsewhere in Asia as they had in Japan. But the immediate threat of communism sharpened the focus of local leaders. That was true nowhere more than in Korea, which had been split into two halves at the end of the Second World War. Farmers in the new communist north were given land in a massive program of redistribution, years before they were violently collectivized. With enthusiastic American support, the new government of southern Korea under President Syngman Rhee overturned the imperial system that had dominated the Korean countryside under Japanese rule. The combination of American military might and the end of Japanese rule made the first stage of reform politically and administratively easy enough: hundreds of thousands of acres owned by Japanese landlords were quickly repossessed and handed over to tenants, with overwhelming support across the political spectrum domestically. In 1949, just a year after South Korea became formally independent, the new government also redistributed the holdings of all landlords who owned above roughly seven and a half acres. The share of South Korea's land owned by farmers who worked their own plots rose from 35 percent in 1945 to 90 percent just six years later.[22]

For Ladejinsky himself, the next stop was Taiwan, where he would try to repeat his impressive feat in Tokyo. In September of 1949, he traveled to the island to conduct field research. The Republic of China, governed by the nationalist Kuomintang (KMT), had taken possession of Taiwan after five and a half decades of Japanese rule. At the same time as Ladejinsky's visit, decades of political division and civil war were coming to an end on the Chinese mainland, and the KMT were rapidly losing ground to Mao Zedong's Communists. Just two months later, Chiang Kai-shek, president of the Republic of China, would flee to Taiwan as his mainland forces were completely routed.

The Republic of China had been an Allied nation, rather than a defeated enemy like Japan, and there was no MacArthur to simply make demands of the defeated nationalists. But among the KMT, Ladejinsky would find easy allies. The party had inherited its political principles from Sun Yat-sen, the revolutionary nationalist who had embraced the ideas of Henry George during his many years traveling overseas. Sun's view had been that the men who tilled the land should be its owners, and long after his death, the principle remained a core part of the political program of the Chinese nationalists. In 1947, thousands of miles from where George wrote *Progress and Poverty* in California, far across the vast Pacific Ocean and long after his ideas had been discarded across most of the English-speaking world, the principles of land value taxation and an equitable distribution of the world's oldest asset—the "equalization of land rights"—were written into the Chinese republic's constitution.

But while the Chinese Civil War was raging, Chiang had abandoned Sun's principles. He had made alliances with the country's powerful landlords, who were natural opponents of the Communists. The act of short-term political expediency transpired to be a dangerous blunder. Just as Lenin had done in Russia thirty years earlier, Chinese Communists urged peasants across the country to turn against the nationalist government by appealing to their desire for independence and land. Farmers who had accepted gifts of land from the Communists faced horrendous violence, torture and summary execution in places where Chiang's KMT won back land from Mao's forces.[23] China's landless rural farmers turned increasingly towards the Communists as the war went on. The promise of land was a politically advantageous one for Mao's revolutionaries. But as in Russia and North Korea, China's peasants would not keep their new land for long before a lethal program of collectivization began.

With the war over, and on its new and much-reduced territory, the KMT revived Sun's teachings on land, both out of principle and for new tactical reasons. The political calculus for the KMT had reversed: while they had sided with the landlords on the Chinese mainland, they had no reason to align themselves with the established class of landowners in Taiwan. The refugees arriving from the mainland, known as *waishengren*, moved mostly to Taiwan's cities, while the KMT was relatively lacking in rural support. Expropriating the island's landlords would help Chiang to build a base of power in the countryside. For the landowners themselves, the only meaningful political alternative to the KMT was a Communist takeover of Taiwan—a deeply unappetizing option. And resistance would have been pointless: Chiang arrived in Taiwan with millions of soldiers and supporters, and instituted a period of martial law that lasted almost four decades.

In the four years that followed the KMT's retreat across the Taiwan Strait, the Republic of China instituted its own radical program of land reform, with support from America's Joint Commission on Rural Reconstruction (JCRR). The first step for the government in Taipei was a cap on rents, which would be limited to 37.5 percent of the yield on a given piece of land.[24] Land owned by former Japanese colonists was appropriated, as it had been in South Korea. On Ladejinsky's recommendation, nationalist bureaucrats visited their contemporaries in Tokyo to learn how they had gone about their model of reforms. He also prodded policymakers to include more tenant farmers on the land committees modeled on Japan's equivalent. "The program designed for the benefit of the great masses of the people is being carried out without the participation of the people," Ladejinsky noted in his observations of Taiwan's rural economy in 1949.[25] Having failed to prevent a Communist takeover on the mainland, American policymakers had no intention of allowing Chiang's island bastion to flounder too. The JCRR assisted in administration, by organizing the sales of land and in building Taiwan's cadastral records—the official accounts of who owned what and where.

As in Japan and Korea, the change was rapid. The cap on rents depressed farm values, enabling tenants to buy plots from their landlords. Agricultural production rose sharply. In 1953, the policy turned to outright redistribution: Land was compulsorily purchased from large owners and offered to tenants at reduced prices. Landlords were paid in land bonds issued by the government, and they were given shares in the Japanese state-owned enterprises that the KMT government privatized. As in Japan, they had no choice but to accept what they were given. In the year the policy was enacted, the number of rural tenants collapsed, from a little over 300,000 in 1952 to fewer than 175,000 in 1953. By 1971, the figure had dropped to fewer than 100,000.[26]

The results of the land reform programs in East Asia are the subject of a lively historical debate. To some, the reforms designed and assisted by Ladejinsky were not just a welcome development from an egalitarian standpoint. They were also the bedrock of the countries' subsequent economic successes. East Asia recovered from its postwar immiseration at incredible speed, and an economic boom in Japan was followed by astounding periods of growth in Taiwan and South Korea. In 2001, Keith Griffin, Azizur Rahman Khan and Amy Ickowitz, three economists then working at the University of California, Riverside, helped to revive the argument for the inverse relationship that land reformers had originally identified—that smaller plots led to higher agricultural productivity and acted as a trigger for further economic growth.

Joe Studwell, a writer and researcher of economic development, makes land reform the crucial first pillar of his three-step recipe for East Asia's economic successes. In his telling, the transformation of rural economies was followed by a combination of export promotion and financial repression, which Japan, South Korea and Taiwan all pursued to varying degrees in the following decades. Boosting agricultural productivity and the incomes of former tenant farmers provided the crucial funding for education and industrialization, propelling the three economies forwards. Studwell makes a powerful case that the division between countries in Asia that have succeeded economically and those that have not began with whether they were able to transform their land economies.

But not all assessments of land reform in East Asia reach the same explosive conclusion. Oliver Kim and Jen-Kuan Wang, respectively economists at Open Philanthropy and Penn State, take a different view.[27] They suggest that only the earliest part of the land reforms in Taiwan seemed to boost agricultural productivity, when Japanese-owned lands were redistributed to citizens of the Republic of China. But the next and larger stage of Taiwanese land reforms, which broke up big estates into small farms, did not increase agricultural yields. In fact, the redistribution might have squeezed farm sizes to the level at which they were no longer viable to run. But whether large-scale redistribution helped the traditional, even backwards rural economies grow much more rapidly is by no means the only metric for its success. Avoiding the bleak outcomes of collectivization in the countries that fell under the control of communists is an enormous point in favor of the programs.

In the nascent world of development economics, Ladejinsky's successes in East Asia made him the closest thing possible to a superstar. His insights were sought out by governments around the world. Across the nations of South and Southeast Asia, in the Middle East and Latin America, nations both new and old courted Mr. Land Reform. Ladejinsky spent much of the rest of his life traveling from place to place, eager to convey the lessons he had learned in Tokyo and Taipei, and keen to undermine the communist threat that he believed an unreformed rural economy would empower. Later in his career, he worked for the Ford Foundation and the World Bank. But almost everywhere for the rest of his life, Ladejinsky encountered political environments that were far more resistant to truly radical reform than the ones he had encountered in East Asia.

Across the newly independent nations that had formerly been colonial possessions, the priority of land reform—and the simplest political option—was to expropriate the former colonists and the domestic power brokers who had served them, as had initially been the case in South Korea and Taiwan. The same logic was true in India, which with the fall of China to communism became the largest unaligned nation in Asia. When the country's new government took control in 1947, the most immediate focus of land reform was to clear out the zamindars, a cohort of local feudal leaders who had acted as intermediaries between the thinly staffed British Empire and the populace across much of northeastern India.

The British had inherited the building blocks of the zamindari system from the Mughal Empire that had previously ruled the country—the word itself is derived from the Persian *zamin*, meaning "land," and *dar*, meaning "holder." The group comprised a wide range of local leaders who were responsible for waging war (on behalf of the Mughals, and sometimes against each other) and raising taxes from subjects far from the reach of the central government. Under British rule, the system was transformed to accommodate a much more powerful state. In the late eighteenth century, the local zamindar leaders were stripped of their arms and armies. But the loss of their military power was compensated with the official recognition of their landholdings, and a powerful and formal financial role as conduits of tax revenue for the British. John Stuart Mill, the English philosopher and economist, later said the English had been "blindly introducing the English idea of absolute property in land into a country where it did not exist and never had existed."[28]

Mill's sentiment was shared widely in India. The zamindars were objects of detestation for the nationalists pushing for independence in the early twentieth century. Harsh Deo Malaviya, a left-wing activist and author on land reform in the mid-twentieth century, said that "the zamindars literally functioned economically as the native garrisons of an alien imperialism."[29] As with almost every feudal system, peasants ran the risks of financial, physical and sexual abuse from their masters. But for the Indian National Congress, the political movement that led the resistance against British rule, opposition to the zamindari system was also the basis of a convenient strategic alliance. Like most of the world's intellectual movements, the Congress was dominated by relatively affluent city dwellers, while India as a whole was overwhelmingly rural. The feudal system in the countryside, inextricably linked with British rule, was a vital area where urban Indian nationalists could build common cause with rural India.

In his zeal for nonviolence, Mohandas Gandhi hoped that there might be a route for conciliation. Before India's independence, he suggested that the class of landlord middlemen might eventually take the role of the beneficent and noble trustees of the land and its tenants, writing that they might become a form of Indian samurai.[30] But most of the nationalists organizing for autonomy and independence were less indulgent. To them, the system was proof that the British neither understood nor cared for the Indian population, having foisted a form of European feudalism on the country. In 1934, Jawaharlal Nehru, who would become India's first post-independence prime minister, wrote damningly about the zamindars.

"He just takes a big share in the produce—his rent—without helping in any way in the work of production. He thus becomes a fifth wheel in the coach—not only unnecessary, but an actual encumbrance, and a burden on the land."[31]

Legislation to abolish the privileged position of the colonial landlords and taxmen came thick and fast in the years immediately after the country's independence in 1947. By the time of Wolf Ladejinsky's first extended trip to India in 1952, the new states of Madras, Bihar, Madhya Pradesh and Uttar Pradesh were among those that had passed their own abolition acts, organizing for the transfer of the zamindars' land and the compensation to the previous owners. At the federal level, amendments to the new Indian constitution were made to ensure the states had the power to dispossess the former lords. Redistribution was underway.

But when it came to the rest of the rural Indian economy, change was frustrated by a combination of ambiguities and limitations. Compared to the rapid shift to widespread land ownership in East Asia, progress in India seemed to be extremely slow. After trips across the countryside, Ladejinsky became pessimistic about the impact of the reforms, and he would remain so for the remaining decades of his working life. Though the feudal elements in the countryside had been abolished, the life of a tenant farmer had hardly changed, he noted, except that they owed their taxes to the government rather than the local zamindar. "The zamindari system, with its absurdities and injustices, was the weakest enemy to attack, because it was imposed by a foreign power which handed out property rights to which neither the British nor most of the recipients had any claim," Ladejinsky noted.[32]

In the two decades after independence, many Indian states implemented land ceiling rules, specifying the limit to what an individual landlord could hold. But the rules were riddled with simple loopholes. Where limits were set at the individual level rather than at the level of the family, holdings could be split over dozens of supposed owners. Research by economists Timothy Besley, Jessica Leight, Rohini Pande and Vijayendra Rao suggests that when tenancy rules were reformed to protect the farmers renting land from large-scale owners, they benefited wealthier tenants who could afford or borrow to buy the land they worked on. The very poorest tenants were more likely to simply be pushed off their plots, ending up in even more precarious positions as landless laborers. The overall redistributive effect was extremely limited. By one estimate, only 1.3 percent of land in India was actually transferred to its tenants between independence and 1992.[33] Writing in the second half of the 1960s, Ladejinsky bemoaned that India's political leaders, the Congress party, had already lost their interest in land reform.

Ending the most egregious symbols of colonialism was much easier than changing the entire structure of the rural economy. The same was true in Kenya, where conflict over the ownership and use of land had already emerged before the country became independent. The Kenya Land and Freedom Army, nicknamed the Mau Mau, was made up of and supported by landless peasants. The group launched a violent campaign against the British government and the white settlers in the country in 1952, a decade before formal independence. Once the country governed itself, the fertile highlands that had been reserved for white settlers were a politically obvious target for redistribution. But divisions emerged almost immediately as to which of the country's ethnic groups deserved what share of the land. President Jomo Kenyatta and his cronies ended up with huge tracts of land themselves.

Late in 1954, Ladejinsky's two decades of service to the American government and his decade as one of the most important Cold War-riors came to a disgraceful end. His position as agricultural attaché in Tokyo was terminated in a misdirected panic during America's Red Scare. The Department of Agriculture labeled Ladejinsky a security risk, on the grounds that in 1930 he had been briefly employed as a translator for the Amtorg Trading Corporation, a trading house used by the Soviet Union for trade overseas. The fact that his sisters still lived behind the Iron Curtain was used against him too. Ladejinsky's firing prompted an uproar. Author James Michener, who had won the Pulitzer Prize in 1948, said Ladejinsky was "known throughout Asia as Communism's most implacable foe" in a letter to *The New York Times*.[34] Walter Judd, a Republican congressman and one of the foremost supporters of Chiang Kai-shek in American politics, called Ladejinsky's work "about the only successful anti-Communist step we have taken in Asia."[35]

Despite the indignity of his ejection from government service, Ladejinsky had no intention of abandoning his chosen fight. In January of 1955, he arrived in Saigon as a reformer for hire. The new government of South Vietnam was in the process of being instituted, and Ladejinsky took up a new role as an adviser to Prime Minister (and then President) Ngo Dinh Diem. The separation between the country's north and south a year earlier was a consequence of the messy end to Vietnam's war of resistance against France, and was intended to be a temporary measure until nationwide elections could be called. In reality, the split would last for two decades, through a brutal civil conflict that became the site of America's first meaningful military defeat.

The circumstances Ladejinsky encountered on his first trip into the countryside presented an immediate and enormous challenge: The prospect that Vietnamese communists, who had retreated to the North when the country was split, would use land to rally peasants to their cause was not a possible threat for the future, but an existing reality. There was a strong degree of appreciation for the Viet Minh across agrarian Vietnam for their resistance against the French. Some of the communists had also taken village land and tax records north with them, frustrating the ability of bureaucrats to establish the reality on the ground. Worst of all, in areas where the Viet Minh had previously run the show, there was limited appetite for any rent-reducing land reform.[36] Tenants had not paid rent at all when the communists occupied the countryside.

With the benefit of hindsight, Ladejinsky's early writings from Saigon and the farmland of Vietnam illustrated that the seeds of the South's eventual loss in the war had already been sown. Many parts of the country had not bothered to elect the land reform committees that the government had supposedly instituted, and those that were operational remained dominated by landlords. Religious movements that combined elements of Buddhism, Catholicism and folk religions held huge sway in various parts of the country. The presence of the state was almost entirely missing in the countryside, which Ladejinsky called a political vacuum. "They are not authorities in the real sense of the word," he bemoaned. "For their power to govern is so limited as to be almost nonexistent."[37]

Ladejinsky helped the government hammer together a program for wider land redistribution in 1956, but even on paper it fell far short of the successful programs he had pioneered in Japan and Taiwan. He pleaded with President Diem to take note of the successes in East Asia, especially when it came to their elected land committees. As in India, the proposals were far too limited to seriously change the agricultural economy. Landlords would be allowed to retain one hundred hectares each, which meant that 70 percent of tenants, Ladejinsky noted, would not qualify for the right to buy any land. In fact, only about 10 percent of South Vietnam's tenants actually ended up acquiring land through the reforms during Ladejinsky's time in the country.[38] He left Vietnam in 1961, as the number of American troops operating in the country began to climb into the thousands. For four years after Ladejinsky's departure, the newly founded US Agency for International Development did not have a single employee concerned primarily with land reform stationed in Saigon.[39]

The government of South Vietnam would eventually scramble to rectify the errors made in its initial land reform program, taking a second swing at the problem in 1969. New rules changed the maximum amount of land that could be retained by landlords, with the ceiling reduced to fifteen hectares. The redistributed land was handed out to tenants for free. The American government even agreed to provide 10 percent of the up-front costs of compensating the owners—a small outlay, given the cost of the almost half a million troops the United States had deployed in the country by then. Given the dire straits in which they found themselves by that point of the war, most Vietnamese landlords were happy to take the deal. "Landowners who have property in Viet Cong-controlled areas are delighted, since the bill will compensate them for holdings they had given up for lost," noted *Time*.[40] The war had already reached its violent zenith, and the South was not winning. In its belated attempt to use land reform to blunt the advance of communist revolution, the government in Saigon had moved even later in the day than Russian Prime Minister Stolypin had six decades earlier.

A recurring theme in India, Vietnam and across Southeast Asia was a reluctance to be as radical as Ladejinsky would have liked when it came to redistribution, and a failure to guarantee that reforms were followed through even when they were passed. Visits by Ladejinsky to the Philippines, Nepal and Indonesia in the early 1960s revealed backwards and inefficient agricultural economies, but little about their limited programs of land reform suggested any meaningful prospect of change. Speaking to a colleague, Ladejinsky said it would require a miracle to transform the Indonesian countryside, given the "voluminous, disjointed, contradictory" agricultural policies of the government in Jakarta.[41] The so-called land ceiling—the amount that a landlord would be permitted to keep after redistribution—was far higher in almost every proposal everywhere in Asia than it had been in Japan and Taiwan. "Any meaningful land reform without a land ceiling programme is a misnomer, while its presence is one of the main causes of the few reforms which have succeeded," Ladejinsky wrote in 1974.[42]

But the politics of land reform were not always a straightforward panacea against unrest. One of the most enthusiastic proponents of meaningful land reform in the developing world was Mohammad Reza Pahlavi, the Shah of Iran. In 1961, mass redistribution of land was a central tenet of the White Revolution, a wave of reforms intended to modernize and industrialize the country at a rapid pace. The plan was decidedly Ladejinskian—turning a class of tenant sharecroppers dominated by absentee landlords into independent small landowners who owed their new prosperity to the Shah. It received enthusiastic support from the Kennedy administration. By one estimate, about 31 percent of Iran's farmland was redistributed to about 18 percent of its farming families, far more than in India or the other half-hearted reform efforts.[43]

Instead of doing what it was meant to, the reforms perversely helped to bring down the Shah in the 1979 revolution that ushered in the Islamic Republic.[44] The campaign of redistribution faced a barrage of opposition from major landowners and from the clerics, often themselves from wealthy landowning families, whose religious endowments of land were under threat. Hossein Borujerdi, the grand ayatollah at the time of the announcement, opposed the Shah's land reforms as un-Islamic, issuing a fatwa against them and stalling their implementation until after his death. Opposition came from below too. Despite the scale of the redistribution, landless agricultural workers and those whose new plots were not large enough for them to subsist on flooded into Iran's cities.[45] Both groups— the clerical elite and the new precarious urban population—became bitter opponents of the land reforms. The former would become the leaders of the revolt that overthrew the Shah in 1979, and the latter the revolution's vital foot soldiers.

For Ladejinsky and the other land reformers, the initial burst of success in East Asia became an increasingly spotty record globally as the years dragged on and support for redistribution from Washington waxed and waned. In the early 1950s, when Ladejinsky's most successful campaigns were underway, the drumbeat for major change from Washington, DC, had been loud. In 1952, Dean Acheson—the official who had deployed Ladejinsky to Japan in the first place and then risen to become secretary of state—said that land reform was the foremost part of America's international strategy. In the early 1960s, the government of John F. Kennedy promoted the Alliance for Progress, a plan for cooperation between the United States and Latin America that included support for major land reform. But on other occasions, American policymakers decided that siding with the major landowners against communism—as Chiang Kai-shek had tried to do in China—was the better option. In 1954, the Eisenhower administration had even supported a coup against the government of Jacobo

Árbenz, the Guatemalan president who was in the midst of promoting his own large-scale land redistribution program. Programs of land redistribution in Brazil and Chile were punctured by US-supported coups in 1964 and 1973 respectively.

But in the end, it was not politics, but technology that took the wind out of the land reformers' sails. A miracle in agricultural innovation known as the Green Revolution rippled across the world through the middle of the twentieth century. Norman Borlaug, a young American agronomist who would eventually receive the Nobel Peace Prize for his work, had pioneered new forms of disease-resistant dwarf wheat in Mexico in the 1940s. By the early 1960s, 95 percent of the wheat grown in the country consisted of his own varieties, and its harvest had risen sixfold in less than two decades.[46] Each passing year brought higher-yielding and more resilient crops to farmers around the world. The shift was nothing short of a miracle in reducing the risk of extreme poverty, malnutrition and famine not just in Mexico, but around the world. By the middle of the 1960s, Indian farmers were planting Borlaug's strains of wheat.

Agricultural yields were at the beginning of a protracted surge, which would bring relief from worries about widespread hunger and overpopulation. Globally, the amount of land used for growing cereal crops has risen by just 13 percent since the early 1960s, while the global population has climbed by over 160 percent.[47] Cereal production, on the other hand, has risen by more than 250 percent over the same period, more than offsetting the number of hungry mouths to feed globally. The improvement in production had unintended consequences when it came to the appetite for radical and politically thorny land reform. Borlaug's strategy was to bet on the strong, testing and demonstrating the new strains of wheat among larger, richer farms. Bigger landowners not only had the best land, but also possessed the capital to invest in seeds, fertilizer and equipment.[48] They were the most likely candidates when it came to demonstrating an ability to produce a commercial surplus. Borlaug had a singular focus on producing more, raising yields and alleviating shortages and hunger. Speaking about his work in India, Borlaug later said that he wasn't "worried a damn bit about equity at that point."[49]

Ladejinsky made the case that land reform and new technological improvements could go hand in hand. "India appears to be on the verge of significant innovations in agriculture," he wrote in 1968. "But India is far from prepared for the organizational, cultural, social and political changes that must accompany the fullest realization of the technological changes."[50] Despite Ladejinsky's best efforts, the sense of urgency around land reform declined as the years passed. Indeed, the capital-intensive improvements in agricultural technology led some economists to wonder whether big farms, rather than small independent owners, should be the future of the rural world.

In 1975, Ladejinsky died at the age of seventy-six after suffering a massive stroke in Delhi, ending three decades of practical work for a single cause. By the time of his death, the intellectual momentum behind redistributive land reform was far past its peak. Just as the politics of land had rapidly dissipated in the Western world, so they did in the new Third World too. In the decade after Ladejinsky's death, an assessment of the land reform program for the US Agency for International Development bluntly laid out the reality: "Redistribution of land to small private farmers has occurred only rarely in the past decade, and then usually on a small scale," the authors explained. "Nor have the political, economic, and social outcomes been uniformly beneficial. Not all land reforms have stabilized the governments that carried them out; sometimes the very rhetoric of reform stimulated revolutionary rather than peaceful change, and produced the destruction of rights that had existed before reform was undertaken."[51]

The combination of the agricultural transformation delivered by the Green Revolution, combined with political pressure from both the left and right, brought Ladejinsky's struggle to a functional end even before his death. The end of the crusade for land reform bore an uncanny resemblance to the one that had smothered Henry George's Single Tax movement at the turn of the twentieth century. But even as the politics of land was fading in the new developing nations, the growth of its economic relevance as an asset—and, with that growth, the threat it posed to nations all over the world—was only just beginning.

SIX

Collateral and Damage

I n the final decades of the twentieth century, the era of land politics in the democratic world was ending with a whimper. From the publication of *Progress and Poverty* in 1879 to the stumbling decline of the land reform movement a hundred years later, political conflict over landownership had rippled across much of the globe, and rippled away again. The era of mass homeownership had arrived in the urban and developed parts of the world, and a boom in agricultural productivity had sapped the enthusiasm for redistribution in the poor and rural parts. In the final decade of the century, the dramatic decline of communism as a global force would reverse most of the disastrous experiments with agricultural collectivization.

But even as land ebbed as a source of political strife, its economic properties remained the same. In fact, as rates of urbanization and homeownership rose in tandem, land gained a new and elevated importance in the final few decades of the twentieth century. In the rich world, the increasingly widespread availability of loans tied to residential property, fostered by a lattice of programs to boost homeownership, was tightening the link between land and the creation of credit in ways both powerful and dangerous. Innovation in borrowing and lending against land and real estate gave the owners of those assets enormous new financial firepower. For young businesses, the growth of mortgage markets would prove to be a particularly vital lifeline. The modern world of land and homeownership was far more than just a social transformation. It was a financial revolution too.

During America's period of rapidly rising homeownership from the 1930s to the end of the 1980s, the proportion of families living in properties they owned rose from just less than half of the American population to about two thirds. In other parts of the world where ownership had been more limited and concentrated, rates of owner occupation had risen even more rapidly. What had once been a rare privilege for a small segment of society became the dominant form of housing tenure in the Western world over a few short decades. But the burgeoning mortgage markets, boosted by programs that subsidized homeownership, weren't just useful for tenants who hoped to buy their own homes. The emergence of easily available credit, secured against housing collateral, meant relatively easy access to loans for many millions of households. Credit was now available to a huge proportion of the population of America and the rest of the developed world, at considerable scale, and at reasonable rates of interest, for the first time ever.

At the very beginning of the modern era of mass homeownership in America, a thirty-five-year-old entrepreneur in Illinois was among the cohort of young businessmen who would tap into the new source of credit provided by mass mortgage lending. Ray Kroc, a small businessman who had previously worked as a paper cup salesman, owned a modest suburban family property in Arlington Heights in the northwestern suburban fringe of Chicago. In 1938, he borrowed against his family home, much to the dismay of his wife, Ethel, for the $68,000 he needed to buy the rights to sell a piece of catering machinery called a Multimixer.[1] The product enabled a restaurant kitchen to blend six milkshakes at a time. He took out a new mortgage, bought the rights to the mixing machine and set about traveling the country to market the gadget to America's food and drink purveyors.

The eve of the Second World War transpired to be a dreadful time to invest heavily in something that relied quite so much on various forms of international trade. After the assault on Pearl Harbor in December 1941, seaborne commerce routes across the Pacific were severed. America was cut off from the sugar plantations of the Philippines, which was occupied by the Japanese military. Cargo ships were requisitioned for war-related transportation. Sugar rationing began in 1942, which put a pause on the market for sweet treats of all kinds. Kroc's manufacturers could no longer get hold of the copper needed for the motors in his machines either. He was only able to return to the Multimixer business in 1945, when trade routes reopened, war production came to an end and the American economy began to recover.

Despite the painful hiatus, Kroc's acquisition of the Multimixer proved to be a fortuitous investment. His work gave him access to the inner workings of all sorts of catering and restaurant businesses, and in 1954, the now fifty-two-year-old salesman met with two of his customers, the owners of a budding fast-food restaurant in San Bernardino, California. Their names were Dick and Maurice McDonald, and their chance meeting with Kroc turned out to be one of the most consequential in the history of American business. Kroc considered himself a connoisseur of kitchens, having seen thousands of catering and restaurant operations while on the road selling the Multimixer. He was enamored with the McDonald brothers' business, which subverted the norms of American dining. The company sold fifteen-cent burgers to drive-in customers, deploying a revolutionary "speedee" system of preparation and cooking that cut production time down to an absolute minimum. Kroc abandoned the Multimixer and became the franchise agent for the McDonald's restaurant, acquiring the rights to launch and sell new units of the company to investors across the country. Kroc soon opened his own McDonald's branch in Illinois. A year later, he founded McDonald's System Incorporated and set about franchising burger outlets around the country. Had Kroc been unable to borrow the money to take control of the Multimixer business in the first place—by borrowing against the value of his property—the American fast-food industry might look very different today.

Kroc called his own tale of borrowing against the family home to launch a new venture his "personal monument to capitalism." It is one that is now familiar to tens of millions of entrepreneurs, small businesses, freelancers and sole traders of all stripes around the world, whose family homes and properties have been used as the collateral to fund their ideas. Land and real estate offer the easiest form of security for bankers, protecting them against the very real potential of default. In most cases, the very smallest and youngest firms would not be able to access formal finance in any other way. In America, unincorporated businesses—the category covering the vast majority of small firms run by a single proprietor or as a partnership—have around $5.6 trillion in loans pledged against real estate collateral as of 2024, making up 72 percent of their total borrowing.[2] Kroc became the driving force behind the McDonald's expansion. Without the combination of an enterprising man with a property of his own and the rapidly growing and government-assisted mortgage market in the late 1930s, the golden arches would likely never have spread across the world. Kroc reminisced that he had "paid tribute, in the feudal sense, for many years before I was able to rise with McDonald's on the foundation I had laid."[3]

For Ray Kroc, the use of land and real estate in business went far beyond the land-backed credit he obtained in 1938. The real revolution in the company's business model only began in 1956, after Kroc hired Harry Sonneborn, a number cruncher working at soft-serve ice cream firm Tastee-Freez. Sonneborn was to become Kroc's first chief financial officer and eventually the McDonald's CEO. He was also the architect of the crucial decisions that turned the company into a corporate powerhouse. The two men launched a company named Franchise Realty Corporation, setting out to find landowners prepared to lease out their real estate, which would host a new McDonald's restaurant, for a period of two decades. With the knowledge of how much money the new restaurants could make, Sonneborn would then sublet the property to a franchisee for a far higher fee, raking in a fat margin between the two amounts. A few years later, Sonneborn began to cut out the landowners entirely, buying the land himself. McDonald's took out mortgages to build the restaurants and rented the properties to their franchisees, who were not allowed to put their restaurants anywhere else.[4]

Ray Kroc was more than just a fast-food king. He was a new kind of American land baron. The early financial engineers at McDonald's could hardly have known at the very beginning of their scheme that their country was in the foothills of a decades-long rise in land prices from which the company would benefit tremendously. McDonald's would surf on the wave of new real estate–backed credit bursting from the country's banks for decades as its fast food grew in popularity. In 1961, Kroc bought the company outright from the McDonald brothers and merged Franchise Realty Corporation back into its parent firm. The business model of the restaurant known to almost everyone on earth was now blended irrevocably with its crucial real estate arm. Sonneborn was emphatic about his view of McDonald's real way of making money: he regularly joked that the company's burger sales were merely a vehicle for its existence as a real estate business.

Even today, as one of the largest corporations in the world, McDonald's makes more money from rent—almost 40 percent of its revenue—than it does from royalties on Big Macs, Happy Meals and all its other internationally famous menu items put together. As of 2023, the company held $40 billion in land and property assets before depreciation, a little more than 70 percent of its total assets.[5] The world's most famous burger company is one of the very largest corporate holders of real estate in the world. Its history is so intertwined with Sonneborn's strategy that it is hard to imagine that McDonald's could possibly be the company it is today if it hadn't decided early on to pursue a parallel existence as a landlord.

It is not just the fact that land is the single most valuable asset in the world that makes it so important as a source of financial power. The fact that it is both immobile and extremely durable means that a lender can extend credit in the safe knowledge that the plot cannot be stolen, knocked down or hidden away. Unlike the multitude of assets that households or businesses might own, real estate can be valued by bankers with relative ease. The asset might go up or down in value (usually up), but banks can confidently lend its owners money over extremely long periods of time without having to worry about the prospect of the collateral deteriorating as the years pass. The ownership of land is not by any means universal, but it is relatively widespread, meaning millions of people have at least a little of it to pledge when searching for a loan.

Though using real estate as collateral is most crucial for small firms getting their start in the world, land crops up on the balance sheets of the world's largest companies too. The single largest corporate holder of land and real estate by value is e-commerce giant Amazon, which owned $105 billion of the stuff in 2023. In the same year, Alphabet, Intel and Apple boasted $74 billion, $51 billion and $23 billion of land and property holdings respectively. The land they own is vital for their enormous logistical networks, and increasingly for sprawling networks of data centers. But for the giants of tech, land usually makes up a very modest portion of their market value. It is much more so their intangible assets—their brands, intellectual property portfolios and their productive and skilled employees—that give them such tremendous valuations.

The world's biggest firms, with long histories of reporting financial results, are far less dependent on land and property as the collateral to borrow money. They can tap the enormous global bond markets for investment from asset managers anywhere in the world. Large banks, with which big and successful firms often have an extended relationship, will also accept a company's inventory and future cash flows as collateral, instead of their land and real estate. But in industries with older and less profitable business models, land takes on far greater importance. Even for some large, listed companies, especially struggling ones, the value of their real estate represents the value of their entire company.

Macy's, the storied American department store, is a case in point. Its market capitalization—the total value of the company implied by its share price—may actually be lower than the value of the land and buildings it owns. Analyst estimates of the value of the company's real estate range from $5 billion to $14 billion, far more than its $4 billion valuation in financial markets.[6] Something similar is true of British supermarket giants Tesco and Sainsbury's. The two companies operate in a ruthlessly competitive industry with profit margins in the low single digits; as a result, their businesses, despite turning over enormous revenues, are not actually worth much in and of themselves—in both cases, the value of their own reported land and real estate holdings is higher than their total value in the market. When old and storied companies flounder, the land beneath them often becomes the center of a financial carve-up. Iconic American retailer Sears stumbled on for almost a decade of negative returns before its bankruptcy in 2018; it was able to hang on for so long by selling and borrowing against its real estate assets.

The link between banks, business and land is a crucial and underappreciated element for understanding how a modern economy works. But to some economists, the connection is more than just a leg up for entrepreneurs setting up operations for the first time. In their thinking, the ability to use personal property as collateral against loans is a vital foundation in development, one that might even explain a huge amount of variation in economic outcomes across the world. Land and its vital role in the creation and securing of credit could even help to explain why some nations are poor and some are rich, shedding light on why capitalism seems to function in some parts of the world while failing miserably in others. Just as the early American colonists discovered centuries ago, the easy flow of credit is the lifeblood of a bustling economy. That makes the collateral—overwhelmingly in the form of land—a vital prerequisite for prosperity.

Even as the postwar burst of enthusiasm for redistributive land reform began to falter, interest in the use of land as an economic tool emerged in new forms. From the early 1970s, the World Bank in particular became more interested in land titling, the process of ensuring that landowners, particularly smallholders, had formal property rights over their holdings. Among other things, official recognition of their assets meant the owners of small farms could borrow against the farms' value. In 1984, the World Bank assisted the government of Thailand with an ambitious effort to formally title and document the country's land, which proved to be a roaring success. The newly titled land was worth between 75 percent and 197 percent more than the previously untitled land.[7] Farmers with property rights got better access to loans, and at lower interest rates. Titled land exchanged hands more often, its owners deployed more investment in materials and equipment, and farmers recorded higher crop yields. The Thai economy began to boom, and it seemed as if the pivot towards titling land was achieving what redistribution had intended to do under earlier land reform programs.

A new market-oriented way of thinking about land and economic development was emerging. The idea had a new standard-bearer too. Four years after Wolf Ladejinsky's death in 1975, a Peruvian businessman by the name of Hernando de Soto returned to his home country after a career in business and banking abroad. Peru had implemented its own messy land reform a decade earlier under a populist military government. The project had been one of the most ambitious undertaken in Latin America: all of Peru's estates were expropriated and huge tracts of land were rolled together into peasant cooperatives. The results of the reform were mixed at best and dismal at worst: during the 1970s, agricultural output grew by just 0.1 percent per year on average, and Peru went from being a significant exporter of agricultural commodities to a net importer.[8]

In a grim irony, the land reforms sometimes seem to have reduced rather than increased human capital where they were most assiduously pursued. A study by researchers Michael Albertus, Mauricio Espinoza and Ricardo Fort suggests that the more widespread distribution of land raised the income that farmers could make with more labor. As a result, they remained in the countryside and put their children to work in the fields, rather than moving to the city or sending their children to school.[9]

De Soto's first book, *The Other Path*, published in 1986, chronicled the difficulty of setting up a small tailoring business in his home city of Lima. Even with the help of a small team of university students, de Soto found that, after the necessary rigmarole of obtaining the right licenses and approvals, acquiring the legal means for his business to operate took an eye-watering 289 days and cost an enormous sum of money.[10] Most Peruvians simply could not afford the process, even if they knew how to go about it. Without the titles, licenses and permits by which they could operate officially, the businesses that de Soto identified were also often unable to access basic utilities like electricity and water, or financial services like insurance. Most simply opened their businesses without acquiring the correct titles and paperwork, avoiding the arduous process by operating mostly outside of the legal system and beyond the view of official institutions. Such firms may only exist at the margins in the richest countries, but they are the predominant kind of business across most of the world. Even today, the informal economy employs about 60 percent of the world's workers, and a third of economic output in low- and middle-income economies is generated in these off-the-books markets.[11]

The arduous process of registration and large shadow economies meant that the property rights of the poor were weak in Peru and across much of the developing world. Local entrepreneurs might possess a farm, a home or a workshop. But unless they could prove it and defend their owner-ship legally, they were unable to make full use of their assets. This, in de Soto's terms, is "dead capital." The assets of a given business were used for their pure economic purpose as they would be in a country like Britain or America—land, buildings and machinery could be used for farming or small-scale manufacturing. But the same assets could not be used for the much more expansive financial role they played in the West. Capitalism relied on the existence of collateral, de Soto argued, a version of the in-sight that inspired American revolutionaries two hundred years earlier. By his estimate, there was over $9 trillion of such dead capital stored purely in real estate value across the developing world at the turn of the twenty-first century.[12]

Though he is neither a household name nor a titan of academia, de Soto has a reasonable claim to be the most influential development econ-omist of the last half century. His work was the primary inspiration for the World Bank's *Doing Business* reports, first published in 2003, that measured countries by a range of metrics relating to their regulatory bur-den and the strength of their property rights. The reports became a bible for national governments, especially those looking to gain ground in the rankings. For the same reasons that redistributive land reform had risen to popularity among American policymakers during the early years of the Cold War, and that the promotion of homeownership became popular in the West, de Soto's ideas had enormous appeal with policymakers around the world. Stronger property rights and access to formal financial mar-kets might not just lift the fortunes of the downtrodden, but, de Soto's fans hoped, also usher in the final defeat of communism.

The Cold War was reaching its final stage when de Soto published *The Other Path*. The title itself was a reference to the Shining Path, a

Marxist guerrilla group waging a war against the Peruvian military in the highlands of the Andes (Peru's attempt at land reform, like Iran's, was not a panacea against revolt). The guerrillas survived with the support of Peru's impoverished peasantry. The formalization of property rights might not have sounded like a world-changing goal in itself, but de Soto's thesis promised something far greater to government officials in Lima and elsewhere. Providing the rural poor with rights to their own land and a stake in the capitalist economy would not just lead to a potential economic boom for them, but also serve as a bulwark against revolutionary sentiment, de Soto promised. He was proposing to do for the developing world what Noel Skelton had been advocating six decades earlier for Britain.

Arguments about the role of property rights and informal economies would roll on for decades after de Soto's first work was published. But when it came to policy across the developing world, the guard had changed. The governments of Egypt, Indonesia, Mexico, the Philippines and Russia, along with those of dozens of smaller nations, consulted de Soto for his insights. Experiments in formalization popped up everywhere. The old land reformers, and Wolf Ladejinsky's ideas, were out. The role of land as a financial asset—as collateral against loans most of all—was in.

The usefulness of land as business collateral, particularly for the very smallest firms, is not in doubt. If Hernando de Soto and the other scholars who have stressed the importance of collateral to economic development are right, the ability to harness land values in finance may even be a crucial foundation for a country's success. But the use of land as collateral has proved dangerous too. The widespread use of land as a security for loans means the asset has a close and intricate connection to the business cycle—the financial rhythm of booms and busts. When land prices climb, they unlock greater and greater volumes of credit, as banks are willing to lend more and more against the newly valuable plots. But when prices fall far enough, and quickly enough, the same lenders find that the collateral backing their loans is no longer worth enough to cover the risk that borrowers might default. At a great enough scale, the effect on the entire financial system can be profoundly damaging. As a result, land has taken a major role in the world's worst financial crises, surpassing any other asset in its ability to do economic damage during a bust.

Examples of the way land fuels such booms and busts are peppered through history. The newly independent Americans who had hoped to unlock the value of their enormous wealth in land were also among the first to discover the asset's role in financial blowups. In 1783, the Treaty of Paris put a formal end to seven years of conflict with the United Kingdom, and land speculators eagerly set about on new commercial ventures and moneymaking schemes. One of the very largest investors—in financial heft and prodigious physical size—was a man named Robert Morris. He had been among the most crucial of the Founding Fathers, known as the "financier of the revolution" for his central role in the commercial and logistical machinations of the Continental Army and Navy. When funds could not be raised, he used his own money to finance the campaigns against the British. At the time of the American Revolutionary War and in the decade that followed, Morris may have been America's richest man, and a national hero to boot.

The business model that Morris and many other speculators pursued in the aftermath of the war was relatively simple. They borrowed huge sums to buy land, with the aim of flipping the plots to European investors, particularly those in the Netherlands. The Holland Land Company, a syndicate of wealthy Dutch investors, was snapping up millions of acres of American soil.[13] Morris and the other large speculators applied the logic shared by every highly leveraged investor before and since. When the loans they had taken out matured, they could simply roll over the debt and borrow more, accumulate more land and sell it on at greater and greater prices. To keep the game going, Morris and his peers simply needed to make sure the returns on their land sales were great enough to stay ahead of the wall of debt repayments as their loans matured. As long as land prices went up, there was no problem. Two and a half centuries later, it is a concerningly familiar scheme for a modern-day reader.

By 1795, Morris had partnered with two other wealthy land speculators, James Greenleaf and John Nicholson, to form the North American Land Company. The outfit was a financial behemoth with six million acres of land assets on its balance sheet, an area roughly the size of New Hampshire.[14] Its holdings included the lion's share of the plots in the new federal capital that would eventually become Washington, DC, but where construction and development had barely begun. The basic business model of the speculators—buying European-financed land across the new United States, selling it on for a higher price and repaying the creditors—had been enormously profitable until the middle of the 1790s.

But the establishment of the alliance between the three men was a gamble, driven by weakness rather than strength. The appetite of European investors to make far-flung financial investments was dwindling, and the highly leveraged business model pursued by Morris and his fellow investors was beginning to flounder. The French Revolutionary Wars had begun. The Dutch Republic, where Morris and the other speculators had borrowed so much money, fell to the forces of revolutionary France the same year Morris and his partners founded the North American Land Company. By the end of the year, when George Washington wrote to Morris in pursuit of payments for his lots in the new capital city, Morris was obliged to reply, "I am not in possession of Money at present."[15] The speculators' humiliation was complete.

The result of the unfurling conflict in Europe was a seizure in trade and credit across the Atlantic. British wartime legislation suspended the convertibility of the pound into gold, an attempt to protect London's financial position as Britain set out on a conflict with France that was to last almost two decades. The North American Land Company could no longer roll over its many debts at home and abroad. Morris scrambled to sell various landholdings to satisfy his creditors, but their letters demanding repayment continued to pile up. In 1798, the man who had been the financial hero of the American Revolution was finally jailed in a debtor's prison, where he would spend the next three years. Beyond the bad luck of individual speculators, Morris and his peers may even have helped usher in the newly independent nation's first recession.[16] American economic activity had boomed in the early part of the decade, with rising land prices, easy credit and industrial production growing by more than 50 percent between 1790 and 1795. After 1796, output slumped and took around four years to fully recover.[17] The land boom, and the bust that heralded Morris's ignominious end, was just a taste of things to come.

Booms in American land turned to busts and economic downturns again in 1819 and 1837. In 1857 and 1873, financial panics followed the roller-coaster surges and collapses in the price of land surrounding the new and growing railroad network. The latter slump provided Henry George with the early support he needed for his fervent campaigns. The precise details of the crises vary. The institutions involved, the specific forms of lending and the scale of the downturn differed in each of the boom-and-bust episodes in America's land markets. Another cycle began at the onset of the First World War in 1914. European agriculture fell into turmoil, creating a huge opportunity for American farmers to export their goods overseas. The price of crops surged—wheat prices in the state of Washington, far from the conflict, tripled between 1913 and the summer of 1920. As European agricultural production began to recover after the war, prices collapsed, dropping by more than half in the space of less than a year.[18] Agricultural land prices in America tumbled, and when farmers could not pay off their mortgages, the banks that had extended them credit were left with the bill. Thousands of rural banks closed through the 1920s, even as parts of the urban American economy were booming.[19]

In the century since, agricultural land has become far less important as a share of land wealth across America and almost everywhere. But three concurrent and interrelated trends have only made land more important as collateral overall. Firstly, real estate has taken on a far greater role in the financial system, given the rise of homeownership and the rapid climb in house prices. In 1900, across fourteen industrializing economies—a list of nations that includes Britain, America, Germany, France and Japan—about 32 percent of total bank lending was accounted for by mortgages. The figure has climbed dramatically since, passing 40 percent in the late 1960s, rising above 50 percent in the 1990s, and reaching as high as 62 percent a decade after the 2007–2008 global financial crisis.[20] Moritz Schularick, Òscar Jordà and Alan M. Taylor, the economists who identified the phenomenon, call it the "Great Mortgaging." The health of commercial banks and their ability to lend are tied irrevocably to the ups and downs of the land market.

The second trend that has reinforced the role of land as an asset is its growing importance in determining house prices across the rich world. Moritz Schularick, Katharina Knoll and Thomas Steger demonstrate that the surge in house prices in fourteen industrialized economies between 1950 and 2012 was overwhelmingly driven by an increase in land prices, which account for 80 percent of the total increase in the value of housing.[21] The actual quality of housing itself has not improved all too much in many developed economies over the past century. In fact, in many places buyers will even pay a premium for older real estate. London's Edwardian town houses are far more sought-after than its bleak and cheaply built postwar housing. The actual cost of building homes accounts for just a sliver of the rampant climb in house prices around the world.

It isn't just the inherent characteristics of land that have made the asset so central to the modern banking system. The third trend that has reinforced its importance is the way in which the world's largest lenders are regulated, which has only encouraged greater exposure to the real estate market. In 1989, thirteen rich nations signed the Basel Accords, a new rule book for banking regulation that determined the level of risk that banks should attach to a range of different assets. The signatories to the deal included the United States, Japan, Britain and the major powers and banking centers of Europe, representing the lion's share of global financial activity at the time. Dozens more countries in the developing world would become signatories in the decades that followed. At first, the Basel rules were relatively simple. They applied risk weightings, which determined how much capital—the buffer between a bank's assets and liabilities— banks would be required to have. The riskier an activity was perceived to be, the higher its weighting.

The rules meant no capital would be required for assets perceived to be practically riskless, like government bonds and cash, which were given a zero rating. Unsecured lending to companies would carry a full risk weighting of 100 percent, while residential mortgages carried a risk weighting of 50 percent. Put simply, banks were able to lend a lot more money when they extended and dealt in mortgage loans, and a lot less when they made ordinary unsecured business loans. The highest-rated mortgage-backed securities, bonds that contained thousands of mortgages, carried an even lower risk weighting of just 20 percent. The next update to the rules, Basel II, was published in 2004 and reduced the risk weighting for mortgages to just 17 percent. Crucially, neither the original rule book nor its update made any distinction between safer and riskier mortgages: a loan worth 100 percent of the value of a home, extended to a borrower with a low income, and one worth 50 percent of the value of a home, extended to a borrower with a much greater ability to repay, were judged to be just as risky as one another.

Not long after the new global rules for the banking industry were introduced, a surge in land prices, likely the most familiar one to many of the readers of this book, was underway. In the decade leading up to the end of 2006, the greatest land boom in modern American history took place. American house prices rose by 59 percent in real terms. In hotspots like Phoenix, Arizona, and Tampa, Florida, prices more than doubled. The pattern of the land boom was similar to that of earlier periods of rapid growth, but the scale of the leverage and financial speculation attached was not. The modern American financial industry was unleashed, paired with a bipartisan political zeal for higher homeownership rates, which reached 69 percent in 2004, the highest level in American history. The volume of mortgage loans across the country rose more than 120 percent during the exuberant decade-long run. Loans to so-called subprime borrowers, those with the most limited ability to pay back what they had borrowed, ballooned in size.

This time, the land boom was no longer a distinctly American phenomenon. Over the same ten-year period, house prices exploded across much of the rest of the developed world and even outstripped those in America. Prices in Canada, New Zealand and Australia climbed by 66 percent, 77 percent and 95 percent respectively. In Spain and France, they doubled. In Britain, house prices rose by 153 percent, and in Ireland, they more than tripled. It was a global explosion, paired with an even larger boom in mortgage lending across Europe and North America. An alphabet soup of mortgage-backed securities (MBSs), collateralized debt obligations (CDOs) and credit default swaps (CDSs) had been produced and sold by investment banks keen to profit from the continued surge in land prices. The parties involved were undoubtedly greedy. Banks, borrowers and policymakers overextended themselves and helped fuel financial bubbles on both sides of the Atlantic. All took speculative and dangerous risks. But the common perception of the financial activity leading up to the catastrophic blowup in 2008 as reckless risk-taking reveals a widespread misunderstanding. At a casino, even customers who feel the overwhelming pull of the roulette wheel are aware of the odds of leaving empty-handed. When it comes to housing booms, it is precisely the perception of safety and reliability that makes land and real estate assets so tempting to use as collateral for greater and greater leverage.

Companies holding real estate benefited hugely from the upswing too. For each one-dollar increase in the value of a firm's real estate assets between 1993 and 2007, companies borrowed and invested six cents in response, according to research by economists Thomas Chaney, David Sraer and David Thesmar.[22] The market value of American real estate owned by noncorporate businesses—a category comprising small and middling firms—rose by more than $6 trillion over that period, providing the new collateral value for hundreds of billions of dollars in investment. Economists at the Bank of England found a similar connection between the value of British business owners' personal residential property and the investment they made in their firms: a one-pound increase in the value of a company director's personal home between 2002 and 2012—not even property actually owned by the company—increased business investment by seven pence and the company's total wage bill by ten pence.[23]

In 2005, *The Economist* called the global run-up in house prices the largest bubble in history, estimating that the total value of housing around the world had risen by $30 trillion, almost doubling in the space of just five years.[24] But in 2006, the upwards march in American house prices finally came to a halt. By the time prices peaked globally in 2007, the mountain of increasingly complex and highly leveraged derivatives that banks had assembled around the mortgage market had begun to wobble. The entire market—indeed, the entire business model of the banks on Wall Street and beyond—had been predicated on a continued rise in land prices. When it arrived, the relatively modest disruption to the trend—not even a drop, but just a stall in prices—was enough to upturn the mountain of debt that had boomed in the previous years. Lehman Brothers, the weakest and most exposed of the major banks, began to book huge losses on its mortgage-backed securities in 2008. Its stock price plunged, making raising equity to offset the fall impossible.

It wasn't just commercial banks that floundered. Fannie Mae and Freddie Mac, the institutions set up in 1938 and 1970 respectively to help boost lending to homeowners, came under near-fatal strain as the mortgage market and the derivatives relying on it froze up. A week before the total collapse of Lehman Brothers on September 15, 2008, both were absorbed by an enormous federal bailout. Today, the two government-sponsored enterprises are still under the conservatorship of the Federal Housing Finance Agency, a short-term measure that has now been in place for almost two decades. Over the full course of the bust, American house prices dropped by more than a quarter in real terms, wiping out many trillions of dollars in paper wealth. That would have at least been good news for those Americans who had not been able to afford to buy homes in the first place—if the link between land and credit was not so strong that it sparked the worst American recession in eighty years.

In Britain, lenders like Northern Rock, Alliance & Leicester and Coventry Building Society, which had grown rapidly in size during Britain's initial attempt to create a homeowning society in the 1920s and 1930s, were at the center of the immense squeeze as house prices began to fall. They had extended mortgages to homebuyers worth not just the full value of their property, but sometimes as much as 125 percent of the price of the homes they were buying. The loans were a demonstration of just how lax the standards of the mortgage writers had become, and how overwhelmingly confident in a continued rise in land prices both borrowers and lenders were. Several banks and building societies collapsed, and some were nationalized by the government in an attempt to prevent a total collapse of the housing market. In the worst-affected European markets, the downturn was deeper and lasted even longer than it did in America. House prices declined more than a third in real terms from their peak in Spain and by slightly more than half in Ireland.

Land is not the only asset that seems to be haunted by the specter of financial mania, but it may be the most damaging. John Turner and William Quinn, two academics at Queen's University Belfast, have studied a range of financial bubbles throughout history, dividing them into a useful taxonomy.[25] Some bubbles are lightly leveraged and triggered by major new technological changes (or fads), like America's dot-com boom in the late 1990s or the bicycle mania in Britain during the 1890s, during which more than one hundred bicycle firms listed their shares in London and thousands of cycle-related patents were issued. The crazes were wounding for the investors that bought into the bubbles towards their end, but had limited economic consequences for the countries that hosted the frenzy. They even had some social benefits: hundreds of thousands of bicycles were produced each year during the mania, and the dot-com boom helped drive investment in the new infrastructure of the modern internet, accelerating adoption by ordinary households. By contrast, the kind of financial frenzies that are both heavily leveraged and lit by political sparks—tax or regulatory change in particular—are disproportionately centered on land. From the Mississippi Land Bubble more than three hundred years ago to the global housing bubble of the early 2000s, land booms are often accompanied by tremendous bank leverage and followed by a painful economic slump when they burst.

The cycles of boom-and-bust recur with disconcerting regularity. Slumps often seem to be an inevitable consequence of the surges that preceded them. But crashes in asset prices may not be the only consequence, or necessarily even the worst consequence, of a protracted increase in land prices. Despite the severity of the financial crisis in 2008 and the long recession and stagnation that followed across much of the world, for many countries the overall effect on land prices seems to have been little more than a speed bump.

Over time, long booms in land prices transform the balance of who can borrow money from banks. Companies and people with large stocks of real estate benefit from the increase in the value of their land, which can easily be used as collateral to borrow. Those who don't have land not only lack the same ability—they also have to pay more to acquire any land they do need for their business. That change in the distribution of who is most able to get hold of new credit seems to have altered the economy for the worse. Research published by France's central bank suggests that a 10 percent rise in real estate prices not only boosts investment by companies with the most real estate but actually leads to lower investment by the companies with the very least collateral.[26] The firms with the most real estate are older and more established. But far more concerningly, they are also less profitable and less productive overall than their land-light peers.

The discovery is not an isolated one. Sebastian Doerr, an economist at the Bank for International Settlements, found that American companies with the largest real estate holdings were less productive than their peers with no land to borrow against.[27] Doerr also noted that when real estate prices exploded in the fifteen years running up to 2008, the additional flow of borrowing by unprofitable companies was large enough to drag down the overall productivity of entire sectors of the economy. Less profitable but land-rich industries prospered at the expense of more youthful and dynamic ones. If Doerr's findings prove true, then even when surging real estate prices seem to be creating a boom in investment, the economy may be robbed of productive potential, as loans and the resources they pay for are deployed by landed firms, and little is left for the others.

Just as the powerful connection between land and finance prolongs the life of some companies well beyond the point at which they might have ended, it also prevents other companies from borrowing at all. In the hottest housing markets, banks neglect the ordinary business lending that was once their bread and butter, extending more and more credit to real estate–related borrowers. Would-be entrepreneurs are "crowded out," in the terminology of economists. The academic economists Indraneel Chakraborty, Itay Goldstein and Andrew MacKinlay found that between 1988 and 2006, companies that borrowed from banks located in the very hottest housing markets had to pay higher interest rates, borrowed less money and invested far less than their peers elsewhere.[28]

Even as the modern economy seems to be getting less and less physical, the rise of the intangible economy—the world of software, brand value, data and intellectual property like patents—may perversely be making land more rather than less important in banking. If banks are reluctant to lend money against a company's physical assets like equipment and machinery, which they may struggle to value, they are even more averse to the idea of lending against new and incorporeal kinds of corporate assets such as intellectual property and software. As the economy becomes ever more high-tech and digital, banks may come to depend on land as collateral even more. Ironically, the crash of 2008 and its aftermath has bound land and finance more tightly together. Over the last fifteen years, banks have become more mortgage-heavy. In an effort to reduce their risks, major lenders repaired their balance sheets by stepping back even further from unsecured business lending. In many parts of the world, mortgage lending has never made up a greater share of the assets of major lenders than it does now.

In places where land makes up a growing share of national wealth, and where the connection between finance and land is becoming ever more intimate, there is a huge economic risk when prices shift in either direction. This is the nature of the land trap that countries around the world find themselves in today. When prices rise, prolonged credit booms follow, giving greater and greater resources to landowners and depriving resources from those who own little of the world's oldest asset. But when prices fall, the sudden evaporation of credit can be worse than painful—it can be catastrophic, leading not just to a financial crisis but years, even decades, of seemingly irreversible economic stagnation.

SEVEN

The Land Standard

n August 1989, politicians in Wellington, New Zealand, were embroiled in an argument over land. It was not a dispute over any domestic real estate, or one of the familiar tussles over what might be built on it. Instead, the argument concerned a particular patch of earth thousands of miles away. It was no grand expanse: The parcel spanned just a few dozen meters in either direction. It didn't host a palace, a military installation or a vital border crossing. It was a tennis court and a public playground, owned by the government, that had been purchased in the mid-1970s.[1] Most crucially, it was a playground and tennis court adjacent to New Zealand's embassy in Shibuya, in the middle of Tokyo. As the 1980s came to an end, Japan's capital city was the center of the greatest bubble in land prices that the world had ever seen.

After two terms in office, the incumbent Labour Party government in Wellington was heading into an election year. The previous two decades had been difficult for New Zealand. Britain joined the European Economic Community in 1973, severing the preferential trade relations between the mother country and its former colonies, which were especially important for New Zealand's agricultural exports. Surging energy prices all over the world followed. Kiwis faced roaring inflation, rampant unemployment and climbing public debt through the 1980s. But by 1989, the government had something to celebrate. Having recorded a persistent current account deficit since the mid-1970s—meaning that the country was borrowing money from abroad—the Labour administration was keen to trumpet a record surplus recorded for the first quarter of 1989.

But the surplus was not all that it seemed. The figures included the sale of the Tokyo tennis court, which netted the country an astonishing 150 million New Zealand dollars, the equivalent of almost a quarter of a billion US dollars in today's prices. The sum was large enough that it made a significant contribution to the country's headline economic data. One quick-witted Kiwi, writing to *The Press*, a New Zealand newspaper, said it was a shame that the government had only had a tennis court at the embassy, since a rugby pitch would have netted an even bigger sum for the country's balance of payments.[2]

One opposition politician asked the finance minister whether his intention was to sell a tennis court every quarter to boost the official statistics.[3] Another accused the government of selling off the family silver. But the administration in Wellington was hardly alone: governments around the world were looking to do exactly the same thing. Australia's sale of its embassy grounds in Tokyo the previous year had already made around 450 million US dollars for the government, over a billion dollars in today's prices. Australia had made a cool 200,000 percent return on the investment it had made in the site shortly after the end of the Second World War, putting a meaningful dent in the country's budget deficit in 1988.[4] China and Cuba sold land adjacent to their embassies too. Argentina and Myanmar followed suit in 1990.

The parcels of land and the enviable returns made by the foreign governments selling them were symptoms of the tremendous bubble in asset prices that emerged in Japan in the 1980s. Between 1980 and 1990 alone, while Japan was reaching its apex as a financial power, the economy grew in size by more than 80 percent. Over the same decade, the value of the country's land more than tripled, and commercial land in Japan's six largest cities—the very center of the boom—rose by more than 500 percent.[5] The rise in land prices remains one of the very largest on record anywhere in the world, and one of the most exemplary illustrations of the critical role that land can play in a financial system—fueling a boom, and worsening the subsequent bust dramatically.

The explosion in land values was driven by the overwhelming belief in *tochi shinwa*—the "Land Myth." Japanese families, investors, companies and financiers held to the deep faith in land and the real estate that sat on top of it, and were completely confident that it would simply keep going up in value. For most of the decades after the Second World War, they were right—land was undoubtedly a much more lucrative investment than almost anything else available to the majority of Japanese citizens, whether they were wealthy or of modest means. The widespread belief that land is always a good investment is hardly particular to Japan. Many countries have suffered from it, before and since. But in Japan, the commitment to land investment, and the manic financing that inflated the bubble, were of an astounding scale—one with few parallels in modern history.

The link between land and the functioning of the economy in Japan was astoundingly close. Some economists and analysts even said the country was operating on *tochi hon'isei*, or a "Land Standard."[6] The framing was apt: Just as economies historically pegged their currencies to the value of gold until the early twentieth century, Japan's economy was effectively pegged to the price of land. Companies could use land as collateral to borrow from banks. As the price of land surged, they were able to borrow more and more. Japanese companies bought up extensive tracts of land from households, not just to use for their own business operations, but to use as backing for loans in the future. Just as the gold standard made the countries that employed it dependent on the price of precious metals, so did Japan's Land Standard make the country's economy particularly exposed to the rise and fall in the price of the world's oldest asset. And just as the application of the gold standard ended in disaster for its adherents in the 1930s, so did the tight link between land and credit prove to be ruinous for Japan.

By 1989, the governments looking to sell the land on which their embassies sat were not selling the family silver. Rather, they were making an extremely well-timed financial decision, cashing in as an orgy of land speculation was coming to an end. The Japanese stock market, which had surged along with the price of urban land and the country's newfound prosperity, peaked on December 31, 1989, reaching a level it would not surpass again for almost a quarter of a century. About a year later, around the end of 1990, land prices began a decline that would continue for over a decade. The slump that followed the boom was not just a long and painful readjustment. The long-burning effect of the fall in land prices brought one of the most promising economic growth stories of the twentieth century to a functional end.

The scale of Japan's retreat from the frontier of global economic performance has been breathtaking. In 1989, the country had the highest per capita income level of any large economy in the world in dollar terms. Even after adjusting for purchasing power, Japan's gross domestic product (GDP) per capita slipped from as high as 80 percent of the US level in

1991 to 61 percent by 2022. By the same measure, Japan's economy is now less prosperous than either South Korea's or Italy's. More than thirty years after the bubble burst, the Japanese economy has still yet to convincingly emerge from that morass. The story of how the bubble emerged, the near-universal conviction that land prices would continue to rise and the wild and irrational heyday of the late 1980s are key to understanding Japan's extended stagnation. The lessons matter far beyond Japan's borders too. The model of economic growth pioneered in Tokyo in the decades after the Second World War became enormously influential across East Asia, changing the direction of travel not just in Seoul and Taipei, but eventually in Beijing too. The meteoric rise and equally rapid decline of the Japanese land market played the central role in turning Japan's economy from one that seemed to threaten the United States as the pre-eminent financial power in the world to one that now appears to be stuck in a state of irremediable decline.

By the time of the 1964 Olympics in Tokyo, not even two decades after the end of the Second World War, and just a decade and a half after Wolf Ladejinsky's immense successes with Japanese land reform, the country astonished visiting Western journalists with its technological prowess and growing prosperity. The YS-11, the first postwar commercial aircraft designed and manufactured in Japan, transported the Olympic flame across the country. The most impressive exhibit was on land—foreign journalists saw the beginnings of the country's famous network of high-speed rail lines, the first of their kind in the world. Japan's economy had already long surpassed its prewar size, but it was still growing at a frenetic speed, expanding by around 10 percent per year on average through the 1960s. Less than a decade after the Olympics, Japan had already become the second-largest economy in the world, surpassing France, Britain and West Germany. No burst of economic growth, either during the Industrial Revolution or after, had ever been so rapid.

By the 1970s, the expansion was becoming impossible to ignore, even far from Japan's shores. The country was not just increasingly prosperous, but a new and influential global player in many corners of the business and financial world. Japanese industrialists were transforming the way manufacturing was done: the system of production instituted by engineers at Toyota that emphasized a crusade against waste, unnecessary inventories and overproduction was beginning to sweep across the world. Japan Inc. went from making armaments for its imperial misadventure to products for markets across the entire globe. The processes the firms used were an object of obsession for managers and executives overseas. For many of America's established manufacturers, the emergence of Japanese competition was about to make for a near-death experience.

The growth at home and the expansion overseas were dependent on enormous volumes of investment. Bureaucrats and politicians in Tokyo tangled with the question of how such breakneck expansion might be financed. The same challenge would eventually bedevil their peers in Seoul, Taipei and Beijing when Japan's neighbors set about on their own whirlwind periods of industrialization. To ensure funding for their new and prized brands at home and overseas, the Japanese government deployed all manner of economic interventions. The yen was kept deliberately weak to promote the country's exports. The Ministry of International Trade and Industry, established in 1949, had facilitated low-interest loans for favored firms and sectors trying to sell their products abroad. To fund that cheap credit, interest rates on bank deposits were kept deliberately low—a policy now known as "financial repression." Investment in other financial assets and purchases of assets from overseas were tightly restricted to keep savings inside the country.

But even by the time that dumbfounded Western journalists were boarding the *shinkansen* in 1964, the unintended consequences of the boom were beginning to emerge. Land prices across Japan's major cities were surging, most of all in Tokyo, which eclipsed London to become the largest city in the world during the decades that followed the Second World War. To a casual observer, the explosion in the value of land might have been attributed to rapid industrialization and urbanization. After all, land prices had surged in Britain and America during their own periods of rapid development. But the value of land was rising even more quickly than the breakneck growth in incomes. With few options for investment in worthwhile financial assets, and miserly interest rates on their bank deposits, ordinary Japanese households found that investing in land and the real estate on top of it was one of the few decent options available to them.

Land was also treated with extraordinary leniency by the Japanese taxman. A range of how-to books on avoiding taxes on land and real estate became bestsellers across the country. While taxes on income captured what a worker had been paid that year, those on land—mostly in the form of property and inheritance taxes—were based on the price of land and structures years earlier, as municipal governments were slow to update their valuation estimates. While prices were rising by double-digit rates most years, the disparity between official valuations and market prices was often wide. By 1990, at the absolute peak of Japan's bubble, real estate taxes ran to just 6 percent of Japan's total tax revenue, compared to 7 percent in Britain and 14 percent in America, despite the fact that Japanese property prices were inordinately more expensive.[7] Similar distortions existed in the taxation of other investments: company dividends paid by the firms on Japan's growing stock exchange were taxed, but capital gains on real estate weren't, an imbalance that made land all the more inviting to snap up.

As the domestic contradictions of the growing land bubble were beginning to emerge, so were the international strains of Japan's financial repression. Japan's new business prowess, the government's management of the yen and its promotion of exports were fomenting a clash with America over trade. Though neither side knew it, the consequences of the trade war across the Pacific would light the fire under Japan's land market, setting the stage for the collapse that followed. From the early 1970s onwards, the effects of rising oil prices and growing competition from manufacturers overseas—particularly Japanese ones—had proved to be a devastating combination for the once world-beating American industry. American academic Ezra Vogel's bestseller *Japan as Number One* was published in 1979, adding to fears that the country might eventually become the world's preeminent power. Between 1950 and 1980, Japan's exports had risen almost a hundredfold in yen terms, making it America's largest source of foreign goods.[8] The growing prosperity of a wartime enemy was a point of increasing soreness in America.

For the incoming Reagan administration, elected in an atmosphere of American depression and malaise in November 1980, enough was enough. The weakness of the yen and Japan's range of industrial interventions in the decades that followed the Second World War had boosted the competitiveness of the country's manufactured goods overseas, but its successes were now major issues in American politics. The Japanese government had begun the slow process of loosening its financial controls in the 1970s, but it now faced pressure from across the Pacific to move much more quickly and allow the currency to strengthen. Deregulation, which would allow capital to flow more freely and the yen to appreciate, was at the top of the Reagan administration's list of demands.

Not everyone in positions of power in Tokyo was opposed to the idea of loosening up the controls under which the Japanese economy had boomed. In 1982, the Americans found an unusual ally in the new prime minister, Nakasone Yasuhiro. Nakasone was an instinctive conservative who was able to build a solid relationship with Ronald Reagan despite the friction between the two countries. But he was also a rare beast in Japanese politics: he was a skeptic of the country's interventionist economic policies who believed that a stronger yen would be a good thing for the country. A more valuable currency would drive growth and create a vibrant consumer economy, which Nakasone believed would give Japan a greater presence abroad than selling manufactured goods to the world at the cheapest prices.

With Nakasone at the helm, and under considerable American pressure, the financial model that had been built up over the previous four decades was steadily dismantled. In 1984, the deregulation of Japan's cloistered banks and markets unleashed its financial system, which the government had protected from market forces and the outside world for decades. One international fund manager, speaking to *The New York Times*, called the sector "the outstanding performer of the year."[9] Many listed bank shares doubled or even tripled in price over the course of twelve months. The changes also meant that the country's largest companies were no longer beholden to domestic lenders. They could borrow money from bond markets and overseas investors, and they quickly set about doing so. Japanese companies issued 5.1 trillion yen in corporate bonds and another 2.8 trillion overseas in 1984, each up by more than 40 percent from the previous year.[10]

The American assault on Japan's financial firewall reached its zenith in 1985. Nakasone had pleaded with Japanese consumers to buy foreign goods in an effort to appease the disgruntled American government. In Ginza, Tokyo's upmarket shopping hub, a giant image of the prime minister's face was erected, looming over consumers and imploring them to "join hands with countries of the world through imports."[11] Asking politely seemed to have little effect: the yen sat largely unmoved at around 260 to the US dollar. In September of that year, the finance ministers of the United States, France, Japan, the United Kingdom and West Germany gathered at the Plaza Hotel in New York and reached a broad agreement to weaken the strength of the US dollar by intervention in foreign exchange markets. For better or worse, the pact was a remarkable achievement, one of the most successful examples of international monetary dealmaking in modern history. The time of the summit more or less marked the peak of the dollar around the world. Less than three years later, at the end of 1987, the greenback had halved in value and the exchange rate fell to below 130 yen to the dollar.

Tokyo's acquiescence was never enough to satisfy its critics across the Pacific. Earlier in 1985, *The New York Times Magazine* carried a cover warning of "The Danger from Japan" by Theodore White, a long-serving American correspondent in Asia who said that his countrymen were about to discover "who finally won the war."[12] The Reagan administration pulled the trigger on wounding new tariffs in 1987, even after Nakasone's liberalization of the economy, including duties of as much as 100 percent on a range of Japanese electronics. Anti-Japanese sentiment was rife. Advertisements were published in American newspapers grousing about the country's trade surplus and demanding that Japan pay for its own defense. "Let's not let our great country be laughed at anymore," wrote the ad's author, an up-and-coming New York real estate developer by the name of Donald Trump.[13]

Despite the continued griping from the United States, the surging value of the yen was hitting Japanese industry hard. The country's export income fell by 18 percent in yen terms in 1986 and would not recover in a convincing way above its nominal pre–Plaza Accord levels for a full decade. Even Nakasone winced at the rapid climb of the currency. A period of *endaka fukyo* (strong yen recession) ensued—the first of several downturns generated by a strengthening currency. The Bank of Japan cut interest rates four times in 1986 and once in early 1987, in an attempt to offset the pain of the export contraction. For nearly three years, the Bank of Japan's benchmark interest rate sat at 2.5 percent, the lowest in the country's history, in contrast to rates of 6 to 10 percent in the United States and 7 to 15 percent in the United Kingdom at the same time.

But even as the export-led economy stumbled, the pillars of Japan's land boom were falling into place. The marriage of deep interest-rate cuts and financial deregulation was lifting the country's real estate market to new heights, tightening the link between land and credit even further. For the country's big banks, the sudden emergence of the corporate bond market in the 1980s meant finding new customers to lend to. That posed a problem. Japan's banks had built valuable, clubbish relationships with the country's big firms, but they were no experts in financial analysis. Working out which new customers were creditworthy, particularly among the growing ranks of the country's small and midsize firms, would be a nightmare. The solution was simple enough. The lenders began to extend far more money against land and real estate that they could repossess. Lending to the property sector itself was a particularly popular new opportunity: between 1985 and 1990, total Japanese bank loans outstanding rose by around 80 percent, with almost 60 percent of that growth consisting of loans to real estate and construction firms.[14]

The result was one of the most astounding increases in land prices anywhere, ever. In a period of just six years, between the end of 1984 to the end of 1990, Japan's GDP grew by around 33 percent, less than half as fast as the rise in land prices, which rose by 78 percent across the country. The surge was concentrated most of all in Japan's largest cities—not just Tokyo, but Kobe, Kyoto, Nagoya, Osaka and Yokohama, where the price of commercial land surged by 333 percent over the same period. The explosion in land prices was paired with an astounding stock market rally too. The Nikkei 225 index of Japanese stocks almost tripled in the second half of the 1980s. But the increase in land values was different in both scale and in nature to the rapid increase that had occurred during the rest of the postwar period. Japan's economy was growing, but at less than half the pace it had grown in the 1960s. The growth was no longer based on a rapid economic transformation or the prospect of urbanization. Instead, it was based on ballooning debt levels.

The rapid climb in values meant the companies that had been fortunate enough to own land before its value surged were conferred with enormous financial power. Debt held by nonfinancial firms grew rapidly, almost doubling between the 1984 deregulation of financial markets and the end of 1990. A vicious cycle was underway: As land prices rose, companies were able to access more and more credit. Much of the money they borrowed was plowed back into purchases of land and real estate, driving values higher and higher. Bank lending standards became more lax, just as the rapid rise in Japanese land prices made the asset an even more advantageous vehicle for avoiding tax. The effective rate of tax on property declined by almost half during the most frenzied years of the bubble era, as prices rapidly outstripped the ability of the Japanese taxman to keep up. The average property tax rate dropped from an already-low 0.19 percent in 1985 to just 0.11 percent in 1989 and 1990, with official valuations lagging even further behind the reality in the real estate market.[15] In Tokyo, the income from property taxes fell to as little as 0.05 percent of the market value of the city's real estate.[16]

Americans who had panicked a decade earlier about the growing presence of Japanese cars on American roads felt the effects of Japan's economic pivot too, as buyers from Japan began to purchase prime commercial real estate across the United States. Newly wealthy Japanese firms, whose landholdings at home had surged in value, snapped up real estate across the Western world while the yen climbed in value. In 1989, the very peak of the overseas binge, Japanese firms spent almost $14 billion on overseas property, more than ten times as much as they had in 1985.[17] The purchase of a majority stake in New York City's Rockefeller Center by Mitsubishi Estate, announced as the bubble was at its very peak in early 1990, was another emblematic transaction. At $846 million, the transaction seemed colossal at the time, but by one estimate it ran to barely more than 1 percent of the buyer's $84 billion unrealized asset value, mostly held in Japanese real estate.[18] The boom pervaded pop culture both at home and abroad. In *Die Hard*, the 1988 action film, Bruce Willis and Alan Rickman conduct their running battle through a fictional building named Nakatomi Plaza; the name was no accident.

But for all the rational explanations for the boom—financial deregulation, the sharp drop in interest rates and the tax advantages of investing in land—the frenzy showed signs of irrational behavior too. Even by 1987, not yet at the peak of the bubble, commercial property in the overheated urban centers of Japan offered a rental yield of less than 1 percent, well below safe Japanese government bond yields of any maturity.[19] In 1989, the cyclically adjusted price-to-earnings (CAPE) ratio of Japanese stocks, a popular metric for assessing whether companies are overvalued, reached almost 100, twice as high as American stocks at the very peak of the dot-com boom a little more than a decade later.

The total value of Japan's urban land reached truly absurd levels. Even in 1987, with three years of the bubble yet to go, a square meter of residential property in central Tokyo cost around 4 million yen, forty times the 100,000 yen it cost in London. By the time the 1980s ended, Japanese land values reached more than five times the level of the country's GDP, from a little more than three times in 1985.[20] In aggregate, Japan's land was worth four times more than all of the land in the United States. Based on the absurd prevailing prices of Tokyo office space, the boom famously made Japan's Imperial Palace and its grounds, which are less than a square mile in size, worth more than all the land in California.

The effects of the land craze went far beyond the balance sheets of Japanese banks and companies. A lucky class of investors who got in at the right time, or who had been in the right place, benefited enormously from the rapid increase in prices. But for a large group who didn't own land in the right places, the prosperity of the new elite was galling. A country that prided itself on avoiding the visible inequality of other industrialized nations was suddenly dealing with the very obvious consequences of disparities in wealth. A new generation of conspicuous consumers came into the public view, in a way they had never done in Japan before. European luxury stores had begun to open in Japan in the 1970s, after companies like Louis Vuitton and Gucci saw the demand from Japanese tourists in Paris and Milan. In 1989, close to the peak of the bubble, Japan took the crown as the largest luxury goods market in the world, despite its population being half the size of America's.

It might have been bad enough if the winners and losers from the asset price boom were selected at random, creating a sudden and arbitrary surge in wealth for a few. But sometimes, the reality was much worse. With land prices surging, would-be buyers were willing to pay through the nose for unwilling tenants and small landowners to be strong-armed into moving out or selling on, leaving the plots to be turned over by major developers. That was a job for Japan's centuries-old organized crime gangs. The practice of *jiage*, the business of threatening and terrifying recalcitrant residents, was becoming hugely lucrative. The typical fee for such a job was around 3 percent of the value of the land in question, an increasingly enormous sum in urban Japan's bubble era.[21] The gangs already had a foothold in the construction industry, which was booming as Japan's major cities developed. In their book on Japan's criminal underworld, David Kaplan and Alec Dubro suggest that between 1 to 5 percent of the total value of public works projects flowed to the yakuza, and cite police estimates that yakuza ran as many as nine hundred construction firms dotted around the country.[22]

Some gangs became even more directly involved with the real estate industry. Ishii Susumu, one yakuza boss, was released from prison in 1984 after a six-year sentence for gambling offenses. He quickly entered the world of Tokyo real estate, launching companies that conducted *jiage*, making millions of dollars and plowing money back into the booming stock and real estate markets. By 1989, Ishii had gained the moniker of the world's richest gangster, sitting on assets of $4 billion in Japan and overseas. At the very end of the bubble era, Ishii captured global headlines after it was revealed that one of his firms had paid a $250,000 fee to Prescott Bush, the elder brother of then–US President George H. W. Bush, to assist with the acquisition of an American asset management company.

If the yakuza and the new luxury-loving financial elite were the antagonists in the story of Japan's bubble era, the country was about to get its white knight. In December 1989, lifelong central banker Mieno Yasushi took the reins as governor of the Bank of Japan (BOJ). Mieno had made his views clear before he was given the top job. He had explicitly warned in 1988 about his discomfort with speculative activity in stocks and real estate. In his new position, Mieno's disapproval was now the official view of the entire BOJ. In his opening press conference as governor in 1989, he stated that the nation was frustrated with surging land and stock prices and the inequality that they were causing. He began raising interest rates, with the explicit intention of bringing the financial mania in the market back to reality.

Mieno and the Japanese people wouldn't have to be frustrated with high asset prices for long. The Nikkei 225 index peaked on December 29, 1989, not even two weeks after Mieno took office and just three days after the BOJ's first interest rate hike. By August of 1990, the BOJ's benchmark interest rate had been raised from 2.5 percent to 6 percent, where it sat for eleven months. Refinancing the borrowing that had fueled the bubble became much more expensive. The slump in urban real estate prices began. In 1991, commercial land prices fell by 4 percent, followed by back-to-back falls of 11 percent in 1992 and 1993.

Mieno was the most obvious and immediate cause of the slump, but the Japanese government was calling time on the bubble too. In March of 1990, the finance ministry had begun placing new limits on loans to the real estate sector. In April 1991, the Japanese legislature increased the taxation on land. The total burden of the tax continued to be low by international standards, but when asset prices had already stopped rising, it placed a new and unwelcome squeeze on landowners—especially those who had borrowed heavily to finance their purchases, or borrowed against their landholdings to make all manner of investments. The country's taxation of land had been damaging in both directions: falling tax rates helped to juice the bubble as it expanded, and rising ones helped to accelerate the collapse when it finally came. Despite the falling value of land, in the five years after the bubble burst, revenue from the country's fixed property tax rose by more than 50 percent.[23]

The understanding of what was happening in Japan was extremely slow to arrive for many commentators. Speaking to *The New York Times* in January 1991, the chief economist of Japan's Long-Term Credit Bank said that the real concern for Japan was the Gulf War, not the domestic economy.[24] The same article aptly described the approach at the time. "Hardly a day passes when Yasushi Mieno, the governor of the central bank, does not deliver another insistent sermon on the need to keep interest rates high to bring sky-high property prices down and cool the economy," the piece noted. "He has said publicly that he would not mind a decline in land prices of 20 percent, a figure that he also said would not cause unmanageable losses for banks."

In 1992, a Japanese bestseller made Mieno's moralistic point with even more gusto. Economist Noguchi Yukio, who gave the name to Japan's Land Standard in the first place, published a new book, *The Economics of the Bubble*. As extreme returns flowed to asset owners, Noguchi argued, the virtues of work and the values of the public were degraded. Whatever the merits of the argument, Mieno and Noguchi really did speak for the nation. The bubble-poppers were cheered on by many international onlookers too. Mieno was named central banker of the year by *Euromoney* magazine in 1991, even once the reversal in interest rates had begun. As late as 1993, the front page of *The Wall Street Journal* credited Mieno as the "Yen Master."[25] In an interview for the piece, Mieno called the economic downturn that was by then well underway "not only inevitable, but desirable," noting the "decline in morals" that he had seen in the late 1980s.

But even as Mieno took a premature victory lap, the consequences of deliberately bursting Japan's land bubble were becoming increasingly obvious and would soon be clear for the world to see. Commercial land in the most bubbly areas would eventually fall in value by more than 80 percent from its peak. A vicious cycle rolled on and on: land prices fell, banks stumbled, credit contracted and companies tried to pay down their debt rather than investing and expanding. When the Bank of Japan's monetary tightening began in 1989, thirteen of the largest twenty listed companies in the world were Japanese. The largest four companies in the world by market capitalization were all Japanese banks. The situation is almost impossible to imagine relative to their modern status: the largest Japanese bank in 2024 did not even make the list of the largest one hundred companies globally.

The first serious signs of the extent of the damage in the financial system arrived in 1992, when the country's *jusen*, the private mortgage lending companies established to facilitate access to the housing market, began to wobble. The lenders were directly exposed to the collapse of land prices, and many had made a shift during the bubble years from the safest forms of mortgage lending to the superior returns available in the commercial property market. A government investigation that year found that two thirds of loans to the largest fifty borrowers from the *jusen* were already deep in arrears. Bureaucrats in Tokyo responded with a ten-year rehabilitation plan. But the government's thinking was still based on the logic of the Land Myth, that prices would bottom out and soon begin to recover again. Instead, collateral values continued to fall, and the volume of nonperforming loans continued to increase. Estimates of the total amount of loans in some form of non-repayment were repeatedly raised, and seven of the lenders were liquidated in 1995. Government funds were needed to cover the large losses. It was the first bailout in the aftermath of the slump, but not close to the last. Japanese financial firms would have to be rescued by Japanese taxpayers again and again in the years that followed.

Policymakers in Tokyo were constantly surprised by the extent of the damage, particularly by the growth in nonperforming loans. Definitions and classifications of loans were changed, and banks that were reluctant to admit the extent of the rot were chided to provide more accurate figures. Many still presumed that they might paper over the problem when land prices rose again, not yet realizing that there would be no meaningful recovery. Japan's financial supervision was a mess too: dozens of poorly managed financial firms were left to go about their business, stumbling into crisis. The country's financial bureaucrats struggled to see the linkages between the institutions that made the whole financial system vulnerable. In March 1992, the Ministry of Finance estimated that the entire banking system was saddled with around 8 trillion yen in nonperforming loans, a large but manageable sum.[26] By mid-1998, with the establishment of the country's Financial Supervisory Agency, that estimate had climbed to 123 trillion Japanese yen, equivalent to about a quarter of the country's GDP.[27]

As the land boom went into reverse at home, the companies that had splurged on international property deals sounded a retreat. For some of the firms involved, the experience was wounding, even fatal. The American subsidiary of Mitsubishi Estate, which had captured American column inches with its purchase of Rockefeller Center in 1989, went into bankruptcy in 1995. Many were forced to sell at steep losses when their debts caught up to them. Shuwa Investments Corporation, one of the biggest foreign buyers of American land and real estate, had bought the Arco Plaza complex in downtown Los Angeles for $620 million in 1986; Shuwa sold the office towers for less than half that value seventeen years later.

Japan's financial sector limped through the 1990s with constant issues rooted in the deflation of the land bubble. In 1991, most of Japan's major banks had double- or triple-A credit ratings with all the major ratings agencies. By 1998, none did.[28] Japan's banks both contributed to and suffered from the Asian financial crisis, which rumbled through 1997 and 1998, devastating the economies of South Korea and Southeast Asia. Japanese lenders were withdrawing from their overseas presence, leaving a sudden shortfall of credit in markets across Asia where they had previously been major players. Regulators showed a failure to grasp the scale of the problem again in late 1997, during the collapse of Sanyo Securities, a middling securities dealer. Because it was not a bank, Sanyo was seen as a company that could be safely allowed to topple without systemic implications. But defaults on its borrowing from banks rippled through the financial system, which froze up. Larger banks and securities houses began to fail in the fretful weeks that followed. By the end of 1998, the Long-

Term Credit Bank of Japan, once the world's ninth-largest lender by market capitalization, larger than any American bank at its peak, had collapsed and been nationalized. The consequences of the bust rolled on for almost two decades in some cases.

The main difference between the aftermath of America's housing bubble and the aftermath of the land bubble in Japan is simply the extent and length of the collapse in asset prices. Japanese banks were still failing and being bailed out in 2003, almost fourteen years after Mieno's initial interest rate increase and nearly a decade after his retirement. An equivalently torturous response to the bursting of the US housing bubble in 2008 would have meant bank bailouts extending into 2022. The value of all US residential real estate and vacant land fell from a peak of $24.1 trillion in 2006 to a low of $18.2 trillion in 2011, a five-year decline of around a quarter in total. The value of all Japanese land took fifteen years to reach its absolute low in 2005, at which point it had fallen by close to 50 percent in value. The slump in the most expensive urban cores was far more extreme. Even today, three decades after the bubble burst, Japanese land prices sit at barely more than half their peak. The best regulators in the world and the most conservative financial institutions would have found it impossible to deal with the miserable financial climate that the country's bureaucratic and political establishment put in place.

The governors of the Bank of Japan, their counterparts at the Ministry of Finance and Japan's political leaders through the 1990s presided over the kind of asset price implosion usually reserved for wars, or perhaps the very worst natural disasters. A precarious financial situation had called for a cautious and delicate approach from policymakers. Mieno in particular instead set out on a blundering moral crusade that his successors did far too little to fully comprehend or address. Between 1989 and

2004, the cumulative capital loss of land alone ran to one quadrillion yen, around 8 trillion US dollars at today's exchange rate.

If the torturous financial consequences had been reserved for the companies that had benefited during the go-go 1980s, the slump might well have been a case of just deserts. But the deterioration of bank and business balance sheets turned into an economic decline that Japan never entirely emerged from. More than anything else, the relentless feedback loop caused by falling land prices is what turned the boom-and-bust into a multi-decade slump. Japan's average GDP growth fell from a little over 4 percent in the 1970s and 1980s to 1.5 percent in the 1990s, and then to just 0.5 percent per year in the 2000s. The policymakers who wanted to squeeze out the financial excesses at the end of the bubble era misunderstood just how embedded land assets were in the financial system. So long as prices continued to fall, and absent a huge change to the structure of the country's economy, a real economic recovery was impossible.

It wasn't just economic growth that slumped in Japan. Inflation stalled too, even more starkly. Between the end of 1993 and the end of 2020, Japanese prices barely budged: consumer prices rose by just 4 percent above where they were at the beginning of that period. Over the same two decades, by comparison, American prices rose by 79 percent. That worsened the problem of nonperforming debts for Japanese companies: when they took out their loans in the 1980s, debtors might have presumed that the principal that they owed would at least be eaten into by inflation over time. That was no longer the case. Banks hardly benefited either. When their borrowers finally defaulted on loans, the land and real estate they handed over was now substantially less valuable than when they pledged it as collateral.

Richard Koo, the long-serving chief economist at the Nomura Research Institute in Tokyo, offered a cogent and revealing explanation of how Japan ended up in its economic mess. The country underwent what Koo called a "balance sheet recession": The downturn was caused by liabilities (the debt owed to banks) suddenly outweighing assets (collapsed real estate values). In response, the households and businesses that had borrowed against more expensive land tried to pare back their spending. That would have made sense for an individual family, or an individual firm, but when such a large portion of the economy tried to refrain from spending and borrowing at the same time, Japan was thrown into a protracted and damaging series of recessions.

In those circumstances, it was impossible for Japan's central bankers to do their job and generate a recovery in incomes, even when they finally decided to try and do so. From the middle of 1991 to late 1995, the country's benchmark interest rate was steadily trimmed from 6 percent, all the way to 0.5 percent. But families and businesses trying to reduce their debts didn't care much: they did not want to borrow at all—at any price. The only way in which monetary policy would revive the Japanese economy, in Koo's view, was by reinflating the very bubble that the central bankers tried to pop in the first place, an unappealing option. Koo's proposed recipe to rescue Japan was fiscal stimulus, which could lift consumption rather than just encourage more and more land-backed investment: when all the other sectors of Japan's economy were paring back their spending, the government's role was to step into the breach and take their place.

But the efforts by the Japanese government to revive the country's fortunes, like the response from its regulators, were timid. The government was borrowing large sums of money, not because it was actively trying to rescue the economy with fiscal stimulus but because the slump had led to a sudden seizure of tax revenues. In nominal terms, Japanese tax revenues dropped by more than a third between 1991 and 2013, and didn't return to their precrisis level until 2019. When the government eventually did announce stimulus packages that might have raised demand meaningfully, it offered misleading estimates of their size. Incentives to companies willing to spend were offered by successive governments, but the sweeteners were extended to firms whose land assets were tumbling in value and who simply did not want to borrow, no matter how appealing the inducements might have been in ordinary times.

In 1997, the Japanese government made the astonishing decision—cheered on by the International Monetary Fund—to raise the country's consumption tax from 3 percent to 5 percent, almost the exact opposite of Koo's prescription. If the Bank of Japan's muddled decisions in the late 1980s and early 1990s were the cause of the bubble bursting and the immediate financial distress that followed, the Ministry of Finance's complete refusal to take the lead in encouraging a recovery afterwards was an even larger contributor to the stagnation that extended deep into the late 1990s and beyond.

The bursting of Japan's land bubble and its roiling economic consequences dragged on through the early 2000s and began to dovetail with another growing economic problem for the country. At around the same time the bubble popped, Japan's median age rose to forty. The generation born during the Second World War, which powered Japan's rapid industrial expansion between the 1960s and the 1980s, was aging. The eldest of the group would soon begin to retire. Japan's fertility rate had dropped to below two children per woman in the 1970s, an international forerunner of the decline in birth rates that has since spread across the world. With vanishingly little immigration, the generations of new workers entering

Japan's labor market each year began to decline in size. In 2005, when land prices finally reached their absolute low, the country's workforce—the population between the ages of fifteen and sixty-four—was in decline, falling by hundreds of thousands each year. Japan's increasingly elderly population may even be the foremost cause of its low growth today.

The country's insularity has not helped either. Japan is still an inward-looking place by the standards of a wealthy democracy, a trait that will always be a hindrance in a modern, knowledge-oriented international economy. The country ranks astoundingly low in terms of foreign direct investment (FDI): according to the UN's trade and development body, FDI in Japan runs to less than 6 percent of the country's GDP, miles below the 53 percent average for developed economies, lagging behind even the autarkic economy of North Korea.[29] Cross-border collaboration in science and technology, the cornerstone of productivity-boosting innovation, is extremely limited in Japan too. Richard Katz, a longtime observer of the Japanese economy, notes how isolated many parts of the Japanese economy are: no developed nation ranks more poorly when it comes to international cooperation in science, and only 2.7 percent of Japanese scientists have spent time working overseas, compared to 6.5 percent in the rich world generally.[30]

But for all of Japan's challenges today, the effects of the land bubble and the troubles brought by its collapse bear the greatest responsibility for derailing the country's once-astounding expansion. The slow-burning decline has made all of the country's other problems more difficult to deal with. Around the world, particularly in Europe and elsewhere in East Asia, policymakers fret about the prospect of "Japanification," the risk of undergoing a similar period of stagnation, and with good reason.

But the experience that Japan has gone through since the 1990s may actually be closer to a best-case scenario relative to what countries suffering from the same land-fueled slump would encounter. Japan bears no signs of deep civil strife. It is still highly developed, unemployment is extremely low and inequality is limited, by the standards of almost any rich country. The country's astounding social cohesion has allowed it to weather a period of relative economic decline that might well have broken others—and may well do so in the years to come.

EIGHT

Learning the Hard Way

Even as commercial property prices were booming in urban Japan in the 1980s, climbing towards their eventual implosion, the decisions that would generate an even larger Asian land bubble were being made across the East China Sea. In the People's Republic of China, land, real estate and everything else had still been the property of the state. Commercial activity had been smothered under the command economy instituted by the Chinese Communist Party, and workers and peasants lived where their state employers housed them. But after four decades of stasis, the market for land was about to be unfrozen.

During the Chinese Civil War, which ended in 1949 after two decades of on-and-off conflict between China's nationalist government and the insurgent Communist Party, land had been at the heart of Chairman Mao Zedong's campaign to overthrow the country's leadership. The Communists made dubious promises to the country's enormous peasantry, vowing to redistribute the holdings of landlords and turn an enormous class of rural tenants into prosperous shareholders. It was precisely the campaign that Wolf Ladejinsky had feared would subsume Asia into Soviet-style authoritarianism.

From the very beginning of the civil war, Mao had grasped just how important China's rural masses would be in any attempt to take power. "Revolution is not a dinner party, or writing an essay, or painting a picture, or doing embroidery," he wrote in 1927, defending an outbreak of peasant violence against landlords in his native Hunan Province. While some Communist leaders believed that the party's future was in China's cities and feared the excesses of rural turmoil, Mao believed that overthrowing the established order in the countryside was crucial for the eventual success of the revolution: "To put it bluntly," he wrote, "it is necessary to create terror for a while in every rural area."[1]

As the Communist forces took more and more ground during the civil war and as his own euphemistically named Land Reform Movement began, Mao fulfilled his promise. Instead of following the path of redistribution pursued in Japan or Taiwan, Mao's campaign was a part of the broader effort to suppress any remaining anti-Communist forces through violence and terror. By the estimate of Frank Dikötter, a historian of modern China, at least 1.5 million people were killed in the Communists' land reform campaign between 1947 and 1952.[2] Many of those killed were small farmers, rather than land barons, and many others were simply peasants who ended up on the wrong end of malicious or panicked denunciations by their neighbors. As part of the campaign, Mao set a soft target, based on his belief that about one in one thousand citizens was a hardcore counterrevolutionary: local authorities should kill half of them—one in every two thousand people—and see how things went.

But the poorer peasants who inherited landholdings that once belonged to their butchered neighbors would not own them for long. Just as

Ladejinsky had suggested, and just as had happened in the Soviet Union, the Communist Party had no intention of building a nation of independent farmers. Between 1956 and 1958, a campaign of outright collectivization was underway across the country, with small, privately owned farms subsumed into huge state-run farms, while personal landownership of all sizes was abolished. Housing was provided by a worker's employer, either an agricultural collective or a state-owned industry. Over the two decades that followed, all land in China was under the ownership, control and administration of the state.

Mao died in 1976, ending his almost thirty years of rule of the People's Republic. The collectivization of land had been part of a disastrous effort to industrialize the country, which failed in its economic aims and killed millions of Chinese citizens in the process. In the final decade of his life, Mao plunged the country into chaos again, out of fear for his own security at the top of the country's political pile. He called on millions of young ideologues, who would be known as the Red Guards, to upturn Chinese society and wipe out the conservative modes of thinking among their teachers, parents and other authority figures. For two years, the fanatics engaged in an outburst of violence and destruction that Mao called the Cultural Revolution. Even after 1968, when the Red Guards were finally reined in by the military, the chaotic political environment of radicalism, backbiting and disorder persisted for another eight years.

In the aftermath of decades of chaos, new leaders were consolidating their power. Deng Xiaoping, a diminutive chain-smoker who had been purged from political life by Mao, managed to outflank his opponents and become China's new paramount leader—the head of both the country's military and its ruling Communist Party. Though a lifelong party member, Deng believed that China had veered badly off course under Mao. He had already been punished for his disloyalty: From 1969 to 1973, like many errant Chinese politicians, Deng had been sent away to do manual labor far from the country's capital. He worked on the shop floor of a tractor factory in Jiangxi Province, cut off from political life. His son, Deng Pufang, was left paralyzed after being crippled during his imprisonment by the Red Guards. Deng Jr. was widely believed to have been pushed from a window by his captors, though his family never confirmed the details of the story publicly.

Deng Sr. and a coterie of like-minded reformers steadily began to overturn decades of state control in China's agriculture and industries, a process that would eventually bring one billion Chinese citizens into the global economy for the first time in practically half a century. China lacked infrastructure for transport, communication and energy. There was an acute shortage of housing, and much of the country's working-age population—numbering half a billion people—was employed by inefficient state-owned enterprises. But they were also young, comparatively well-educated and full of untapped entrepreneurial promise. China's economic production was still lower than India's on a per capita basis, though Chinese citizens were twice as likely to be literate as their Indian neighbors. If the simple building blocks of infrastructure could be improved, China's enormous potential might finally be tapped.

To do that, Deng needed capital that he did not have. Much of the investment that had been made in the previous decades was deeply unproductive, the result of decades of misguided economic planning. The country's immiserated workers and farmers were in no position to finance an economic revolution, nor were its backwards financial institutions. Borrowing money from overseas at any scale was out of the question: Deng's grip on power was tenuous, at risk from Communist hard-liners who would jump at any opportunity to smear him as an agent of foreign interests.

After decades of collectivization, the question of land, who owned and used it and how it could be used to raise money was about to return to the center of China's political economy. Within Deng's clique of supporters, Zhao Ziyang, who served as China's premier from 1980 to 1987 and general secretary of the Communist Party from 1987 to 1989, was among the most fervent, a reformer even among the reformers. He had been a party member since the age of eighteen, and like Deng, he had rebuilt his political career after a dangerous period of exile during the Cultural Revolution. Driven by a fanatical commitment to Chairman Mao, the young Red Guards had attacked Zhao for his family history as a landlord's son. He spent several years at work in a factory in political exile before being rehabilitated during Deng's resurrection. Zhao was made party secretary of Sichuan in the mid-1970s, and the market-oriented reform program in agriculture that he piloted in the massive Chinese province was credited with rescuing Sichuan from its depression.

Zhao played a vital role as one of the architects of China's modernization, helping to establish the mechanism that would eventually become the cornerstone for China's rampant economic growth. He credited Henry Fok, a Hong Kong real estate tycoon who would later sit in China's rubber-stamp legislature, as the inspiration for how urban development might be accelerated outside a limited number of industrial zones. "If you have land," Fok asked Zhao in a meeting in the mid-eighties, "how can you not have money?"[3] Zhao was initially confused by the statement. But he quickly caught up. In Hong Kong, which would remain a British colony until 1997, the government owned all of the land and funded its own capital expenditures with an extensive land-leasing program. Henry Fok was offering Zhao a version of the same understanding that the American colonists had established two and a half centuries earlier: deployed correctly, land could be made liquid and turned into a flowing spigot of money.

Hong Kong—a city of around five million, the last true outpost of the British Empire and a symbol of freewheeling capitalism—was about to take on an outsize role in the financial future of the People's Republic of China. At the time of Zhao's meeting with Fok, the real estate magnate's suggestion presented a huge opportunity for China's development. But the idea would also prove to be the seed for a gargantuan bubble, one that would end in the country's current economic malaise. China's reformers were taking lessons from a city that, while an economic miracle in some ways, boasts some of the world's very highest house prices and some of its steepest inequality today. Hong Kong is a place where wealth and the lack of it are almost entirely based on how much property a family owns, and where the ranks of the city's very richest people are overwhelmingly made up of real estate titans. More than any other place, the city has come to represent the poisonous role that land can take in a modern economy. The story of Hong Kong, and the vital role of land assets since its earliest days as a colony, is the key to understanding China's deeply troubled housing market today.

When Henry Fok and Zhao Ziyang sat down in 1985, Hong Kong's use of land as a means of public finance was already almost a century and a half old. The practice of selling long-term rights to use land dates back to the earliest days of Britain's occupation of the island. Facing defeat in the

Opium Wars that had begun in 1839, the Chinese government ceded Hong Kong to the British Empire on January 20, 1841. Six days later, HMS *Sulphur* arrived on the barren and mostly empty island, and the Union Flag was hoisted in what is now the city's Sheung Wan district. The rock's new administrators wasted little time: the first sale of land began less than five months later, before the city even officially became a Crown colony in 1842.

On June 14, 1841, imperial merchants gathered in Macao—which, unlike Hong Kong, was already an established port throbbing with traders and travelers—to bid on parcels of land across the harbor front of Hong Kong Island. Some of the plots, sold as nonrenewable seventy-five-year leases, went to buyers that are still familiar names in the world of business and finance today. Three of the parcels went to Jardine, Matheson & Co, a multinational conglomerate worth almost $12 billion in 2024, which is listed on the London Stock Exchange. In total, the lots sold for the collective sum of £565, a little less than £50,000 in today's money.[4] The merchants were just as eager to buy as the new colonial government had been to sell, and immediately began throwing up their godowns, the ramshackle trading warehouses, which would soon be filled with goods from China bound for export to Europe.

For Britain's Colonial Office, established in 1768, sales and auctions of land leases were the perfect means of providing an income to build up a new trading post. The tenets of British imperial finance meant that any new colony's finances had to be self-sufficient. No subsidies would be coming from the British Treasury, but nor would the new territory be milked as a cash cow by London. Taxation on incomes or sales within the territory required too much management by the limited administrative staff. Land sales were comparatively simple: plots could be easily identified, and buyers could be easily registered. The length of the leases was stretched and clipped back over the subsequent century, but the basic principle remained in Hong Kong throughout its period as a British colony, and indeed, long afterwards. Auctions of land have been Hong Kong's largest single source of revenue since it was handed over to China in 1997.

In 1841, the city's historical foundations were being set in place, both physically and metaphorically. Hong Kong had been declared a free port by Captain Charles Elliot, the new superintendent of trade. No customs duties or other taxes would be levied on trade, and merchants trading on the island would fall under the protection of the British Empire. At the time, it was a grand proclamation about a very modest place. The island was home to a few thousand fishermen and their families, living in villages scattered around the island, with no towns, cities or meaningful commerce to speak of. Not everyone in Britain was happy with the Empire's new possession. "You have obtained the cession of Hong Kong, a barren island with hardly a house upon it," the foreign secretary and subsequent prime minister Lord Palmerston told Elliot. "It seems obvious that Hong Kong will not be a mart of trade."[5] It was a spectacular historical misjudgment. Hong Kong was not just to become a major port, but eventually the world's largest. Elliot was given no time to prove the Foreign Office wrong: in August, he was stripped of his post and returned to England.

Henry Pottinger, the new administrator of Hong Kong who would eventually become its first governor, arrived at the head of a new expeditionary force to resume the war with China. The British government was unsatisfied with the rocky outcrop of Hong Kong but had much higher hopes when it came to opening the existing metropolises like Guangzhou, Shanghai and Xiamen to trade by force. With the future of the new island territory uncertain, Pottinger left clear instructions to his subordinates not to go overboard in expanding Hong Kong too quickly.

He returned in January of 1842 to find that his orders had gone almost entirely unheeded. A contingent of Royal Engineers had constructed four miles of road—the beginnings of what is now the city's famous Queen's Road—for the population of fifteen thousand, probably more than twice the Hong Kong population before British ships had arrived in the bay a year earlier. The burgeoning settlement of Victoria boasted a number of stone houses, a new hotel, tailors, doctors, a canteen, more warehouses, a brothel and a jail, where previously it had been a jumble of tents and makeshift huts. Pottinger found himself apologizing to his superiors for the growth of the city. "I have done as much as I could to retard, without injuring this settlement," he told Lord Ellenborough, then the governor-general of British India. "The disposition to colonize under our protection is so strong that I behold a large and wealthy city springing up."[6] Palmerston, Pottinger and the British government had underestimated the attractiveness of a free port to merchants across southern China, who were flooding into the new trading post.

From its earliest days, the value of land has been crucial to Hong Kong's smooth governance. As the territory boomed, demand for land was driven higher and higher, and the revenues from land sales with it. The opening of a land registry was announced in March of 1842, where the owners of leases could register if they sold their plots to other investors. When the Treaty of Nanjing was signed in August, five Chinese ports would be opened to international trade, including for the drug the British East India Company was desperate to sell into China's miserable opium dens. But Hong Kong would be ceded entirely to the British Empire. When the deal was ratified in June 1843, Hong Kong officially became a British

Crown colony. Administrators and merchants now had the certainty they needed to expand even more rapidly.

Pottinger also received instructions on how to conduct land sales in the new colony. The idea was not to hand over the land permanently to new private owners. The imperial administrators wanted to make sure that the revenue source would continue in perpetuity. In 1843, the Earl of Derby, colonial secretary and a future prime minister, made clear to Pottinger that no land was to be auctioned "for any time of greater length than may be necessary to induce and enable the tenants to erect substantial buildings, etc."[7] Leases could be sold, but the Crown was to retain outright ownership of the land. When the contracts were finished, the land would be returned to the government, ensuring that the profits from sales kept flowing. As Hong Kong grew as a trading entrepôt, the model worked perfectly. Land prices rose, auctions took in more money and the local authorities could develop the city without resorting to either heavy taxes or subsidies from London.

In the century that followed, the British colony continued to expand in size, both geographically and by population. The Kowloon Peninsula across the bay from Hong Kong Island was annexed in the aftermath of the Second Opium War. By 1886, when the Hong Kong government was assessing the future use of land in the colony, the rents from land leased by the government had risen to over 150,000 Hong Kong dollars.[8] In 1898, the British government strong-armed the wavering Chinese imperial court yet again, securing a ninety-nine-year lease of its own for the New Territories, the land stretching from Kowloon to the Sham Chun River, and for the hundreds of islands surrounding the area. From the beginning of the twentieth century to the outset of the Second World War, Hong Kong's population more than quadrupled in size. In 1911, the collapse of the ailing Qing dynasty ended millennia of Chinese dynastic rule and ushered in decades of civil strife and political chaos, guaranteeing a constant flow of refugees to the safety of the British port and driving the value of land ever higher.

As the middle of the twentieth century approached, decolonization was underway for most of the colonies of European empires in Asia, Africa and the Americas. But Hong Kong was to remain a British outpost for another five decades, the country's final overseas colony of any meaningful size. Hong Kong's population had collapsed during the war, falling from 1.6 million to just 600,000, with hundreds of thousands of residents fleeing to the mainland or later expelled there by the Japanese.[9] Many were made homeless by American air raids on the occupied city. But the effects of China's brutal civil war and Chairman Mao's victory quickly put the city's population on an upwards trend again, quickly climbing back to and surpassing its prewar levels. By 1951, Hong Kong had a population of two million, as refugees flooded south from the chaotic mainland. The population would climb by around a million per decade over the subsequent forty years.

The rest of the world was in the process of being transformed. New left-wing governments were on the march around the newly independent developing world. Within Western nations, the dry principles of nineteenth-century finance that had dominated when Hong Kong was founded—low taxes, light regulation and free trade—were no longer in vogue. Two world wars and a wounding global depression in Europe and America had ushered in a new world of massive government intervention in the economy. All manner of industrial policy, management of economic demand and government controls on imports, exports, wages and prices prevailed for the thirty years that followed the peace in 1945, and beyond in some places.

But Hong Kong was an unusual outlier, not just in remaining a colony, but also in retaining most of the old distaste for economic meddling. Geoffrey Follows, who became the colony's financial secretary immediately after the war, was responsible for rebuilding the city's economy from the devastation of Imperial Japan's brutal occupation. Rather than pursue the interventionist policies in vogue in Europe, Follows prioritized the accumulation of currency reserves to make the city resilient against future economic shocks. When it came to tax and regulation, the light-touch principles that had made Hong Kong so popular with traders remained in place. The Chinese business community in the city was also vociferously opposed to new and modern systems of economic management, resisting the introduction of any taxes on income when they were proposed.[10]

From 1961 to 1971, Hong Kong's financial secretary was John James Cowperthwaite, a Scotsman who was unambiguously devoted to the principles of Hong Kong's earlier administrators. Cowperthwaite was an advocate of free trade, budget surpluses and a limited role for government. His ideological commitment stretched as far as refusing to make primary-level education free and compulsory, which only began in 1971 after Cowperthwaite left office, almost a century after the act that made schooling mandatory in Britain. Philip Haddon-Cave succeeded Cowperthwaite as financial secretary until 1980 and subsequently served as Hong Kong's governor. Haddon-Cave governed more or less in the same classical liberal vein, pioneering what he called "positive non-intervention" in the economy.[11] Each of the three men shared a disdain for government borrowing and stressed the need for Hong Kong to retain its financial independence from London.

Hong Kong's financial leaders may have been out of step with the mood music in their home country, but with most of the Empire gone, successive British governments were largely happy to let the colonial administration go its own way. Hong Kong was a bastion of low taxes with a night-watchman government, which free-market economist Milton Friedman singled out for commendation. "The power of the free market," Friedman mused in his 1980 PBS series, *Free to Choose*, based on his book of the same name, "has enabled the industrious people of Hong Kong to transform what was once barren rock into one of the most thriving and successful places in Asia."[12] Friedman was not wrong. The city was booming again. Between 1960 and 1980, Hong Kong's real GDP per capita more than tripled, even as the chaos of the Cultural Revolution raged on the Chinese mainland. Hong Kong industrialized rapidly, expanding a large production base in textiles into toys, watches, electronics and radios for export, mostly to the Western world.

But as it was developing its reputation as a free-market nirvana in a world drifting increasingly towards economic intervention, the importance of land to the government's fiscal health that had existed since the first months of Hong Kong's colonization was growing again. Indeed, the government's reluctance to either raise taxes or borrow more gave it an incentive to deliberately boost land prices. No matter the pain for residents hoping to buy the city's modest apartments, or to operate businesses on its scarce square footage, rising land values made the life of the government far easier, while any fall in prices would pose an immediate strain on them. The poisonous relationship between land and the government's bottom line gained a name in the 1970s: the "high land price policy." The government stood accused of deliberately boosting land prices to greater and greater levels, despite the painful expense for residents trying to buy apartments or operate businesses. The city's leaders—both those in the British colonial administrations and the Chinese leaders who succeeded them decades later—have repeatedly and vociferously denied the charge.

Hong Kong's growing prosperity and exploding population were having a predictable effect on the price of land, in a city that had relatively little of it. As early as 1963, one British MP noted that the city's frothy market "put London's land prices quite in the shade," though Hong Kong was then barely a third as rich per person as Britain, let alone its wealthy capital city.[13] With the surge in prices, the government was becoming more and more dependent on the income from land. In 1950, when the city was still recovering from the effects of its occupation, the land revenues made by the government—a combination of income from land sales, property rates based on the rental value of properties and the rents on land sold long ago—accounted for less than 15 percent of the city's total budget revenue.[14] The figure steadily climbed, passing 20 percent in 1956, 25 percent in 1961, and climbing to a full third of the government's revenue by the early 1960s, roughly where it remained on average for the rest of the twentieth century.

The government could not always keep prices propped up. Hong Kong's land market was about to undergo a slump that would set the tone for the city's modern history. A banking panic in 1965 was followed a year later by the chaotic violence of Chairman Mao's Cultural Revolution on the Chinese mainland. Hong Kong was separated from the Red Guards in

Guangdong Province by just a few meters of water. Political madness spilled across the border: In 1967, the city was wracked by riots. Combative trade unionists organized large-scale demonstrations, and leftist groups with connections to the Chinese Communist Party began a campaign of violence, littering the city with improvised explosive devices. The venerable headquarters of the Bank of China, still owned by the Chinese government, was festooned with banners and loudspeakers calling on Hong Kongers to revolt against their British rulers. Rumors circulated that Mao might even use the opportunity to invade the colony, which the modest British garrison would have had no hope of defending. By the end of the year, land prices in the city's Central District collapsed to between 200 and 300 Hong Kong dollars per square foot, down from 1,000 to 1,200 dollars three years earlier.[15]

But the turmoil of 1967 proved to be a vital turning point for modern Hong Kong too. For the previous one hundred and twenty years, the city's propertied establishment had been largely British. It was represented by the storied trading houses with names like Jardine, Swire, Wheelock and Wharf, some of which had been among the buyers of land in the territory's very earliest auctions. Another group of elites, like the immensely wealthy Hotung and Fung families, were part of a small Anglo-Chinese cohort that had prospered with close relations to the colonial government. But Hong Kong's old stalwarts were losing confidence in the city and winding down their investments. The moment of uncertainty proved to be an opening for a group of enterprising and ethnically Chinese businessmen, who used the brief opportunity in the chaos of the 1967 protests to snap up huge quantities of land and begin to replace the city's old elites. Among them was Li Ka-shing, a young manufacturer of cheap plastics. In the mid-1960s, Li had three real estate holdings. Cheng Yu-tung, a jewelry magnate, also took the chance to buy up land at its lows; he too became a property mogul in the process.

The new property titans positioned themselves on the winning sides of some of the best land deals in history. Li and Cheng were among the businessmen snapping up the paper promises known as land exchange entitlements. The Hong Kong government had begun to issue the certificates in 1960, which were to become the foundation of the wealth of the city's real estate tycoons. Hong Kong's need for new housing for a growing population was exacerbated by the flood of refugees still arriving from mainland China, numbering in the hundreds of thousands. The still largely rural areas relatively close to the border with the mainland were the most obvious spot for intensive development of new satellite towns, which would be filled with both public and private housing. The holders of land in the New Territories were offered an enticing choice by the thrifty Hong Kong government: they could take a nonnegotiable cash payment, or a land exchange entitlement that gave them the right to choose a plot of land in the newly developed towns of the New Territories sometime in the future.[16] Every five square feet of agricultural land could be swapped for two square feet of new residential land.

The British colonial government had been disciplined in the extreme when it came to keeping its budget balanced, but it proved to be absurdly generous when it came to its land swaps. The entitlements were transferable, and the new developers snapped up thousands of them from farmers who did not entirely understand their huge value. Three years before the policy was ended in 1983, the contracts amounted to thirty-six million square feet of agricultural land for development to the holders, about seven hundred and fifty football fields' worth, in what was rapidly becoming the world's most expensive city.[17] It was a colossal windfall to the developers, who had now assembled the foundation of their enormous land banks. The astute deals were one of the biggest factors in the companies' astounding profitability. By the middle of 2024, Sun Hung Kai Properties and Henderson Land held around about 4.5 square miles in their land banks together, enough to house hundreds of thousands of people at Hong Kong's famous population densities.[18]

In an ordinary year, a company based anywhere in the world would be considered financially solid if it was able to turn about 10 percent of its revenues into profits, after the cost of goods, salaries, taxes and all its other expenses (a measure known as a "net income margin.") But for astoundingly successful firms, especially those that have captured a niche in a booming new industry, higher profits are possible. Microsoft, America's largest company by market capitalization, has recorded a 28 percent net income margin on average over the last thirty years. Taiwan Semiconductor Manufacturing Company, the company with a technological lead in making the world's most advanced semiconductor chips, has made a net income margin of 34 percent on average since 1992. Both of the two firms spend tens of billions of dollars each year on research and development in defense of their technical advantages: falling behind the curve, even for a short period of time, would be a death sentence for the companies' whopping profits.

But the highly profitable technology giants of the corporate world pale in comparison to Hong Kong's property developers when it comes to making money. Sun Hung Kai Properties, the largest of the city's real estate giants, has recorded a net income margin of 48 percent on average since 1990. It ranks, along with some of its peers, as one of the most profitable firms not just in the city, or in Asia, but anywhere in the world. Hong Kong's largest real estate developers and their immensely wealthy owners have not unlocked a special new way of building property that has eluded the rest of the world. Their enormous profits, sustained over decades, are rather the symptom of a powerful oligopoly that persists in the city.

The real estate companies originally founded by the men—Li Ka-shing's CK Asset Holdings Limited and Cheng Yu-tung's New World Development—became half of the city's Big Four developers, along with Sun Hung Kai Properties and Henderson Land. Some of the storied British hongs, like Wharf and Wheelock, two real estate developers, and Hutchison Whampoa, a port and telecommunications operator, were swallowed up in acquisitions by the new titans of Hong Kong's real estate world in the 1970s and 1980s. Despite the city's reputation as a hub of trade and entrepreneurship, among the ranks of the city's very richest men, those who made their money in Hong Kong itself are almost all real estate developers or their children. Li Ka-shing's astute decisions at the nadir of Hong Kong's land market made him Hong Kong's richest man for most of the city's modern history. Lee Shau Kee—a founder of Henderson Land—comes not far behind, followed by Henry Cheng, the eldest son of Cheng Yu-tung.

The biggest real estate firms have benefited too from the way the government's land auctions have changed over time. During the nineteenth century when Hong Kong's land sales were pioneered, and leading up to the middle of the twentieth century, plots sold by the government had small up-front payments and higher annual ground rents—the stipend the developer would pay to the government through the course of its tenancy, usually over seventy-five years. But over time, rents had been held at low nominal levels by the government, chewed away by the sometimes-rapid inflation of the twentieth century. That means today, almost all of the cost of purchasing land from the government is done up front, rather than in annual increments. Hong Kong investor David Webb has illustrated the point with the example of Pacific Place, an enormous mall in one of Hong Kong's priciest districts.[19] When the site was sold to Swire, a storied Hong Kong conglomerate, the development set the company back about $1 billion, an even larger sum forty years ago. The lease came with an annual rent of just 1,000 Hong Kong dollars, less than 150 American dollars, to be paid for seventy-five years. With almost all of the cost of the land now in the initial payment, only the very largest buyers with the most bountiful capital supplies can compete for the top projects.

The surging price of land has transformed Hong Kong's economy and changed the types of business that thrive in the city. As early as 1965, the International Council for Scientific Management noted, "High land prices have taxed the ingenuity of Hong Kong industrial entrepreneurs."[20] The squeeze on more land-intensive industries became more and more severe over the subsequent decades, and businesses that needed significant space saw their costs surge far faster than their sales could keep up. The industries that had powered Hong Kong's rise to prosperity found bases elsewhere. Manufacturing shrank from 20 percent of the city's economic output in the middle of the 1980s to just 5 percent by the end of the century, and 1 percent today. In fact, bank lending to most kinds of businesses has declined as a share of all credit. Fifty years ago, manufacturing made up a fifth of Hong Kong's bank lending, and loans to the wholesale and retail industries made up another third.[21] Today, those categories make up less than 10 percent combined. Most of the loss in share among physical industry has been replaced by lending to households—overwhelmingly in the form of mortgages—and by borrowing on the part of property developers. Those categories collectively make up 60 percent of the total today, from as little as 20 percent fifty years ago.

Some of the city's leaders have understood quite well the noxious role that extortionate land prices play in its governance, but have been unwilling or unable to address them directly. Chris Patten, Hong Kong's British governor at the time of the handover and a persistent critic of the Chinese government's increasingly illiberal grip on the city today, says that he would have liked to smother the "grotesquely large profits" made by the real estate developers and to bring an end to the high land price policy.[22] His desires were stymied by a fear that squeezing developers could have crushed the stock market and that a major change to the city's fiscal model was impossible to achieve given the proximity of the handover.

The city's first post-handover leader, Chief Executive Tung Chee-hwa, pledged to release the land needed to build eighty-five thousand new apartments per year in order to finally bring down the city's exorbitant property prices. But the effects of the Asian financial crisis, which began in 1997, were painful for property-owning Hong Kongers and put an end to the plan. Apartment prices dropped and didn't stop falling until 2003, at which point they had declined by 60 percent and wiped out all of the gains of the 1990s.[23] But even at their lows, property was still hardly cheap by international standards: a piddling fifty-square-meter apartment on Hong Kong Island might have still commanded a price of a little more than 175,000 US dollars at the time, almost eight times the median Hong Kong household income.[24] Land sales by the government were curtailed, and few tenure conversions—which allowed land zoned for agriculture to be used for residential property—were permitted. Sales were restarted in 1999, then suspended again in 2002. It would take until 2011 before the revenue from sales and tenure conversions returned to its 1998 level.[25] When prices dropped, the government hardly even tried to disguise its intentions: it was deliberately throttling the supply of available land in an effort to keep prices from falling further.

In some ways, the consequences of the tight link between land and Hong Kong's economy have been obvious. In other ways, things are even worse than they might appear. Most obviously, the city's high land prices have made it even more exposed to the ups and downs of the real estate cycle than other major financial centers. The decade that followed the Asian financial crisis was a period of immiseration for Hong Kong's land-rich elite, but what was about to come would be the bonanza of a lifetime. In 2008, while property markets in much of the rest of the world were still reeling from the effects of the global financial crisis, Hong Kong's real estate market was about to boom, as China's economy exploded in size. The port city's role as the gateway to the biggest economic growth story in history made it not just a trading entrepôt, but a financial lung through which China's companies, and 1.3 billion increasingly prosperous citizens, were able to breathe the air of the outside world. Hong Kong's property prices exploded, rising by around 150 percent, even after accounting for inflation, between the end of 2008 and the end of 2018.

By 2019, the price of an average residential property in Hong Kong had climbed to 1.24 million US dollars, according to global real estate agency CBRE, around 40 percent higher than the equivalent level in Vancouver and 80 percent higher than in London.[26] Even that figure understates just how wildly expensive real estate had become in the city, since Hong Kong's flats are far smaller than homes in most parts of the world. In the same year, residents paid $2,091 per square foot for their property, nearly four times as much as in New York City. The importance of land and property in Hong Kong's total wealth sits at extraordinary levels: by the estimate of economists Thomas Piketty and Li Yang, both of the Paris School of Economics, the share of housing in the aggregate wealth of the city's households ran to at least 75 percent in 2018, compared to less than 35 percent in America during the peak before the global financial crisis.[27]

Even as prices boomed, the last fifteen years have been a miserable stretch when it comes to Hong Kong's housing supply: between 2010 and 2024, developers completed a little more than fifteen thousand new domestic residences on average each year, less than half of what they were building in the last decade and a half of the twentieth century, and not even a fifth of what Tung Chee-hwa had once promised to build. When confronted with their enormous profits, and Hong Kong's astoundingly high real estate prices, developers gripe that the costs imposed by the government to convert rural plots to housing and commercial property is what drives them to hold such enormous stocks of land. But regardless of how the blame should be apportioned between the developers and Hong Kong's government, any would-be buyers of the city's inordinately pricey properties have felt the consequences of the shortages.

There may be no smoke-filled room where bureaucrats, politicians and real estate titans conspire to make the city's housing deeply unaffordable to its residents. Many members of the government profess—perhaps even sincerely—that there is no high land price policy and that it is not the government's intention to keep real estate prices at astronomical levels. But at its core, the evidence of Hong Kong's problem is simple and clear: it is a city where all the land is owned by the government, where land prices are among the very highest in the world and where the plutocrats that own its real estate firms are by far the city's richest men. Whether that is by accident or deliberate design, for malign or corrupt reasons, the high land price policy is a simple point of reality. The incentives of a group of developers, the city's wealthiest homeowners and its bureaucrats and politicians have made it so.

Even Hong Kong's famously low tax levels are somewhat illusory, given the reality of the high land price policy. Residents pay low tax rates on their personal and corporate income, and there is still no direct sales taxation. But they also pay the rents on its extraordinarily pricey real estate. The city's eye-popping land prices—the highest in the world per square foot of residential property—are the mirror image of its low tax rates. Alice Poon, an author and former employee of Sun Hung Kai Properties and Kerry Properties, two of the city's leading property developers, calls this Hong Kong's "hidden tax."[28] If property prices were lower, revenue from land sales would tank, and there is no way the city would be able to maintain its combination of rock-bottom tax rates and low government debt.

Hong Kong's property market has entered a period of gloom again in recent years. The city's earthshaking protest movement in 2019, the authoritarian turn of Hong Kong's government, the slowdown in the Chinese economy in recent years and the sudden rise in interest rates around the world have all weighed on the market. In real terms, residential property prices have dropped by more than a third since their peak. Still, at the end of 2024, an average fifty-square-meter apartment on Hong Kong Island would have set a buyer back around 900,000 US dollars, more than twenty times an average Hong Kong household income now. The downturn has left the city economically depressed, but without making housing particularly affordable.

The huge divisions between Hong Kong's haves and have-nots in the markets for land and housing were not the cause of the enormous protest movement that engulfed the city in 2019. Hong Kong's feistily indepen-dent local identity and the increasing encroachment on the city's civil and political rights by the central government in Beijing are more than enough of an explanation for the enormous support for the pro-democracy move-ment. Handed from one distant power to another in 1997, the city has never been afforded the right to govern itself in any meaningful sense. But all the same, the gargantuan gaps in wealth generated by the inequi-ties of the housing market give Hong Kong's youngest residents no inter-est in conserving or defending the existing political arrangement either.

If there is a single avatar for the case that persistently high land prices can damage a place that otherwise has almost all of the necessary compo-nents of success, Hong Kong is the most obvious candidate anywhere in the world. It has an entrepreneurial and innovative population, low taxes and light regulation and an unimpeachable position as the gateway to one of the world's biggest bazaars of consumption and production in main-land China. But through its broken land and property markets, Hong Kong has managed to turn these enviable advantages into pitfalls. Incomes in Hong Kong now lag well behind those of Singapore, the Southeast Asian city-state with which it is inevitably compared.

The consequences of Hong Kong's problems with land are far greater than even its acute economic and political struggles would suggest. When Zhao Ziyang met Henry Fok and listened to his ideas about land and wealth, Hong Kong became the proving ground for the way China treats land, housing and government finance. The conditions that have smoth-ered Hong Kong's innovative spirit and made it so economically unequal have been transmitted to the world's second-largest economy too—without much thought for the consequences.

Land auctions captured the imagination of Zhao Ziyang and China's other reformist leaders in the 1980s for much the same reason that they had appealed to Hong Kong's colonial administrators in the 1840s. Using the world's oldest asset as a way to generate income for the government was administratively simple and almost impossible to avoid. At its best, it could be a way to allocate the land to the most productive causes. It also assuaged some of the worries that the hardline Communists had about inviting foreign capital into the country: investors might suddenly change their minds about China and pull their money out of China, as they had in many other emerging markets around the world. But land was an asset they couldn't take with them.

The Hong Kong system had an ironic ideological appeal too, since the government of the colony owned the land itself. That gave the People's Republic, ostensibly still a communist country, the ability to blur some ideological lines. Leases known as land-use rights could be sold without technically making private landownership legal. Whatever discomfort more hardline Communist Party functionaries might have had with the sudden changes, most of them quickly came to understand that the new model didn't mean giving up either their privileged positions or political control. Indeed, the new wealth offered by the sales could even accentuate their power, not to mention the opportunities it provided for corruption and self-enrichment. Forty years after its violent extermination, China's landlord class was back.

Zhao Ziyang was not the first or only policymaker in China who grasped the potential for land assets to become the bedrock for the government's finances. The petri dish for mainland China's first experiment with land auctions was found within sight of the British colony, across the river that separates it from the Chinese mainland. In 1980, the city of Shenzhen was made one of the country's first special economic zones (SEZ). It was the focal point of Deng's plans, the vanguard of the new Chinese economy. In 1981, foreign investors could already apply for new land-use certificates within the confines of the SEZ, for which they would pay the local government an annual fee. The contracts could not be otherwise transferred, borrowed against, bought or sold, but a crucial taboo—the exchange of land for money—was already being broken at a small scale.

By the middle of the 1980s, what had once been a backwater on the coast of Guangdong was a thriving commercial hub, bustling with entrepreneurs and reformist officials. Shenzhen's population had exploded from a few hundred thousand in the late 1970s—less than a twentieth the size of Beijing—into one of China's largest and most prosperous metropolises in the space of just a couple of decades. Today, it is the headquarters to China's corporate giants—globe-trotting tech firms like Huawei and ZTE call the city home, as does BYD, a giant in the booming electric vehicle ecosystem at home and abroad. Shenzhen is a symbol more than anywhere else of the country's transformation from a handicapped command economy to a financial world power. It is also the most obvious symbol of how the shifting role of land and property have changed the entire country.

When the moment came, Shenzhen's model of financing itself through land sales was adopted practically wholesale from the British colony it bordered. In December 1987, eleven years after Mao's death, the first private auction of land since the establishment of the People's Republic was conducted in Shenzhen City Hall. The city leased a piece of land measuring 8,588 square meters—a little bigger than a football pitch—for a term of fifty years, bringing in a little more than a million US dollars.[29] Nestled among the Chinese officials, reporters and municipal leaders at the auction were dozens of Hong Kong economists and businessmen. The gavel used by the auctioneer had been gifted to Shenzhen by the Hong Kong government. Just as in Hong Kong in 1841, the sale was not even entirely legal yet. It would be another six months until a Chinese constitutional amendment removed the legal barriers to owning and selling land-use rights, opening the door for auctions to be conducted nationwide. But the stage was now set for the revolution in China's land use.

One by one, other Chinese municipalities began to copy Shenzhen's model, beginning their own land auctions to raise revenue. Likely very few of the party bureaucrats organizing the sales, or the buyers of the new land leases, realized that the system was a hand-me-down, passed rung by rung from the United Kingdom's War and Colonial Office in the early nineteenth century, and that they were inheriting a system of finance designed by a distant empire a century and a half before. Nor would they have known that along with that system, they would inherit all of its flaws—flaws that would not become immediately obvious, but would without a doubt emerge.

NINE

The Biggest
Bubble in History

By 1992, Deng Xiaoping was eighty-eight years old. His crusade for economic reform had been stalled for three years. The bloodbath that he had presided over in Tiananmen Square had put all forms of liberalization in China, whether financial or political, on hold. The world had reacted to the massacre with horror, and China's leadership had turned inwards, back to what they knew best. The fall of the Berlin Wall later in 1989 and the dissolution of the Soviet Union that followed had convinced hard-liners within the Communist Party that opening up was a dangerous gambit that threatened their grip on the country. The greatest supporters of Deng's economic transformation found themselves sidelined by conservatives. Deng had stepped down from his official positions in November of 1989, succeeded by Jiang Zemin. China's reform and opening-up measures had not been reversed, but the advocates of any further change were on the defensive.

Unlike most of the cabal of reformers around Deng, Premier Zhao Ziyang was a political liberal too—at least by the standards of the leadership of Communist China. He found himself purged from public life in

China for a second time, not by Maoist hard-liners but by Deng himself. On May 19, 1989, one day before martial law began in Beijing, Zhao had stepped out into Tiananmen Square to call on the students on hunger strike to disperse, promising to continue to listen to their demands. "You are not like us," Zhao said. "We are already old, and do not matter." It was to be Zhao's last public statement. When he died in 2005, the former premier had spent the final fifteen years of his life under house arrest in Beijing. Zhao's candid diaries on the reality of governing in China in the 1970s and 1980s were smuggled out of the country in the form of audio recordings and published after his death.

China's political apparatus had turned against reform in the early 1990s, but Deng had one final campaign left to wage. On January 19, 1992, the former paramount leader arrived in Shenzhen, the site of China's first experiments in land auctions. Reform had been hampered by the new leaders in Beijing, but the city was still bustling with unsuppressed activity. Accompanied by Shenzhen's mayor and the secretary of the provincial Communist Party, Deng buzzed across Splendid China, one of the country's first amusement parks, in a golf cart. He visited the headquarters of a company producing laser discs.[1] After Shenzhen, Deng would travel across the Pearl River Delta to nearby Zhuhai and Guangzhou, giving a series of speeches. He argued not only that reform was irreversible, but that those who were not committed to it should lose their positions in government. It was only because of the fruits of the reform policies, Deng argued, that the country had been able to survive the chaos of the Tiananmen protests at all. Without them, he claimed, the country would have been plunged into another disastrous civil war.

When they heard that Deng was speaking just over the border, journalists from Hong Kong rushed across to cover the story. But media outlets across the mainland were controlled by Deng's political rivals. News of the tour was suppressed at home and did not appear in print, radio or on television. That might well have remained the case, had an unauthorized report not appeared in a local Shenzhen newspaper two months after Deng's visit. Chen Xitian, the deputy editor of the *Shenzhen Special Zone Daily*, had been asked in strict confidence to attend Deng's trip. On March 26, more than two months after the tour, the paper published a series of articles covering the details of Deng's speeches and tour at length. Deng's message proved popular among officials around the country, and his venerated status gave other Communist leaders the courage to break ranks and endorse the further modernization of the economy. Later that year, Jiang Zemin weighed in behind Deng. At the fourteenth National Congress of the Chinese Communist Party, the top meeting of senior officials, Jiang introduced the world to the idea of the "socialist market economy," which entered the Chinese constitution in 1993. Reform was back.

Today, Shenzhen is at the vanguard of the modern Chinese economy, and is the most startling symbol of the country's entrepreneurial prowess. Far more than Beijing, Shanghai or Guangzhou, China's other wealthy megacities, it is a product of Deng's project, intertwined completely with the decision to open China to the world. Almost nobody lived in what is now Shenzhen before it was made a special economic zone. While China's other megalopolises boast of hundreds of years of deep history, in its southern commercial hub, almost every resident is a migrant or the child or grandchild of one.

When Deng was speaking in southern China in 1992, the country's real estate market was still in its infancy. It would be several years before most of the country's citizens got the opportunity to own their own homes, and more than a decade before their rights to own and inherit were enshrined in the constitution, which had once forbidden private property entirely. But the changes made over the years that followed Deng's tour would transform China at an astonishing pace. As the economy exploded in size, it quickly began to exhibit some of the worst problems associated with land as an asset. China would eventually produce the largest land bubble by value anywhere in the world, making the American exuberance in the run-up to the 2008 financial crisis look staid and sensible by comparison. Land affects every aspect of China's economic and political model, and the asset is the source of all too many of the country's greatest problems today.

Shenzhen is still the emblem not just of Chinese entrepreneurial and technological skill but of its challenges with the land market too. It is regularly ranked not just as one of the most expensive cities in the country when it comes to real estate, but as one of the most expensive anywhere in the world. At their 2022 peak, house prices in Shenzhen ran to around 70,000 yuan per square meter, or a little less than $1,000 per square foot.[2] At the same time, San Francisco prices ran to more like $750 per square foot, though incomes there are far higher. In fact, Shenzhen is one of the only places on earth that makes Hong Kong's real estate market look cheap. Unlike most of urban China, where homeownership runs to extremely high levels, Shenzhen's is lower than many Western megacities, with only around 30 percent of the population owning the properties they live in.

Two powerful propellants of China's new real estate boom would emerge by the end of the 1990s. One of the crucial decisions that supercharged the market for land was installed unintentionally, two years after Deng's southern tour. In 1994, the Chinese government changed the distribution of tax and spending responsibilities between local governments around the country and the central government in Beijing. For decades, China's economic management had been highly decentralized. Provincial and local governments owned the means of production in their own jurisdictions, running the state-owned enterprises and supervising collective farms. Most tax was raised in the provinces and kept by local governments, who also had the lion's share of responsibilities when it came to spending. A portion was then sent back up the chain to the central government. But from 1994, Beijing took full fiscal control of the country's revenues. Instead of keeping most of the revenue they raised, as they had in the past, provinces and cities would have to remit a far larger share to Beijing and accept whatever they were given back in return.

The decision to deprive China's local governments of an enormous proportion of their income might have otherwise been a dry and dusty fiscal amendment, interesting mostly to the country's bureaucrats and a clutch of international China-watchers. But paired with the early opening-up of markets in land in a previously planned economy, the decision became something far more momentous. The share of revenue kept by local governments fell from 78 percent of the country's total to 44 percent in a single year, but the spending responsibilities of the provinces and cities were barely changed at all.[3] In 1993, the revenues collected by China's local governments had been enough to fund all of their spending; in 1994, the measly revenues they were allowed to keep covered less than 60 percent of their expenditure, leaving them desperately in need of a new source of income to fund their obligations.[4] More than any other single policy decision made by the Chinese government, the reshuffling of the country's tax and spending responsibilities in 1994 lit a fire under the market for Chinese land that would burn for almost three decades afterwards.

The power grab by the central government left China's local government leaders in a bind. In the same situation, an American state or municipal government might have borrowed from banks or bond markets (wisely or otherwise), but that was banned by Beijing. Faced with the sudden shortfall, local governments got creative, turning to a range of murky off-budget revenues, sometimes known as the "little golden box." Residents, especially those in rural areas farthest from the view of the central government, faced a barrage of informal, unreasonable and often flagrantly illegal administrative fees, levied on anything that moved. The charges were not just a mechanism for raising revenue, but for enabling massive local corruption too. The further any such shadowy revenue was from Beijing's view, the easier it was for local governments to raise. But by the end of the 1990s, China's central government had gotten wise to the fact that residents of the countryside were being shaken down for inventive new forms of local government income. Beijing moved to curtail the deeply unpopular practices.

But even as their dubious avenues for revenue-raising were being closed off, local authorities found a better way to wriggle free from the fiscal straitjacket. Revenue collected from the kind of land sales that had first been pioneered a decade earlier in Shenzhen were classed as separate off-budget incomes, which, like the fees they had tried to impose, did not have to be shared with Beijing. Land sales became a vital plug for the yawning hole in local government budgets, often the only tool local authorities could use to balance the desperate mismatch between their incomes and spending obligations. By the end of the 1990s, land sales were now not only legal and highly profitable, but encouraged over any other way of raising revenue. Receipts from land revenues rose from less than 10 percent of local government income at the end of the twentieth century to two thirds in 2010.[5] The pressure put on local Chinese governments from Beijing meant they had even more incentive to boost prices than the government had done in Hong Kong: they had been strong-armed into making as much money from land sales as they possibly could.

The second source of fuel for the multi-decade housing boom came from the growing prosperity of Chinese families heading into new forms of industrial and white-collar work. Many millions had money to spend and invest for the first time in their lives. In 1994, just as Beijing's unfortunate tax changes drove local governments into a scramble for off-budget revenues, the employees of state firms gained the right to buy their existing homes, the first step in the accumulation of property for many Chinese families. The private provision of housing finally became official in 1998, when a new law permanently severed the link between government employment and the provision of accommodation. During the last decade of the twentieth century and the first decade of the twenty-first, China's GDP grew by around 10 percent per year on average. Residential real estate investment surged at an even more rapid pace, growing by more than 20 percent each year.

Even in land-frenzied Hong Kong, local savers at least had access to a bustling financial market and faced no restrictions on deploying their capital overseas if they liked. The ability to choose other assets puts some limit on how detached from fundamental investment reality the property market can get. But in the mainland, citizens had very little else to invest in other than property. Just as Japan had done in its period of rapid growth, the Chinese government engaged in financial repression to direct the country's savings towards its industrial champions. Interest rates on bank deposits were kept deliberately low to ensure that banks could offer low-interest loans for China's prized state-owned enterprises. Though the Chinese economy was growing almost more rapidly than practically any other economy in the world, the returns on holding money in a bank were often negative, after accounting for inflation.

The alternative options for China's household savings were pitiful. In 1990, Shanghai's stock market opened for the first time since the end of the Chinese Civil War. But Chinese stocks have made for a volatile and miserable investment ever since, for households and professional investors alike. And even as Chinese leaders opened their economy to the outside world, and Chinese goods began to flood from ports across the country's eastern coast into every trade lane on earth, the Communist Party leadership had no intention of allowing ordinary citizens to shuffle their money out into overseas investment products. They kept the country's strict capital controls in place. The government has maintained its grip on the value of China's currency, controlling the flows of money in and out of its borders. For the very richest citizens with international business connections, there have always been ways to sneak money out of the country, in the guise of inflated corporate investment overseas or fictitious bills for imported products. But for ordinary households, getting much of their money out of the country was and remains extremely difficult. For most investors, real estate—as much of it as they could get their hands on—became the only alternative, and the best method of benefiting from the rapid growth of the Chinese economy.

As the new land-financing model was on the rise in China, the need for households to save was growing too. As the country's communist structure was dismantled piece by piece, the old forms of social welfare provided by state-owned workplaces went with it. China was still a communist country in name, but the government assistance available to workers and retirees had become far stingier. According to the International Labour Organization of the United Nations, the average Chinese pension was worth about 170 yuan per month in 2020, less than $25, a figure that does not go very far even in poorer parts of China.[6] Mass migration has made life for many Chinese workers even more precarious: the country's *hukou* system of household registration and welfare makes citizens born in one part of the country eligible for benefits there, and there alone. Since 1990, hundreds of millions of Chinese citizens have moved from their small towns and villages to the country's most productive cities for work, losing access to even the limited welfare they might have been entitled to at home. Chinese households have determined, quite rationally, that saving huge sums for expensive housing assets is their safest alternative form of security. A Chinese family's financial future is stored in their homes, as much or more than it is anywhere else in the world.

After decades of communist dogma, the old connections between social status and landownership reasserted themselves too, almost as soon as the legal restrictions on property ownership were dropped. As in Europe, owning land in imperial China was a marker of status, and the acquisition of generational wealth was a prized goal. The old pre-communist social norm that a man seeking a bride should own a home for the new couple to live in came roaring back as soon as the private sector took control of the housing market. The newly emerging household demand for more and more property, the desire of local governments to sell as much of it as possible and the roaring Chinese economy were the bedrocks of the new market, and of the frenetic decades of speculation about to unfurl. The conditions were in place for the biggest housing boom in history.

One of the millions of Chinese workers about to join the enormous wave of internal migration was Xu Jiayin, a thirty-four-year-old manager at the Wuyang Iron & Steel Company. Xu had worked at the enormous state-owned enterprise for a decade after graduating from university. Like many of his peers, he was unsatisfied with his station in life and his role in China's old economy. According to his own account, after being passed over for a promotion, he took inspiration from Deng's southern tour speeches and left his job, heading south for bustling Shenzhen. He took on a Cantonese name, Hui Ka Yan, and looked for employment in the blossoming private sector. He initially worked for a trading company, climbing the ranks to become a manager. But the promise of a somewhat more comfortable life as a middle-class, white-collar professional was not enough for Hui. In 1996, he decided to fulfil the promise of the new Chinese economy and struck out on his own as an entrepreneur. Hui borrowed almost a million dollars from his former employers and founded a real estate developer called Hengda. It would be known to the world as the Evergrande Group.

As China's local governments were becoming hooked on the revenues from their land sales, the country's budding real estate developers were growing rapidly alongside them. The companies would be the intermediaries that linked local governments desperate to sell land to would-be buyers desperate to make secure investments. Even by 1997, before the legal responsibility for Chinese employers to house their workers was abandoned,

Hui was relatively late to the party. China Vanke, one of the country's largest real estate developers, was among the very first companies in the country to float its stock in public markets, snapping up the identification code 000002 on the Shenzhen Stock Exchange after the market opened in December 1990. Country Garden, another behemoth developer today, was founded in 1992.

China's decrepit, crumbling housing stock had been built next to communal farms and state-owned enterprises, convenient locations in the top-down Mao-era economy. That world was on the way out. Buyers wanted modern, urban apartment blocks near the new private sector companies emerging in China's growing cities. To the companies building the new units, speed was the name of the game. Rapidly growing urban China was effectively virgin land for new housing developments, as inviting to the real estate developers as the bountiful expanse of earth had been to the English settlers landing in New England in the early decades of the seventeenth century. Capturing the best available land as rapidly as possible, before competitors could arrive, was an overwhelming imperative. Even relative to the speed of China's relentless economic expansion, the developers grew at an astonishing pace. In 2000, Vanke, which was already one of the country's largest housebuilders, made 3.7 billion Chinese yuan in revenue selling property to hungry Chinese buyers. By 2021, the company booked sales of 452.8 billion yuan.[7] Over a period where total Chinese GDP rose by around 1,100 percent, it has been possible for real estate developers that were already among the largest in the country to grow more than ten times as quickly.

For such breakneck expansion to work, investing the proceeds of real estate sales back into land purchases would not have been enough: the companies needed to borrow heavily as well. Between 2000 and 2020, the liabilities of China's real estate development firms rose from around 2 trillion yuan, equivalent to 19 percent of China's GDP at the time, to 86 trillion yuan, equivalent to 85 percent of the country's total economic output.[8] Household debt, overwhelmingly in the form of mortgages, rose from around 25 percent of China's disposable income in 2006 to more than 130 percent in 2020.[9] By some estimates, residential housing now accounts for 80 percent of household assets in China.[10]

Evergrande would grow faster and borrow even more rapaciously than any of its peers. The company's first development in Guangzhou, built on cheap land on the site of a former pesticide plant, was snapped up by frantic buyers in a matter of hours. Hui's business model was simple: the company would accumulate an empire of cheap land, often buying up marginal plots overlooked by other investors, financed with the proceeds of an even more dramatic borrowing binge. The best spots in China's richest cities— Guangzhou, Beijing, Shenzhen and Shanghai, the enormous and wealthy "tier one" megalopolises familiar to foreign businesses and travelers— were quickly exhausted. In response, Evergrande and other developers began to expand farther out into China's smaller and less prosperous tier two and tier three cities, away from the most developed parts of the eastern coast. The company's assets—overwhelmingly in the form of land-use rights purchased from local governments—rose from about five billion yuan in 2004 (less than $1 billion at the time), to a peak of 2.3 trillion yuan in 2020 (more than $300 billion), recording an average growth rate of more than 50 percent per year. The firm's debts exploded to acquire the assets as the company borrowed more and more money from any source available to keep grabbing up land.

In October 2009, even as the Western world was nursing its wounds in the aftermath of the global financial crisis, China's housing market was booming and Evergrande's stock floated on the Hong Kong Stock Exchange for the first time. But the government in Beijing was already becoming uneasy about the amount of money that China's state-owned banks were lending to real estate developers. House prices climbed by more than 20 percent the same year. The government placed restrictions on bank lending to real estate developers, which only drove the companies towards international bond markets, where they became some of the largest borrowers of US dollars in Asia. Interest rates around the world had been slashed as the Great Recession unfolded, making the high yields on bonds issued by Chinese developers appetizing to hungry fund managers around the world. Evergrande and the bond market proved to be a match made in heaven. Between 2010 and 2020, the firm's bond debts rose from less than 9 billion yuan to more than 230 billion. For a long time, it paid its creditors handsomely: the company's bonds regularly offered yields of between 10 percent and 20 percent.

By the time its stock was listed in Hong Kong, Evergrande wasn't just expanding rapidly to snap up more and more land in the best locations. The company now needed to grow at a breakneck pace just to stay ahead of its ballooning debt interest payments. The company had established the basic structure of a Ponzi scheme: new debts were being taken on to pay off the old ones. A slowdown in fundraising would be deadly. Not long after Evergrande's shares were listed on the Hong Kong Stock Exchange, a coterie of skeptics began to take interest in the firm. Analysts and short sellers believed that Evergrande's model of highly leveraged land speculation was not only unsustainable, but that it might also be hiding all manner of financial misbehavior. In 2012, Andrew Left, the founder of short-selling firm Citron Research, claimed that Evergrande was already insolvent and accused the company of fraudulent accounting and bribery, pointing to a history of creative accounting. Hui came under fire from Left, who said the company's founder had "secured his Doctorate from what is essentially a mail-order program at the University of West Alabama."[11] Left was sued for his research, and in 2016 he was banned from the Hong Kong stock market for five years after a judge ruled that he had published misleading information.

Developers searched relentlessly for more and more sources of leverage. They borrowed from their own suppliers and contractors, paying in IOUs where possible and delaying any transaction that required cash for as long as they could. Eventually, they found an even better form of borrowing. "Pre-sales" allowed companies to take money up front from would-be homeowners for the promise of new apartments in the future. Buyers received a modest discount, and developers received a wad of cash at the earliest possible opportunity. Between 2015 and the end of 2019, on the eve of the Covid-19 pandemic, bank lending by real estate developers rose by about 18 percent, and bond issuance by around 19 percent. In the same period, pre-sales rose by an astounding 103 percent, becoming the most popular single source of funding for developers in China. This method of financing was smart on the part of the eager developers, but it also proved to be their most dangerous form of leverage.

Pre-sales are by no means unique to China: property developers all over the world use the proceeds from a pre-sold project to pay for its construction. Buyers pay a deposit, take out a mortgage and receive their home on an agreed-upon timescale. But in China, there was no official system of escrow, the agreement between buyer and pre-seller that stops the developer from spending the money to finish other uncompleted projects. And that is exactly what Chinese real estate firms did. In the laxest jurisdictions across the country, sellers could begin marketing properties to new buyers as soon as a foundation stone was set in place, with no controls preventing them from using the funds from homebuyers' payments on other projects in the meantime.

When new buyers paid for their unbuilt properties, their cash was instead used to build estates that had been promised to previous groups of homebuyers months or even years earlier. Pre-sales made for the perfect form of financing. Compared to banks or asset managers, Chinese households were disorganized and unsophisticated creditors. Their lump sum payments effectively made for an interest-free loan to developers that could be extended indefinitely if the would-be homeowners were guileless enough to fall for the developer's excuses. By the eve of the Covid-19 pandemic, only 15 percent of Chinese property sales were actually completed homes, with almost 85 percent sold ahead of time. Before the music stopped, developers were selling twice as much floor space as they were actually building.

At the same time that the Chinese developers' financial excesses were reaching a crescendo, the speculative behavior on the part of buyers was peaking too. In the earliest days of China's housing boom, most purchases were made by first-time buyers who had previously lived in employer- or government-provided accommodation. But by the 2010s, China's home-ownership rate had already climbed to over 80 percent. Many of the buyers snapping up housing were buying second or even third homes, on the expectation of continued capital gains and a lack of alternative ways to park their money. By the beginning of 2018, the Survey and Research Center for China Household Finance at the Southwestern University of Finance and Economics at Chengdu said that around 44 percent of house purchases were made by buyers who owned another home already, and another 25 percent to buyers who owned more than two.[12]

Evergrande had reached the absolute peak of its fortunes by 2017. The company's stock hit its record high that year, giving the developer a market value of over $50 billion. Hui Ka Yan was China's richest man, standing ahead of technology giants like Jack Ma, founder of Alibaba, or Pony Ma, founder of Tencent. Guangzhou Evergrande, the football team that the company's founder purchased in 2010, had topped the Chinese Super League in every season since. Evergrande had subsidiaries in banking, insurance and health care. The following year, it would make an investment in an American electric vehicle company, Faraday Future, the first step of an effort by Evergrande to build its own battery-powered cars. The company that Hui Ka Yan had was the most extreme, even absurd, specimen of the real estate bubble that was by then a quarter of a century in the making. But both Evergrande, and the bubble that made its ridiculous and debt-burdened business model possible, were coming to the end of the road.

China's leaders were not completely blind to the astonishing buildup of debt and frenzied financial speculation underway across the country. But for local government leaders, the challenge of holding down house prices was the political equivalent of looking directly into the sun. Real estate had become vital to their economies, even beyond the land revenue they needed to sustain their spending. The rampant increase in real estate wealth was and remains the cornerstone of middle-class prosperity in China. Even beyond the importance of housing as an asset, construction contributed over a fifth of China's annual GDP growth. Stalling that increase would threaten the underpinning of China's entire economic and political model, something which no municipal leader would dare to seriously attempt.

Like Japan before it, China's rapid growth created its own Land Myth.

The perception that property prices would continue rising indefinitely was almost universal. It was not just an irrational faith in the magical properties of the property market. Many homebuyers took the cynical view (for a long time, correctly) that the government would simply not allow prices to fall. Buying a second or even a third apartment to leave empty seemed an entirely rational decision for Chinese families, no matter how ridiculously expensive housing became. For developers, the logic was equally straightforward: no amount of money could be too large to borrow if it meant acquiring more of an asset that could only ever rise in value.

At the end of 2016, Chinese president Xi Jinping introduced a new mantra for the real estate market: "Houses are for living in, not for speculation." The instruction came directly from the top, and it was quickly picked up and repeated by party functionaries across the country.[13] But for several years, the phrase seemed to be a platitude. Chinese cities occasionally squeezed the ability of buyers to access mortgages for second homes or required steeper down payments when the market was particularly heated. But any time a city's crucial targets for GDP growth looked like they might be missed, or regional banks and developers got into financial trouble, local governments would scramble to boost activity in the housing market, offering a quick boost to the economy. Popular cities like Shenzhen and Guangzhou occasionally experimented with price limits based on the floor space of apartments, which sellers tried to circumvent in spirited and desperate ways. One agent in Shenzhen touted million-dollar bananas and durians in an attempt to hide illicit black-market property sales.

But for the first time since Deng's southern tour, things were about to change in a serious way for China's land and real estate market. In August

2020, senior officials at the People's Bank of China and the Ministry of Housing gathered representatives from the country's major property developers together. Xi's mantra was about to be applied for real. The punch bowl was dry, the lights were coming on and the party was over. The bureaucrats issued new restrictions on what developers could borrow, based on their liabilities, the ratio of their debt levels to the value of their equity, and their cash reserves. The regulations were named the "Three Red Lines," coming into force at the end of the year. Under the new rules, very few major developers were permitted to borrow more from banks or bond markets except to roll over existing loans. Some were not even allowed to borrow to refinance loans they had already taken out. Evergrande was the most heavily indebted of all.[14]

The new rules meant companies had to tighten their belts in an unprecedented way. But what was happening to the real estate developers would certainly not end with them. Firms like Evergrande, China Vanke and Country Garden were not just large companies, but vital middlemen in China's entire economic model, matchmakers between local governments desperate to sell land and households desperate to invest in an asset that could hold its value and offer the potential for solid capital returns. With the Three Red Lines, China's leadership was hoping to pull the tablecloth from below a feast and keep all the plates above it in place.

For the first time, buyers were seriously shaken. Those who had made large pre-sale payments had reason to believe that the money they had paid to developers could disappear and that the apartments they were owed might never arrive. The companies that supplied real estate firms with everything from copper and concrete to marketing services panicked that the IOUs they had accepted in the hundreds of billions of dollars would never be paid. Just as the debt-driven land speculation schemes pursued by early American financier Robert Morris had run out of road more than two centuries ago in the early days of the new republic, Evergrande's adventure was coming to an end. The company's bills, and those of other developers, collapsed in value as the company's woes became clear. Where buyers could be found for them at all, their debts traded at a rapidly increasing discount to their face value.

When the Chinese government finally slammed the brakes on the rapid expansion of the property developers, the behemoth that Hui Ka Yan had founded in Shenzhen was in the process of building 798 different developments—at least, it said it was. Evergrande held around 231 million square meters of land in reserve across the country, an area four times the size of Manhattan or London's Zone 1, with the potential to house several million people. The company limped on for less than a year after the Three Red Lines were introduced. In September of 2021, Evergrande failed to make the payments due to international bondholders who had once eagerly snapped up its high-yield debts. The companies that supplied the raw materials Evergrande needed to build went unpaid, and it begged for loans from its own employees. On December 9, 2021, just short of twenty-five years after the company had been founded, credit rating agencies said Evergrande had defaulted.

Protests against all manner of real estate–related injustices began to pop up across China. Buyers besieged Evergrande's headquarters in Guangzhou after the company defaulted on its bonds. Developers cutting house prices on new developments faced uproar from residents who had bought at the earlier, higher prices. Some buyers of pre-sold housing who saw their developments suddenly stall in the midst of construction moved into the deserted estates, squatting inside the shells of the homes and investments that were meant to be theirs. Hundreds of boycotts of mortgage repayments were announced by disgruntled buyers across the country, who were already making payments to banks for apartments they worried they would never receive.

Evergrande was not alone. The company had always been the most risk-tolerant player in the dangerous game played by Chinese property developers, and it was known internationally for its astounding debts and reckless expansion. But by the end of 2023, even giant companies like China Vanke and Country Garden, which were once thought to be relatively sure bets and had been able to borrow from international bond markets at low-interest rates for years, were battling to avoid default. Yields on bonds issued by Chinese developers had exploded to levels that suggested a collapse was imminent. The financial straitjacket imposed by the government had become increasingly visible not just at the company level, but in macroeconomic data across the entire country: real estate investment plunged. By 2024, investment had declined by around a third from its peak in 2021.

China's housing bubble managed to produce some of the worst symptoms of a housing glut, and the worst symptoms of a housing shortage, all at the same time. Responding to rapacious demand from buyers, developers produced a ridiculous excess of real estate in some places, and with it an enormous number of empty homes. By the estimate of Gan Li, who directs the China Household Finance Survey, over a fifth of China's urban housing stock sat empty in 2017, the consequence of properties purchased on the expectation that prices would simply continue rising.[15] The tens of millions of unoccupied apartments across China are monuments to the immense waste of human labor and physical resources required for their construction—an ocean of copper, concrete and steel has been assembled to build them. They are a physical symbol of a tremendous economic misstep.

Even with the huge surplus of housing across the country, prices are extraordinarily high, defying the common understanding of supply and demand. By the time the Chinese government finally decided to act against the real estate developers who had facilitated the boom, the average price-to-income ratio was 13.4 not just across the most expensive cities in the country, but across its fifty largest urban areas.[16] Chinese house prices make those in San Francisco and London (with house price-to-income ratios of around 10 and 9.1 respectively in 2024) look cheap by comparison. Buyers must save huge chunks of their income for decades to have any chance of affording them. Indeed, China's savings rate is among the very highest in the world, at 46 percent of its GDP, far above even the 34 percent in South Korea and 28 percent in Japan—two relatively high-saving countries—and more than twice the British and American levels of less than 20 percent. The lion's share of China's immense pile of savings is funneled back into the market for land, which is what makes real estate so astonishingly expensive.

From overseas, the absurd excesses of the Chinese housing market made it look as if the bubble was popping, in rapid and spectacular fashion, as it did in the Western world in 2008. Painful experiences all over the world suggest that what goes up must come down, devastating the borrowers and lenders who fueled the boom. But that presumption does not really hold true in China. Even as Deng and his successors transformed the Chinese economy in the 1980s and 1990s and beyond, opening the country up to global trade, the government kept a tight grip on the country's financial system. Today, it is one of the least reformed, most government-controlled parts of the economy. Loans are still overwhelmingly made by banks, and the country's largest banks are still largely owned by the government. Much of the lending goes to thousands of Chinese state-owned enterprises, whether they are creditworthy or not. Targets for the volume of loans and targets for economic growth are handed down from Beijing to local governments and banks. Tight control of the financial system is combined with a strict web of capital controls that still prevent most ordinary citizens from pulling their money out of the country. The government has an extensive toolbox that it can deploy to halt financial blowups.

That means if Beijing wants to prevent the bubble from bursting entirely, holding the housing market in a sort of suspended animation, it may well be able to do so. But that does not mean the government can hold back the financial tides without heavy cost. Even as enormous profits have been made in the land and real estate markets in China over the past three decades, the relentless boom means that financial and material resources have surged into the property market and away from other places. A growing stack of research by academics in China and abroad comes to an alarming conclusion: the astonishing excesses in China's real estate market have seriously damaged the productive potential of the economy, across sectors and sometimes in very unusual ways.

Chinese banks deployed more and more credit to the real estate market, either to real estate developers or to new homeowners looking for mortgages, just as regional banks in America did during the house-price boom that led up to the global financial crisis in 2008. The Bank of China, the venerable state-owned lender that had blared the slogans of the Cultural Revolution across central Hong Kong in 1967, is a prime example. In

2002, when the behemoth's shares were first listed in Hong Kong, less than 20 percent of its total loans went to real estate in one form or another, with the vast majority of loans going to industry—in particular, state-owned industry. By 2019, over 40 percent of the bank's total lending went to the property market in one way or another.

The rampant growth of the housing market and the surge in real estate prices have been a problem for companies looking to borrow, especially in parts of China where smaller, local banks are the dominant financiers of both households and businesses. One piece of research by economists Harald Hau and Difei Ouyang shows that in cities where land has risen most rapidly in value, borrowing costs for small manufacturing companies have surged too.[17] Capital constraints on banks limit how much they can lend in total, and mortgages—as in the West—are inevitably seen as a safer bet than riskier unsecured business loans. Across 172 of the cities the academics looked at, in the places where real estate prices increased most rapidly, the credit crunch for local businesses reduced corporate investment by 21 percent, total output by 36 percent, and overall productivity by 12 percent.

The most productive companies in other parts of the Chinese economy also seem to drift into real estate over time, according to Yu Shi, an economist working in the research department of the International Monetary Fund.[18] Her research, published in 2018, shows that the most productive manufacturing companies in China have reduced their spending on research and development and their overall investment in their usual business when local real estate markets have boomed, moving instead into the land speculation game. Without the real estate boom, Yu estimates that productivity in the manufacturing sector between 1995 and 2010 would have been 0.5 percent stronger per year. In the short term, the effect—like many of the productivity-sapping effects of a real estate bubble—is hardly noticeable. But when a land boom lasts for a quarter of a century, the compounded impact is impossible to ignore.

When it comes to entrepreneurship, the vital component of dynamism in any economy, the tremendous surge in house prices has been bad news too. Young would-be entrepreneurs are discouraged by high property prices from setting up their own companies, according to Lixing Li and Xiaoyu Wu, two Chinese economists based in Beijing. While homeowners enjoy the surge in prices, young people who do not yet own a house are faced with the growing size of a potential mortgage to repay, and the fact that they need a home for any prospect of marriage. Between 2000 and 2010, the research notes that the rise in residential house prices averaged 9.4 percent, while the average rate of return made by Chinese companies was 5.6 percent. The more rapidly house prices rise in a major city, the fewer entrepreneurs are found.

The Ponzi game played by China's fastest-growing developers was a symptom rather than a cause of the bubble that was inflated across the country—not just under the nose of the government but with its enthusiastic participation. During a period of incredibly rapid income growth, China made land a linchpin asset that facilitated its entire national development model, sending prices surging to higher and higher levels. China has become even more dependent on ever-rising land prices than Hong Kong, the city from which it copied its model.

China's rampant land boom has been so enormous that it puts the examples from elsewhere around the world in the shade. Even five years after the government called time on the multi-decade bubble, the consequences of the freeze in the housing market are not over. State-owned developers have bought up land in some parts of the country, taking the place of private developers. Real estate in China is still among the most expensive in the world. The boom may have been curtailed, but the bust has been incredibly slow. As in Japan, the government has moved to stem the bleeding with various support measures but stopped short of aggressive fiscal stimulus to boost incomes. In place of the enormous volume of lending once directed towards real estate, bank loans to manufacturing companies have exploded, helping to drive a surge in exports. That explosion in outbound trade has been met with hostility from not just America but countries all around the world whose own manufacturers fear being undercut.

In China, as in Japan before it, the market for land as an asset has become almost completely divorced from the actual uses that are supposed to give land value. That makes the situation markedly different from those in the priciest Western housing markets, where housing shortages are a serious issue in the most prosperous and productive urban areas. For a populace with little else to invest in, the high-rise apartments dotted across urban China, from prosperous Shanghai or Shenzhen to the poor and globally anonymous cities in the country's interior, represent bank accounts in the sky as much as they represent homes to live in. The belief that land prices could only go up has encouraged rampant speculation, detached from the question of where people actually need to live.

Today, China's income growth has slowed markedly. By the end of the 2020s, the economy will likely be growing at something more like 3 to 4 percent, nowhere near the double-digit boom under which the housing market grew, when people established their expectations for how prices should rise. The country's rapidly shifting demographics will cause huge problems too. The largest generation of Chinese citizens is now in its early fifties. The population aged between thirty and sixty years old is large, but younger generations are shrinking in size. When China's middle classes, some of whom are sitting on two or three properties, want to liquidate their investments to fund their retirements, who will be buying?

More than anywhere else in the world, China is pinned in the jaws of a land trap. Allowing house prices to truly tumble would be the greatest test that the government's control of the financial system has ever faced, even if it did not shake the Communist Party's support from middle-class Chinese homeowners to its core. The social contract between China's authoritarian leaders and the country's population exchanges their political and civic freedoms for the promise of rapid economic development. But the consequences of China's extraordinarily high house prices are already painfully clear. If they are permitted to rise again, or even to stay at their current elevated levels relative to incomes, the dynamism from the country's once-flourishing economy will be sapped. The middle path—the road on which China finds itself today—is one of protracted stagnation.

TEN

Singapore Fever

The dismal consequences of China's overwhelming financial dependence on land are now on display for the world to see. The asset has been intimately connected to the country's economic model for the last three decades and the subject of huge speculative activity and leverage, just like Japan during its boom years. The slump in the property market has left China's economy in a protracted economic slowdown. The lesson learned from Hong Kong—that government-owned land could be turned into liquid cash—was the kernel of modern China's misadventure with land.

But if China's leaders had instead taken notes from another example, things might look very different today. In November of 1978, two months before he was installed as China's paramount leader and began to slowly open the country to foreign investment, Deng Xiaoping landed for the first time in the Southeast Asian nation of Singapore. Zhao Ziyang was still plugging away in Sichuan, reforming the province's tightly controlled agricultural system. It would be another decade until Shenzhen's formative land auction set the ball rolling, and twenty years until the wholesale privatization of China's housing market.

When he landed at Paya Lebar airport in Singapore, Deng was collected from the sweltering runway by Singaporean Prime Minister Lee Kuan Yew, who had governed the city-state since 1959, before its existence as an independent nation. He would continue to do so for another fourteen years, and remained a titan in the country's politics until his death in 2015. The two men had little in common. On the tarmac, Lee stood almost a foot taller than his Chinese counterpart. Deng had been an active Communist Party member since the early 1920s, spending decades as an armed revolutionary on the run from the authorities. In the space of three decades, he had fought against Chinese nationalists, the Empire of Japan, and then Chinese nationalists again, before the People's Republic was eventually founded. Lee, on the other hand, was a Cambridge-educated lawyer who had suppressed leftist movements in his own country, accusing them of fomenting an insurgency against the new nation.

Singapore in 1978 had a population of not quite two and a half million people, while China was the most populous country on earth. Even the shared ethnic background between the two men was an illusory point of similarity. Lee's ancestors had left China's eastern coast several generations earlier, and he had been raised speaking only English; he did not begin learning Chinese until his thirties, when he had already entered politics, and even wrote a book about his struggle to master the language. Deng, on the other hand, had grown up in China's Sichuan Province and spoke Chinese with a heavy regional accent. He had learned French while studying and working in Paris in his early adulthood, but he spoke no English.

When the two men met, China was barely yet beginning to emerge from its decades of domestic turmoil and isolation from the rest of the world. When Chairman Mao died in 1976, he had not traveled internationally for more than ten years, during which time the bloody and chaotic Cultural Revolution had devastated China both economically and socially. The most urgent order of business between Deng and Lee was to begin cleaning up the explosion of communist fanaticism that had spilled out far beyond China's borders. Ending Beijing's continued support for communist insurgents in Southeast Asia was at the top of Lee's list of requests. In return, the new Chinese leadership hoped to establish basic diplomatic relations with Singapore, an increasingly influential power broker in the region.

But Deng had bigger ideas for the relationship between Beijing and Singapore too. Just as China's reformist leaders were learning from Hong Kong, they wanted to understand how the increasingly prosperous Singapore functioned. Both cities, along with South Korea and Taiwan, were among the emerging handful of rapidly industrializing "Asian Tigers." As Deng began seeking out sources of foreign investment for China, the wealthy, ethnically Chinese businessmen overseas were an obvious port of call. Both Singapore and Hong Kong had become hubs of commerce and finance, almost synonymous with international capitalism, and had embraced free trade even during the postwar decades when support for open markets was at a low ebb internationally.

To Lee, the prospect of an enormous new trading partner for Singapore was inviting. He made a simple argument to Deng. Chinese emigrants had been arriving to the tropical island for a century and a half, fleeing despotism and chaos at home. They had worked as coolies, unskilled laborers living in desperately poor conditions. Most were illiterate and engaged in backbreaking labor for very little money. If Singapore had been populated by this segment of the Chinese population and become so prosperous, Lee argued, imagine what China, still populated by the heirs of its mandarins and philosophers, could achieve if the country were truly unleashed.[1] Deng visited Jurong, one of Singapore's blossoming industrial centers, the home of steel mills, electronics manufacturers and petrochemical plants. He also paid a trip to the city's Housing & Development Board, the government agency tasked with providing shelter to the city-state's population.

But Singapore was interesting to China's leaders for more than just its growing prosperity. Lee Kuan Yew had found a political niche in the world, establishing a government that fell somewhere between Western liberalism and authoritarianism. Singapore's society was, and still is, far freer than China's. But it remains less free than those in the Western world. Elections are held, and minority parties contest, but Singaporean politics is dominated by the People's Action Party (PAP), which Lee helped found. At the time of Deng's visit, the PAP had all the seats in the country's parliament, and it retains the vast majority today. Singapore was ethnically diverse but employed strict laws against speech that might upset the feelings of ethnic or religious groups. It was (and remains) one of the least corrupt countries in the world, an even more unusual feat in a region where graft was commonplace.

Over the decades that followed, Deng would travel to Singapore twice more, in 1983 and 1989. On his epoch-making southern tour in 1992, he singled out the city-state as an example of a social order to follow. China's leaders caught a case of what would come to be known as "Singapore fever." Hundreds of bureaucrats and up-and-coming party members visited Singapore to understand how the city was governed. In the decades that followed, tens of thousands of mid-level Chinese officials visited the city on research expeditions—including, in 1992, a thirty-nine-year-old regional party secretary by the name of Xi Jinping.

But the visitors failed to apply the most important lessons that Singapore had to offer. When it comes to land and housing, China's leaders would have benefited from following the city-state's example far more closely. Singapore is a low-tax financial hub, one of the very richest countries in the world on a per capita basis, and the second most densely populated nation on earth. It inherited almost all of its legal and financial framework from Britain, just as Hong Kong did. Almost every piece of information about the Southeast Asian city-state suggests it had the perfect conditions for the kind of affordability crisis plaguing many of the most prosperous nations, and for the financial instability that tends to come with it. Singapore stands out relative to other rich cities and countries. It has managed to avoid the kind of problems with land and real estate that throttled the once-thriving entrepreneurial spirit of Hong Kong, rattled the Western world in 2008, stalled Japan's growth story in the 1990s and plague modern China.

Singapore today is a nation of ownership. Almost 90 percent of resident households live in their own properties, a rate far above the equivalent in almost any developed economy.[2] Homeownership rates in countries like Britain, America, France, Australia and New Zealand range between 60 and 70 percent. In the world's vibrant and densely populated financial hubs, rates are even lower—about half of Hong Kongers own their own homes, as do roughly the same proportion of Londoners. In New York City, the rate of owner-occupation is more like 30 percent. Not only is homeownership widespread in Singapore, but compared to the other major international hubs of the world, housing is remarkably cheap. An average home in the city costs around 3.8 times a typical annual income, a third as high as the equivalent level in Los Angeles, and less than a quarter of the level in Hong Kong, the city with which Singapore is so often compared.[3] Singapore's properties are as cheap as or cheaper than those in places like Tulsa, Oklahoma, or Glasgow, Scotland, relative to local incomes. Indeed, housing in Singapore is by some distance the cheapest of any meaningful international hub in the world.

More than perhaps anywhere else, Singapore has avoided the risk of being trapped by land. The country's cheap housing and its widespread ownership rates are the fruits of an unusual model that the Singaporean government has pursued for the last sixty years. Its unique way of managing land and housing has yielded enormous benefits for its citizens, and for its financial stability too. Had Deng and Zhao taken a dimmer view of Hong Kong's growing real estate oligopoly, or recognized the squeeze that high land prices were already putting on the territory's businesses by the late 1980s, modern China might well have looked very different today. But the lessons offered by Singapore hold relevance far beyond a what-if case for Beijing. All across the developed and developing world, the decisions made by the tiny city-state bear close examination—for the countries that have barely yet begun to exploit their land wealth, the issues are not too late to fix.

Though the modern Singaporean system of landownership and housing has been in place for just sixty years, it has been more than two centuries in the making. The city was founded in its modern form two decades before Hong Kong, and in a relatively similar fashion. Sir Thomas Stamford Raffles, an administrator employed by the East India Company (EIC), arrived on the island on the 28th of January in 1819. The company was not just an enormous force in Asian commerce, but also the preeminent power in politics across much of the continent for most of the eighteenth and nineteenth centuries. The EIC had its own army, larger than Britain's, and it was the largest corporation anywhere in the world. It was an early public-private partnership that had been granted a monopoly on British trade across South Asia—a monopoly it intended to defend against any foreign competition.

When he arrived on the island, the thirty-seven-year-old Raffles was the lieutenant governor of British Bencoolen, a hub of pepper plantations stretching along the coast of southern Sumatra in modern-day Indonesia. Raffles had previously been governor of the neighboring island of Java, the home of modern Jakarta. He came from a family of colonial administrators: he was born in the Caribbean, where his father had been a ship's master, ferrying sugar and molasses back to Britain from the island plantations. Raffles Jr. had begun his career for the EIC as an adolescent clerk at the company's headquarters in London. By the time the young bureaucrat landed in what is now Singapore's Boat Quay, today a buzzing area of bars and restaurants, he was already knee-deep in the operations of the British Empire. It was the role in which he had served for his entire life.

The Singapore on which Raffles arrived was not so buzzing. Hundreds of years before the arrival of the European empires, it had been a trading post known as Temasek. But by 1819, it was sparsely inhabited, its population consisting of perhaps a few hundred villagers and fishermen from the neighboring Malay Peninsula. But Raffles had high hopes for the island. He aimed to establish a free port on the Strait of Malacca, the body of water that separates Indonesia's Sumatra from what is now western Malaysia, which Singapore straddles.[4] In 1819, as today, the route was a bottleneck for seaborne trade. China, Japan and the thousands of islands that now make up Indonesia lay to Singapore's east. To the west, the strait opened into the Bay of Bengal, and beyond it the riches of both India and Europe. At its narrowest point, the channel spans less than two miles. In 2019, about $3.9 trillion in goods were estimated to transit through the strait each year; almost everything the industrialists of East Asia ship to Europe goes through the waterway, heading westward, while oil and gas from the Middle East is shipped in the other direction.[5] The route saves sailors hundreds of miles of travel and avoids the risks of traversing the shallow waters of the Sunda Strait farther south.

Many others saw the same opportunities that Raffles did. Five years after he established the simple trading post, the population of Singapore had risen to over ten thousand.[6] There was an influx of immigrants from what are now Indonesia and Malaysia; Chinese immigrants quickly began to arrive too, disembarking from Fujian on the earliest junk boats in 1821. Indian migrant workers also came, following the East India Company, as they did everywhere the outfit went. The three groups still make up the modern Singaporean ethnic mix, which is predominantly Chinese with large Malay and Indian minorities.

Raffles's most urgent task was to find a source of revenue for the trading post, which could be used to build the necessary infrastructure for a commercial hub. The incoming governor had already been experimenting with methods to raise public finance for more than a decade across the Indonesian archipelago, with little success. In 1808, when the Napoleonic Wars were raging not just at home but all across the colonial possessions of the European empires, Raffles had detached the island of Java from its Dutch occupiers, who were aligned with France. The island's paper currency, issued by the Dutch, had collapsed in value to the point of being almost worthless. Java's previous imperial rulers had relied on forced cultivation, in which particular crops were demanded by the authorities in lieu of taxes. In an aim to kill two birds with one stone, Raffles had tried to institute a land-based tax system in Java. In his grand vision, farmland would be leased out to Javan princes and other nobles for Spanish dollars, on the understanding that they would cultivate the land with whatever they deemed fit and would not subsequently levy any other taxes of their own on the peasants that lived there.[7]

In his own account of his time in Southeast Asia, Raffles repeatedly referred to Adam Smith's treatise on economics, *The Wealth of Nations*, which may have provided the intellectual ammunition for his project. Smith had been an early advocate of land value taxation, a century before Henry George published his magnum opus. But Raffles's ambitions reached far beyond public finance. He wanted to change the way Javanese society worked at a much deeper level. He outlawed the slave trade on the island, which he viewed as interlinked with the damaging system of forced cultivation. "This nefarious trade, which has desolated this island," he wrote, "driven by the monopolies of the Dutch, which have, in a great degree, driven the fair merchants from the seas, and left the main to kidnappers and pirates."[8]

At the end of the Napoleonic Wars, Java was returned to the Dutch, and Raffles's system was still half-baked. The paper currency he had aimed to abolish was still in circulation, despite its near-total devaluation. When Java's old administrators returned, they found that the British land sale system was bringing in rents far lower than those Raffles had bragged to his superiors about. Even though the system had not worked on its own terms, the new Dutch assessors saw its promise. "There are still many defects to redress," said J. de Bruijn, the administrator who took over one Western Javanese town in 1816.[9] "Nevertheless the late British administration, by the first introduction of the land rent system, has rendered to the Netherlands Government a principal and essential service, from which in future the most salutary results will originate." The kernel had been planted.

In Singapore, Raffles was far more successful in bringing his ideas about land and public finance from theory to reality. The use of land for revenue would become one of the foundations of the modern city. Two treaties signed in 1824 solidified Singapore's status as a permanent British possession in the eyes of both the Dutch and the Johor Sultanate, the Malay kingdom that was separated from Singapore by just a few hundred meters of water. As in Hong Kong, Singapore's administrators had not waited for the island's final status to be settled before they began to sell it off. "Land has already assumed a high value, and a few lots of about sixty feet front, in a convenient situation for mercantile purposes, realized at public sale upwards of fifty thousand dollars in the course of half-an-hour," Raffles boasted to a friend in January of 1823. Buyers of land leases paid a sum to the new governors of Singapore and an annual ground rent. "I have established a revenue without any tax whatever on the trade, which more than covers all civil disbursements, and which must annually increase in future years," he added.[10] Henry George would not be born for another sixteen years, but the sentiment would surely have met his approval.

Raffles is still considered Singapore's founding father—his name adorns the square in the city's central business district, right next to the spot where he landed in 1819. Raffles College remains one of the country's most elite secondary schools, and hospitals, malls and streets named after the colonial bureaucrat still pepper the island, despite the fact that he actually spent less than a year there over just three brief visits. The most extended of his trips was eight months long, running between October 1822 and June 1823, after which he left the trading post he had founded, never to return. But he had created the foundations of something that would become highly unusual in the world, especially when it came to land and housing.

For the next hundred years, the cities of Hong Kong and Singapore followed an all but identical path as Asian trading posts of a distant British Empire. Officials between the two ports regularly hopped from one to the other, rotating between the similar bureaucracies. At least three of the governors of Hong Kong were previously or subsequently governors of the Straits Settlements, the grouping that included Singapore, the towns of Malacca and Dindings on the mainland of what is now Malaysia, and Penang, an island off its western coast. Land leases by the colonial government, like those undertaken in Hong Kong from the 1840s, would continue to be a pillar of Singapore's fiscal management over the century that followed.

Until the early twentieth century, both cities were crucial facilitators for the export of opium from British India to China, the lucrative trade Britain went to war twice to retain. Like Hong Kong, Singapore boomed: the city's population rose to over two hundred thousand at the turn of the twentieth century, and to more than half a million by 1931. In February of 1942, Singapore—considered at the time an impregnable fortress of the British Empire—fell easily to the rampaging forces of Imperial Japan, just seven weeks after the surrender of Hong Kong. It was, according to Winston Churchill, "the worst disaster and largest capitulation in British history."

Beginning in the aftermath of the Second World War in 1945, when the modern world was forming and the old European empires were breaking up, the fortunes of the twin trading cities began to diverge. In Singapore, the experience of Japanese invasion became a foundation stone for a new national identity. The perception that the city had been abandoned by the British Empire and left to its own devices, vulnerable and alone, sowed an anxious insecurity in the city's governing class that persists today. Singapore was quickly on the road to independence. It became part of the Federation of Malaysia in 1963 and eventually became an independent nation in 1965, while Hong Kong would be governed by Britain for another five decades before its 1997 handover to China.

The fragile pact between the leaders of Singapore and Malaya that created the newly independent country of Malaysia lasted for less than two years before the union broke apart. Disagreements about tax and spending contributed to the split, as did unresolved racial tensions. Singapore had a Chinese ethnic majority, while Kuala Lumpur's Malay leaders wanted to offer their own people preferential treatment. At the time of its sudden independence in 1965, Singapore was poor and vulnerable. The country's economic output ranked below Mexico's and South Africa's on a per capita basis. In the divorce, Singapore's businesses lost their hopes of preferential access to a large domestic market across the strait. The new island nation had no hinterland for agriculture, and its two million people mostly lived in squalid slums and kampongs, the rural villages that dotted the island. Singapore had no natural resources of any note; it could not even supply its own water. It was also under threat from Indonesia, which had waged an undeclared war known as the Konfrontasi against Malaysia from 1963 and which was fifty times larger than Singapore by population. Just months before the city-state became independent, undercover Indonesian marines had bombed buildings in the city.

Lee Kuan Yew had been among the greatest advocates of the merger with Malaysia. He dabbed his eyes in a rare display of public emotion while announcing Singapore's split from the federation on television in August of 1965. But in a moment of deep uncertainty about the survival of a tiny country without obvious wealth or powerful allies, Singapore's government would forge the path to its subsequent economic success. Land and its ownership were at the center of Lee's new plan for the country. Speaking in 1964, before Singapore had made the leap to complete independence, the prime minister laid out his principles. "No private land-owner should benefit from development at public expense," Lee argued. "I said I would introduce legislation which would help to ensure that increases in land values because of public development should benefit the community and not for the land-owner. Land is becoming a scarce commodity and with the mounting pressure on land at present, we must try to control land values for public purposes."[11]

Despite Singapore's long history of using land to raise revenues, the powers available to Lee when Singapore became independent did not go far enough. The city was still growing rapidly in population, and with little space to expand outwards, the new government intended to build upwards to accommodate it. The Land Acquisition Act was passed by the newly independent government in 1966. It would become the linchpin of

Singapore's modern land and housing system. The law was a steamroller enabling Lee's government to snap up land far below its market price from the private owners who owned freehold plots and to end the long leases sold by earlier administrations, whether the owners liked it or not. Singapore's authorities instituted a "seven-year rule" that meant that when the government bought a piece of land, it would disregard any increases in its value caused by government investment—nearby roads, schools or other infrastructure—that had occurred over the previous seven years. Owners who objected to their land being swept from under their feet had almost no recourse to resist. Using the new law, the government was able to accumulate most of the country's land and bring it under public ownership. The Singaporean state today owns around 90 percent of the city-state's land, twice what it held in 1960.[12]

The legislation could not have been passed if Singapore had remained part of Malaysia. The bill had been discussed in 1965, before Singapore's independence, but stumbled at the first hurdle. Article 13 of the Malaysian constitution enshrined—and still enshrines—the right to be adequately compensated for any deprivation of property by the state. Under the protection of the constitution, the payouts the Singaporean government wished to offer to landholders would almost certainly have been judged far too measly and been overturned by the courts after a cavalcade of legal proceedings. When Singapore became an independent nation, it copied the fundamental rights already listed in the Malaysian constitution, save for one: Article 13.

Lee wrote several books about his own life and experiences governing Singapore, but left relatively few clues about the philosophical or historical influences he may have imbibed when it came to land. The American firebrand Henry George receives no mention in any of Lee's writing. Anne

Haila, a Finnish academic with a research focus on land, suggested that Lee's fondness for Britain's Fabian socialists may instead have been the source of his attitude.[13] Lee encountered the Fabians during his time in Britain in the late 1940s and warmed to their commitment to egalitarian and progressive ideas. During his brief time at the London School of Economics before studying at Cambridge, Lee spoke fondly about attending lectures by Harold Laski, a moderate socialist academic.[14] The British left had been heavily influenced by Henry George and his ideas from the 1870s onwards, and the Fabians continued to advocate for land value taxes even after the idea lost its political verve in the West.

Goh Keng Swee, Singapore's finance minister at the time of independence, was clearer about his influences. Goh had met Lee two decades earlier, when both were students at the city's elite Raffles College, and Goh tutored the future Singaporean prime minister in economics. Goh studied at the London School of Economics, eventually gaining a doctorate in the subject in 1956. He had an admiration for the earliest generation of land-taxers—Enlightenment thinkers like Adam Smith and David Ricardo, the same figures that Stamford Raffles had drawn inspiration from more than a century earlier. Goh argued that the classical free-market economists of the late eighteenth and early nineteenth century had more to offer his home country than the modern ideas of John Maynard Keynes, whose work he had also studied at university in London. In an article published in 1961, Goh made his negative view of Asia's landowning classes quite clear: "In many of these traditional societies, we find a small but powerful class of landlord who often stand in the way of economic progress," he wrote. "Very often, it is found that the landlord does not have the spirit of innovation or the grasp of modern management to be able to launch and manage the new enterprises that are needed for economic development. The traditional landlord is not an entrepreneur and hence the wealth he accumulates, often by exploiting the peasantry, is not used for economic expansion."[15]

Viewed from the Western world, Singapore's methods of acquisition and compensation in the decades after its independence were stingy at best, and confiscatory at worst. Sometimes the discounts that the government demanded relative to the market value of land have been enormous: In 1973, during a period of rampant inflation, compensation levels were frozen in place. They would not be adjusted upwards again for another thirteen years, even as prices surged and the economy almost tripled in size. During that period, swathes of land were acquired at a tiny fraction of their real market value from owners who had no means of refusal. The government used it to build the city's new public rail, the Mass Rapid Transit system, and constructed hundreds of thousands of Housing & Development Board units to house Singapore's growing population.

Singapore's land acquisition system has become gradually less painful for existing owners who find themselves in the way of the government's appetite for land. After years of large-scale land purchases, the government's enormous landholdings mean it can afford to be less stingy. Since 2007, owners have been fully compensated for any purchases by the government at the current market price of their assets. The system is still far less generous than in many countries in the West, where existing owners are often compensated generously, at rates deliberately higher than the obvious market value of their land. The principle remains: in Singapore, land is treated differently than other assets, and is under the ever-present risk of being snatched up for housing or infrastructure by the government.

If the Land Acquisition Act provided the fuel for Singapore's unique housing system, its engine has been the government-owned Housing &

Development Board (HDB), which Deng visited on his first trip to the city-state. The board was instituted in 1960 and charged with designing and building housing estates on the land purchased by the government. In the years since, it has become a crucial leg—perhaps the single most important part—of Singapore's political economy. The three-letter acronym "HDB" is now the universal shorthand for the apartments that are thrown up all across the city. The homes make up almost 80 percent of Singapore's housing stock today.

When the board began churning out apartments, the city's dearth of homes was a political emergency. The condition of slum housing in Singapore was dire, and communicable disease was rife. In 1961, a fire in Bukit Ho Swee, a large settlement of rickety squatter housing, had rendered tens of thousands of residents homeless overnight. Sparse, utilitarian units were built quickly and rented out cheaply to their new residents. The very first HDB projects were a mirror of what was happening across the developed world at the time. Private slum accommodation in inner cities was being demolished at speed, replaced by new social housing owned and operated directly by national and local governments and housing associations. Housing projects were built in cities across America, and the construction of council houses surged in Britain, France and West Germany.

But unlike the socialists and social democrats across Europe with ambitions for large-scale government ownership, Lee had no interest in Singapore's citizens living as tenants. In 1964, before the country's independence, his government launched Singapore's Home Ownership for the People Scheme. Households earning less than 800 Singaporean dollars per month, a figure that covered a large majority of the city, were now eligible to buy rather than rent the new HDB units with a modest down payment.[16] They were not buying freehold properties, in which the owner also holds the land forever (or, in apartment buildings, a share of the land). The apartments were sold with ninety-nine-year leases, after which the land would be returned to the state. That meant the owners of HDBs could purchase a secure tenure for their lives, and often for the lives of their children, who could inherit the property from them. But the land could not be held and passed down forever, as was the norm in most of the rest of the world.

Just as Lee would pioneer a political model that fell somewhere between democracy and one-party rule, the system of housing he established was to be an unusual hybrid too. Despite his university-era admiration for Britain's moderate socialists, his views on homeownership were more aligned with Noel Skelton, the early-twentieth-century Conservative architect of Britain's "property-owning democracy," and even with those Margaret Thatcher would espouse in the 1980s. Lee believed that owners would take care of their estates in a way that renters simply would not. Singapore was no longer just a colony, but a nation; owning their own homes would give the new citizens a real stake in the success of their country. Nationhood had demands too, like the requirement (still in place) for all able-bodied men to serve two years of National Service. The men and their families deserved something in return.

The share of homes owned by their occupants climbed rapidly. In 1970, just a few years after the ownership policies began, the share of Singaporeans living in their own homes was just 29 percent, a proportion that tripled over the subsequent two decades.[17] As the years passed, the quality of the housing available improved by leaps and bounds. HDB buildings are no longer the predictable near-Soviet slabs that were hastily thrown together to rescue the city from slum living. New estates are essentially indistinguishable from high-quality multifamily developments anywhere in the world, featuring swimming pools, open-air gardens, malls and some of the city's famous hawker centers below.

Over time, the government steadily allowed room for a market in Singapore's hybrid housing system too, letting owners exchange their units. But there are still significant restrictions in place that make it very different from a fully private housing market. Foreigners without long-term residency rights cannot purchase HDB units. Singaporean households may only own one unit at a time. Owners must wait at least five years before they can sell a property they have received from the board, preventing any attempts at the kind of property-flipping seen in other countries. Singapore's unique housing system also allows the government to micromanage the ethnic makeup of individual housing estates: quotas established at the end of the 1980s require that sales maintain the rough balance of the country to prevent the emergence of ghettos or ethnic homogeneity across the city.

The Singaporean system of housing finance also developed very differently from those elsewhere in the world. First-time buyers of HDBs can access mortgages worth up to 75 percent of the price of the property from the Central Provident Fund (CPF), the city's compulsory savings scheme. Households with the lowest incomes are eligible for grants to help cover the remaining quarter of the cost. As of 2024, Singaporeans paid interest of 2.6 percent on these CPF mortgages, a far cry from the average rate for new borrowers of American thirty-year home loans at more than 6 percent. At the same time, the tax and financial system is deliberately stacked against anyone who aims to accumulate multiple properties in Singapore's small private market, which accounts for just over a fifth of the country's total housing stock. For purchases of second homes, a stamp duty of at least 20 percent is applied, a figure that rises to 30 percent for any additional properties. Commercial banks may not lend more than 45 percent of the value of a second property to a borrower, and no more than 35 percent for the third or more. It is a system that has made being a homeowner easy, but being a landlord much more difficult.

It is hard to argue with the results. While the state domination of Hong Kong's land market has been used as a revenue-raiser and a source of enormous wealth for a small cohort of real estate developers, Singapore's has been put to the task of housing its citizens at reasonable cost and ensuring widespread asset wealth. Singaporean economist Sock-Yong Phang, an expert in the city's land-use policies, notes that 25 percent of Singapore's housing wealth is owned by the bottom 50 percent of asset owners.[18] In major financial centers like Hong Kong, London and New York, with homeownership rates of barely 50 percent or even lower, the share of housing wealth owned by the bottom 50 percent is effectively zero. Singapore's system, by contrast, has allowed for extremely high rates of homeownership, but without turning homes into investments through which owners can easily get rich at the expense of future buyers.

If the government of Hong Kong has a high land price policy—by accident or design—then Singapore has deliberately engineered a low house price policy for its citizens. Both governments used the tools left to them by their British administrations, but they headed off in remarkably different directions in the second half of the twentieth century. Singapore's rigorously controlled system of land has shielded its citizens from the less comfortable realities of being an international commercial hub with extremely limited space to grow. Despite the city's extremely high rate of homeownership, Singaporeans are paradoxically far less exposed to the ups and downs of the housing market than the residents of Hong Kong.

Residential housing, in both HDBs and private housing, makes up 44 percent of the wealth of Singaporean households.[19] Hong Kong's statistics department doesn't publish the same data, but economists Thomas Piketty and Li Yang estimate that housing makes up 75 percent of household assets, at the very least.

Singapore's use of its land, and its method for ensuring widespread, limited and equitable housing wealth is unique. Without the deep interest of three men—Stamford Raffles, Lee Kuan Yew and Goh Keng Swee—it likely would not have happened, and Singapore would look very different today, sharing much more in common with the ultraexpensive cities all over the world with which it competes for business and capital. A glimpse of what might have been can be found in the city's relatively small private housing market. Around a fifth of homeowners in the city live in private apartments, condos and so-called landed properties, single family homes on privately owned land. For the very wealthy, these homes are an opportunity to take on more space than even the larger executive HDB flats offer. These are the houses and apartments that many of Singapore's foreign white-collar workers rent from landlords, since foreign ownership of property is strictly limited. Even with the constant threat that the government will snap up the land beneath them to build public housing or infrastructure, Singapore's private market is one of the most expensive anywhere in the developed world, with a price-to-income ratio of 13.5.[20]

In Singapore's Katong, a leafy suburb between the central business district and Changi Airport, a single, elegant white home can be found, nestled between looming housing developments and hotels on every side. The house offers another lesson about the city and its use of land. The single-story home dates from 1898, long before the advent of the Housing & Development Board estates. It is known in the city's unique official parlance as a "good class bungalow" or GCB, one of the rare relics of the past in a city that is often unsentimental in tearing down the old to make way for the new. For over a century, the house belonged to the Choa family, a wealthy Chinese dynasty that arrived in Singapore in the middle of the nineteenth century and used the house as a weekend getaway property. The land on which the bungalow sits, with space for hundreds of apartments, was sold in 2011 for just over 100 million Singaporean dollars.[21] But the name of the bungalow is more interesting than its current use. The house sits at 37 Marine Parade Road, and "Seabreeze" is emblazoned on a pillar at the house gates—a fitting name for what was once an ocean-front property. Today, though, the house sits across from a bustling shopping center and housing development, and is more than half a kilometer from the nearest waterfront.

Singapore has managed to bend one of the fundamental rules that makes land such an important and unusual asset: it has made more of it. The island has a history of land reclamation dating back to its very earliest days under the East India Company, but the scale of the effort to expand the city's physical footprint since the 1960s has been particularly astounding. Around a quarter of the country's land area today did not exist at the time of its independence. Thousands of Singaporeans now live in the HDBs of Marine Drive, between the Seabreeze bungalow and the sea itself. Eventually, the popular East Coast Park that now spills into the Strait of Malacca will be just one side of an enormous freshwater reservoir, surrounded by more artificial land and even more housing. In fact, any visitor who has landed at Changi Airport or looked out from the

Marina Bay Sands towers that form part of the city's iconic skyline has stepped foot on Singapore's reclaimed land.

The Singapore that most foreign visitors see, close to the city's central business district and its bustling residential areas, is dense with housing, office buildings, malls and hawker centers. But the city-state also finds the land for the kinds of industry that were smothered in Hong Kong, recognizing that land can be not only an extremely valuable asset for its owners, but also a heavy input cost for companies. As a result, manufacturing accounts for about 20 percent of Singaporean GDP, compared to Hong Kong's 1 percent. The country finds space for science and industrial parks that host domestic and international industrial firms conducting research and development. In Tuas, at Singapore's western tip, thousands of hectares of land have been reclaimed from the sea for industrial use. The Tuas port, still under construction on newly created land, may well be the world's largest automated port when it is completed in the 2040s.

It is tough to know just how much of Singapore's good fortune should be attributed to its system of intervention when it comes to land, but the contrast between the city-state and Hong Kong is now stark. While Hong Kong lags deep in the rankings when it comes to both exports in high-tech goods and income made from intellectual property rights, Singapore comes first and fifteenth respectively in the global rankings for each. The country has more than twice as many workers per capita focusing on research and development than Hong Kong.[22] Singaporean companies and residents have filed between four thousand and seven thousand patents each year over the last decade or so, compared to a few hundred per year in Hong Kong.[23] The difference between the two cities is clear when it comes to the banking system too, which in Singapore is much less exposed to the land market. Loans for the real estate industry in Singapore account for about 28 percent of credit, while household mortgages account for another 22 percent.[24] In Hong Kong, even after a multi-year slump in the housing market, bank loans to real estate developers account for 35 percent of domestic lending, and mortgages for households another 43 percent.[25]

The long-running competition between the two cities has produced a clear winner as far as economic performance goes. Singapore's more equitable model for land and housing has not come at the cost of economic dynamism, and may have even helped it. As recently as the turn of the century, Hong Kong and Singapore's household incomes were roughly similar to one another. But today, Singaporean incomes are about 70 percent higher than Hong Kong's. The only people for whom Hong Kong has clearly been a better bet are those who have reaped enormous returns through its ballooning land prices.

What Singapore has done, more successfully than any similarly space-constrained city, perhaps more successfully than any other country anywhere, is to separate the ownership of housing assets from the land beneath them. The system balances the overwhelming popularity of homeownership—to possess a place of one's own, a valuable investment and a symbol of maturity and security all bundled into one—while preventing massive increases in wealth through housing at the expense of those who do not yet possess any. Henry George would not have approved of the effective government monopoly that Singapore has engineered. But in an upside-down way, the country has achieved a version of what he had hoped for a century and a half ago, perhaps more closely than any other nation in the world.

Back in China, further outbreaks of "Singapore fever" have occasionally erupted among regional politicians and bureaucrats. During their many visits to the city, some officials have even taken home grand ideas about changing China's housing market to something more closely resembling the Southeast Asian city-state's. Two Singaporean academics, Hong Liu and Ting-Yan Wang, conducted surveys of mid-level Chinese officials who had visited Singapore, shedding light on what they found to be the best parts of the Singaporean model. Three quarters of the bureaucrats identified the city's housing system as one of its most attractive elements.[26]

Huang Qifan, the mayor of Chongqing, saw the flaws in the country's real estate sector as early as 2010, making the case that private commercial housing was no longer enough and that the government needed to learn from Singapore and participate more actively in the housing market. He introduced one of China's first property taxes in 2011, a modest levy of 0.5 to 1.2 percent on a handful of highly priced homes and some second homes. But Huang's political affiliations proved to be a barrier to any more adventurous policymaking. He had been a close ally of Bo Xilai, the Communist Party secretary of Chongqing and former Chinese minister of commerce. Bo was embroiled in a corruption scandal in 2012, for which he was eventually convicted of bribery and corruption. Bo was not just an ambitious politician. He had been perhaps the greatest political rival of Xi Jinping, the new paramount leader of China, and his allies kept their heads down in the years that followed his downfall.

Even the biggest boosters of Singapore's model of managing housing and land concede that emulating it would be a tremendous task. When Singapore launched its unique model, homeownership was uncommon, and perhaps three quarters of the country's population lived either in urban slums or shabby villages. For countries that have already set about on a path of widespread private landownership, replicating Singapore's successes may well be impossible, requiring the expropriation of a large class of landowners. The only alternative, to compensate the same owners at the full market value of their real estate—or more—would be inordinately expensive.

But the unusual city-state, with its tight control of land and its hybrid housing market, still provides a valuable lesson for the world. It is an especially vital one to learn for the developing nations that have not yet begun to fully exploit the value of their land. It has managed to retain the welcome features of a healthy market economy in many ways, while preventing either the sorts of inequality or financial risk generated by land markets all over the rest of the world—and especially in global cities with similar international appeal. Singapore has bent or broken the rules that seem to apply almost everywhere else when it comes to land—to the country's clear benefit.

ELEVEN

Falling Stars and Superstars

On January 17, 1956, copies of the *Detroit Free Press* landed on doorsteps across the city whose name it carried, bringing the news that the nation's auto production had hit yet another record level. More than nine million cars and trucks were produced in American factories in 1955, and most of them were rolled out of factories across Detroit.[1] There was another reason why that day was a landmark occasion for American industrial capitalism and the city that served as its emblem. A few hours after the *Free Press* hit newsstands, the Ford Motor Company floated on the New York Stock Exchange for the first time. It was the biggest offering of stock in the history of the United States. The sale of shares was underwritten by 722 banks, raising $657 million for Ford, more than $7 billion in today's money.[2]

It was a good time to be in America's Motor City. The American car industry was at the height of its strength, a totem of the country's economic power. Ford was the third-biggest company in the world, with revenues that ran to around 1 percent of American GDP. Investors had waited a long time to get hold of a stake in the iconic company: Henry

Ford Sr., who founded the firm in his home state of Michigan in 1903, had been a relentless opponent of a public listing. The pioneering industrialist, philanthropist and virulent anti-Semite had died nine years earlier, having once told his son that he would "take every factory down brick by brick before I let any of those Jew speculators get stock in the company."[3] His successors had different ideas about the merit of capital markets.

There were few signs of rust on America's gleaming industrial belt in 1956. Almost a third of the country's working population was still employed in manufacturing of one form or another. Detroit's "Big Three"— Ford, General Motors, and Chrysler—were the titans of the country's unparalleled auto industry. The city had exploded in size during the early decades of the twentieth century. Black men and women from the American South and white farmworkers from rural Michigan and beyond moved to Detroit to take up new industrial employment. Greeks, Macedonians, Italians and Armenians stepping foot in America for the first time made the Midwestern city their home. The Big Three played a vital role in transforming America into the military-industrial powerhouse that decisively changed the course of the Second World War. Until 1940, Chrysler had only ever made a modest range of light trucks for the American military. But within just a few years, the company was making hundreds of thousands of incendiary bombs, millions of rounds of ammunition, all manner of aircraft parts and more than half of the US military's M3 tank fleet. Chrysler's main plant in Detroit churned out more tanks in five years than most of the countries involved in the war.

America faced no real challenge from any other corner of the world when it came to automaking, or anything much else. During the 1950s, the country made up just 6 percent of the global population, but it accounted for about four in every five cars manufactured anywhere on earth. The Japanese car companies that would pose a terminal threat to the American auto industry in the 1970s and 1980s were still minnows: Japan's entire auto industry had produced perhaps just twenty thousand passenger cars in 1955, not even 1 percent of the American total. Few people in America had yet heard of Honda or Nissan, and when Toyota made its first venture into the American market with the Toyopet Crown in 1958, it was a dismal flop. The car was slow, wobbly and unsuited to American roads—the residents of Detroit and its neighboring Midwestern industrial powerhouses, at the absolute height of their sway in America and abroad, had no reason to see Japanese manufacturers as a serious threat to their dominance.

When America's industrial belt was at its peak, homeownership was still rising rapidly. Each month between 1940 and 1960, an average of about seventy-three thousand new households became owner-occupiers. The share of American families that owned the property they lived in climbed from 44 percent to 62 percent. An average house in the city of Detroit cost around $9,379 in 1950, equivalent to about three and a half years of the salary of a janitor at Ford.[4] Nationwide, an American house cost on average a little more than two times a normal household income, compared to around five and a half times the median household income today, despite the fact that modern-day households are far more likely to have two incomes rather than one.[5] In today's money, the median American home cost about $97,000 in 1950, less than a third of the $355,000 price tag for a middling property in 2024.

Economic geography—our understanding of where economic activity takes place and why, which areas are productive and unproductive and whether they can be changed—governs a huge amount of political discussion the world over. The debates are often the source of rancor and resentment. Once-mighty places believe they have been abandoned, and successful ones feel that they are left to subsidize distant parts of the country. But America's economic geography in the middle of the twentieth century was astoundingly even in its distribution. The price of housing across the country's urban cores was much of a muchness—the major cities of the East Coast were mature, large and economically diversified, the industrial hubs in the Midwest were booming and Los Angeles was sprawling outwards as surging car ownership made farther-flung suburbs possible. The cost of a typical home in Detroit was not all that different from the price of one in the metropolitan area around San Francisco ($10,704), Chicago ($11,383), or New York City ($12,387).[6] A working family that owned a typical home in any large urban area in America could afford to sell up, move and buy another—perhaps a little larger or a little smaller—in any of the other major cities across the country.

In 1956, the world Henry George had lived in and written about, a world of burgeoning land monopolies, widespread desperation and yawning inequality, seemed very distant indeed. The unemployment, urban strife and radical politics of America's Gilded Age had been comprehensively replaced by mass homeownership, industrial plenty and the ambitious new social security net constructed in the aftermath of the Great Depression. The suburbs were booming, facilitated partly by the expansion of ambitious public transport networks like Detroit's streetcars and even more so by the massive growth in private car ownership. The American frontier had been closed six decades earlier, but for the new industrial middle class, it had effectively opened again as cities sprawled out across their horizons. The era is now unfamiliar to anyone much younger than eighty, but the combination of industrial strength, relative regional equality and ample, low-priced housing has helped it retain its position as the brand image of the American Dream.

In that world, the workers who were literally buying into Detroit's industrial swagger had very little way of knowing that they would never be so comparatively prosperous or confident again. A decade and a half after the Ford IPO and the peak of American industrial pomp, Detroit and America's other manufacturing powerhouses were in the midst of a protracted tailspin from which they have never completely recovered. By the late 1960s, foreign automakers (and especially the champions of Japan's industrial renaissance) were beginning to break into the American market: auto imports went from less than 1 percent of new American passenger automobiles in 1955 to 24 percent in 1970.[7] When the oil-rich nations that made up the Organization of the Petroleum Exporting Countries (OPEC) unilaterally raised oil prices in 1973, the cost of energy for American households and businesses alike exploded, putting a new and painful squeeze on those who were making energy-intensive goods like automobiles.

Just as foreign competition against Detroit was ramping up, it became one of the cities hit hardest by the racial violence of the late 1960s. In 1967, riots in Detroit were put down not just by the Michigan National Guard but also by two US Airborne divisions. Depopulation to the suburbs surrounding the city accelerated: Detroit went from 1.8 million residents in 1950 to fewer than a million by the turn of the twenty-first century. For landowners who had bought into the city at its industrial peak, the downturn was a disaster. At the end of 2024, the value of an average house in Detroit ran to around $73,600, just over half in real terms what it was in 1950, and around a fifth of the American average of almost

$345,000, according to data from Zillow, an American online real estate marketplace.[8]

Asking an American to predict what was coming for the country's economic geography in the second half of the 1950s—not just to predict the competitive threats to US automakers from Japan, but also the oil crises of the 1970s and the new industrial revolution in communication technology that would follow—would have been an unreasonable request. Indeed, many of the era's technologists, financiers and businessmen were unable to foresee the trends that would shift American industry and the distribution of wealth across the country, let alone an ordinary citizen.

Yet this is precisely the kind of forecast that most families across the world, whether they know it or not, are asked to make. Decisions made by a person's parents and grandparents on where to live, work and, most important, buy a home—which in most cases will be a family's single largest investment in their lifetime—have determined much of the difference between families with little to no asset wealth, those with many millions of dollars in assets and everyone between. It is hard to attribute much of the massive accumulation of wealth from the rise in land prices to merit on the part of its beneficiaries, just as it reflects no failing on the part of those who have lost out where prices have collapsed. The story of Detroit's decline is not just one of industrial decline and immiseration for the people who bet on the place in question. It is also an example—a particularly drastic one—of the transformation of economic geography not just in America but across the world over the past half a century. The shift of economic growth and economic activity towards a small handful of colossally productive cities is a vital part of why land has become more rather than less important in the modern world.

Even before the decline of the West's industrial heartlands truly began, a few farsighted observers could already see how the industrial world was about to be transformed. It wasn't just the patterns of global trade or energy costs at work, but a seismic technological change too. Arthur C. Clarke, the British futurist and the co-author of the screenplay for the film *2001: A Space Odyssey*, was among the group of prognosticators. Speaking in a BBC broadcast in 1964, he explained the looming revolution to his audience. "The incredible breakthrough which has been made possible by developments in communications, particularly the transistor and above all the communications satellite, these things will make possible a world in which we can be in instant contact with each other wherever we may be," he said.[9]

But Clarke's forecast didn't just concern technology. "It will be possible in that age, perhaps only fifty years from now, for a man to conduct his business from Tahiti or Bali just as well as he could from London." That shift, he believed, would fundamentally reshape humanity's urban existence. "When that time comes," he said, "the whole world will have shrunk to a point, and the traditional role of the city as a meeting place for man will have ceased to make any sense . . . I only hope that when that day comes and when the city is abolished, the whole world isn't turned into one giant suburb."[10]

The technological breakthrough Clarke described was underway in San Francisco Bay. In 1955, before the Ford IPO and during Detroit's glimmering industrial zenith, the industrial structure of the world was being remade in a nondescript office on San Antonio Road in Mountain View, California. William Bradford Shockley, a physicist who would later win the Nobel Prize for his research on semiconductors, was setting out to try and make a commercial success from the transistors he had helped invent.

He founded a company named Shockley Semiconductor, the first West Coast firm working on new silicon-based semiconductor chips.

Just as Detroit's decline was not obvious to its residents, the economic geography that would make the Californian city the ground zero of the global technology industry was hardly apparent either. Shockley almost founded the company under the wing of defense manufacturing firm Raytheon, which would have placed him and his venture on the East Coast—a far more obvious location for access to finance and expertise at the time.[11] Fullerton, several hundred miles south of San Francisco, was another serious contender for the firm's location, and so was a site in Florida. In some tellings of Shockley's story, he chose the location because his aging mother lived in nearby Palo Alto. When Shockley finally did settle on Mountain View, convincing skilled scientists and technicians to move from the existing American technology industry based overwhelmingly in the northeast of the country was one of his earliest struggles.

Just two years later, in 1957, eight of Shockley's most ambitious young employees set out on their own with a new firm and cemented the San Francisco Bay Area as the nexus of the tech sector. At the time, even seasoned investors were blinkered to the opportunity at hand in the budding semiconductor industry. Arthur Rock, a young MBA graduate who eventually corralled funding for the new breakaway company, was shot down by dozens of firms during the search for investment—Ford and Chrysler among them.[12] Sherman Fairchild, an inventor and businessman whose father had cofounded IBM, eventually agreed to fund the company, and Fairchild Semiconductor was born. The engineers who left Shockley Semiconductor would eventually become known as the "Traitorous Eight."

By 1959, Fairchild had produced the first commercially viable integrated circuits, the building blocks of the world of modern electronics. By

1966, less than a decade into its existence, it employed eleven thousand people.[13] Among the Traitorous Eight were Robert Noyce and Gordon Moore, who would go on to launch American electronics giant Intel in 1968. Dozens of tech firms, which came to be known as the "Fairchildren," were subsequently founded by Fairchild's early employees. Just as Henry Ford had cemented Detroit as the home of his entirely new industry half a century earlier, the pioneers of what would eventually become America's world-beating technology industry were making the foggy corner of California the home of a new and flourishing industry. In the era of mass production, industrial cities in the Midwest had been the capitals of the second Industrial Revolution. The new Silicon Valley would be the capital of the third, reaping the benefits of a boom in electronics, digital technology and eventually the blossoming of the internet.

In 1969, five years after Arthur C. Clarke's forecast and ten years after the founding of Fairchild Semiconductor, the first rudimentary electronic messages were sent between researchers in different parts of California, across the US Advanced Research Projects Agency Network (ARPANET). Researchers at the University of California, Los Angeles, attempted to share the word "login" with a team at Stanford University to their north. A crash meant only the first two letters were transmitted, resulting in an unintentionally appropriate first message: "lo." The snippet was the earliest precursor to online communication. Clarke had presciently identified the transformative potential that new electronics would have for communications, the instant access it would give people in one corner of the world to every other corner and more or less the timing of the shift.

It is easy enough to see how the transformation of communication technology led Clarke to his prediction that the city was about to die. For millennia, questions of distance had been the most crucial determinant of economic geography. Before the advent of coal, cities had to be close to forests to collect the fuel they needed to function. In the nineteenth century, the ability to travel quickly by rail across much greater distances revolutionized the size and shape of cities. Since proximity—to productive employment, resources and major population centers—is precisely what makes urban real estate so valuable, the technological changes Clarke foresaw would transform the world just as urbanization had a hundred years earlier. Indeed, the future that Clarke imagined would have reversed the trends that began in the era of Henry George. The end of the city, until then the organizing unit of human civilization, would have ended the smothering inequities of land too.

But for all his farsightedness when it came to changes in technology, Clarke could not have been more wrong when it came to the future of the city. Of all the gargantuan shifts in the ways that we live, work and play that were being born at Shockley Semiconductor in the 1950s, the end of urban life was certainly not among them. Even as major industrial cities—like America's Detroit, Buffalo and Cleveland, or England's Liverpool, France's Lille, Belgium's Charleroi and Italy's Turin—have experienced protracted and painful periods of economic decline, the largest and most productive cities around the world have only become more economically vital, and the land beneath them more expensive. Distance has not declined in importance; indeed, in crucial ways it is more important than ever.

Rather than the abolition of the city as the organizing unit for human civilization, the direct application of modern communication technology—the growth of computing, the widespread use of the internet and the rise of mobile phones—has coincided with an enormous rise in house prices across much of the Western world, especially in a specific group of immensely successful and desirable cities. The gap between the world's most successful urban hubs and their laggard peers has only grown and grown. The former, which includes global capitals like London and New York, have boomed as centers of creativity and innovation, even as the economy has become increasingly dominated by intangible digital services. The rise of knowledge work, by engineers, financiers, tech workers, academics—or indeed, sometimes journalists—has lit a fire under the importance of this handful of specific locations, where the world's most productive workers cluster together.

The group of immensely productive and desirable metropolises was given a name in 2006 by economists Joseph Gyourko, Christopher Mayer and Todd Sinai. They are the "superstar cities."[14] The researchers recorded an enormous disparity in the growth rate for house prices in different parts of America between 1950 and 2000. Over that period, prices in San Francisco had risen at a 3.5 percent annualized rate. Prices in Seattle and Portland, Oregon, had risen by 2.7 percent and 2.4 percent respectively. But in places like Cleveland, Dayton and Rochester, New York, parts of America's now-rusted industrial belt, prices had risen by less than 1 percent. Small differences in annual growth rates have become yawning chasms over time. During the second half of the twentieth century, the authors noted, gains in income across America had skewed notably towards high-income households. Such households clustered together, outbidding lower-income groups for scarce land and housing, and allowing house prices to surge. In the years since the three economists gave the phenomenon a name, the cities and their importance have only grown.

The result of the decline of industrial cities and the rise of the superstars means the days when house prices in the large cities of America were more or less equivalent are a distant memory. The median price of a home in San Francisco is more than three times the national level, at $1.26 million, as of the end of 2024. Homes in Los Angeles come in close behind, at just above $995,000. Prices in both Californian cities have risen by around 300 percent since the turn of the century, much faster than the increase nationally. The slump that followed the global financial crisis in 2008 proved to be more of a speed bump than a brick wall in America's most expensive housing markets. In contrast, in some of the least expensive metros where the economy has stagnated—like Decatur, Illinois; Charleston, West Virginia; and Enid, Oklahoma—house prices have not even doubled over the past quarter of a century.

In a nasty irony, Detroit's progressive municipal history made declining land prices particularly painful for its fiscal health. Between the 1890s and the beginning of the city's decline in the early 1950s, the property tax had been Detroit's only source of revenue. The tax had been instituted by mayor Hazen Pingree, an ally of Henry George's, who had been mayor of Detroit and subsequently governor of Michigan. As Detroit began to shrink in population and investors downgraded its financial future, the property tax revenues that had provided such a tremendous windfall shriveled up rapidly. The population declined by roughly 40 percent between the late 1950s and the middle of the 1990s. But property tax revenues fell much faster, tumbling by almost 80 percent over the same period as Detroit's bleak economic future was priced into the city's land values— even as the municipal government repeatedly raised property tax rates.[15] The engine that had powered the city's government spending had gone into reverse. During the early 2000s, as America's housing bubble inflated, Detroit's property tax base recovered a fraction of its value, before crashing again in the aftermath of the global financial crisis in 2008. The sudden slump in property values played a leading role in the city's bankruptcy in 2013, the biggest municipal collapse in American history.

Just as the plummeting land prices in Detroit magnified its slump through tumbling collateral values and tax revenues, the long rally in house prices in the superstar cities has amplified their economic boom. Any homeowner with an idea for a business or a project to pursue has been able to access a large and growing pile of real estate collateral. Research by Federal Reserve economists Arun Gupta, Horacio Sapriza and Vladimir Yankov suggests that more than a third of American employment growth between 2013 and 2019, when the economy was still recovering from the effects of the global financial crisis, could be attributed to real estate values rising.[16] That effect has been concentrated in the parts of the country where real estate collateral was rising in value.

While Detroit's dependence on property taxes eventually proved to be a municipal nightmare, in California's priciest cities it has made governing much easier—even when the quality of governing itself has often been terrible. Since 2012, the value of land in California has risen from $1.94 trillion to $4 trillion in 2024, according to the tax base assessments made by the state government.[17] Without raising San Francisco's 1.17 percent property tax, the local government has nevertheless been guaranteed a steadily growing stream of income. According to the Lincoln Institute of Land Policy, a Massachusetts-based think tank, the property tax rate in Detroit would have to be twenty times higher than the rate in San Francisco to raise the same amount of money to fund local spending.[18]

The economic fortunes of cities, regions and nations have always been subject to change throughout history. That has been even more true in the past three centuries, in which economies have been far more dynamic and growth much more rapid. A variety of important factors to the functioning of a large city—access to water, fuel or food, the availability of transport or human capital—have shifted in relative importance over time, with changing technological and economic conditions. With those conditions, places have risen and declined in their advantages and importance. The record of efforts to promote the places that have fallen behind is spotty, at best—more often than not, the only successful way to balance the stakes has been when governments have deliberately tried to restrain the winners.

But the rise of the superstar cities since the late twentieth century has heralded a huge problem too, one that has slowed the adjustment. Most have systematically failed to expand their housing and infrastructure nearly enough to meet the burgeoning demand to live there, to accommodate those people who would otherwise have moved from places on the decline. Gyourko, Mayer and Sinai, the three economists who gave the superstar cities their name, identified the supply of land and housing—specifically, the fact that little to nothing is built in response to surging house prices—as the major factor driving the wedge between the superstars and the rest. The change in economic geography that emerged during the late twentieth century was profoundly different from the one that had taken place in the late nineteenth century, when places like Detroit were growing rapidly. The growing importance of the superstars was focused on existing cities, which were already populated, with land that was already in use.

Expanding cities either upwards or outwards has become far more difficult in the superstar era. Henry George fumed at landowners who left their plots fallow and empty, simply waiting for them to rise in value. But in the most productive parts of the Western world today, the inability to build is a result of government diktat and the difficulties of local politics, rather than the avarice and laziness of landlords. Long gone are the days in which owners were broadly free to build anything they liked on their land. In the years before the Second World War, the popularity of zoning—restrictions that determined what could be built in a given area—had grown in America since the early twentieth century. The new methods encouraged single-family homes and blocked the multifamily options and taller apartment buildings that would have permitted greater population density in the most popular—and valuable—plots of land. The new land-use restrictions were a boon not just to urbanist dreamers, but to local administrations who wanted to organize their cities by class and race too. For decades after openly race-based zoning was struck down by the Supreme Court in 1917, cities across the country pursued policies that effectively enforced racial segregation. America was not alone. Forms of urban planning had grown in popularity among municipal bureaucrats across the rich world.

Other restrictions make it impossible to expand cities outwards too. In 1947, the British government introduced the Town and Country Planning Act, which instituted the modern system of planning permission in Britain and gave local governments power to institute their own green belts—rings of land around their cities that would be free of development. In the nineteenth century, the growth of new industrialized cities had been accompanied by new railway networks and tramways, and later by the mass ownership of automobiles, transforming where people could live and work. But no similarly momentous change in the technology of transportation accompanied the shift to the superstar cities. A combination of technological limitation and tight legal restrictions has made it far more difficult to utilize the newly valuable urban centers more productively and to the benefit of the many millions of people who might otherwise live and work in them.

The failure of housing growth to keep up with demand is common to all of the West's richest cities. But San Francisco is the modern icon of the inability of the world's most productive and innovative cities to expand in size—somewhat ironically, given the city's pivotal role in the development of the modern communication technology that Arthur C. Clarke believed would abolish city life. According to the state government of California, the city should be building around ten thousand new housing units per year.[19] The city's record of actual housing construction has fallen well below that incredibly modest goal: in its modern history, there is only a single year on record in which San Francisco has seen the completion of five thousand homes, an increase of a little over 1 percent in the city's housing stock.[20] In reality, even ten thousand new homes a year is a gross underestimate of what would be needed to actually match demand. Given the extraordinary cost of local housing—the average rent in San Francisco runs to over $3,400 per month, more than half the median American wage—it is no exaggeration to say that the city could very easily be twice its current size, if densification and expansion were permitted.

The inability to build is visible across the immensely expensive cities of the Western world. Mile after mile of single-story bungalows spill out beyond the center of superexpensive Sydney, a city where land is extraordinarily pricey despite Australia's physical abundance. London is surrounded by thinly populated suburbs that would house millions more people at greater densities. Toronto's "Yellowbelt," which makes up the vast majority of the city's land area, permits a single property per lot. All these cities, where housing is immensely expensive, are characterized by a "missing middle"—the gentle density that falls between detached single-family homes and super-tall commercial and residential towers.

This book is about land, rather than the supply of housing specifically. But the two issues are now inextricably connected, especially in the Western world, and especially where housing is most expensive. The failure to build makes land all the more important, and its unique attributes all the more binding. Data produced by the American Enterprise Institute, a Washington, DC–based think tank, illustrates the stark effect that the inability to build has had. Land makes up about 40 percent of the property value of the median urban area in the United States. In New York City, where land is scarce but the city was at least once permitted to build upwards, the total share of land in house prices is 56 percent. In San Francisco, Los Angeles and San Jose, some of the most expensive cities in America, the share of land in house prices runs to an extraordinary 69 percent, 74 percent and 77 percent respectively.[21]

The problem of housing supply is only getting worse. Research by economists Knut Are Aastveit, Bruno Albuquerque and André Anundsen established that the supply of American housing has become far less responsive to house prices—a relationship known as the elasticity of supply—since the global financial crisis in 2008.[22] Between 1996 and 2006, during the long boom in house prices that preceded the crash, the authors note that a 1 percent increase in house prices was typically followed by a 2.8 percent increase in building permits. But between 2012 and 2017, a 1 percent increase in prices meant a rise in permits of just 1.8 percent. Elasticities in the most restrictive 10 percent of metropolitan areas—places like San Francisco—have plunged, and a 1 percent increase in house prices results in a pathetic 0.4 percent increase in building permits.

The failure to build anything like enough housing has caused all manner of dismal consequences. In their essay "The Housing Theory of Everything," researchers John Myers, Ben Southwood and Sam Bowman explore and expound on the many less-understood consequences of the restrictive supply of housing.[23] Expensive homes help to drive everything from the world's low fertility rates, since young families cannot afford the additional space to raise children, to rising levels of obesity, since sprawling cities in which greater densification is impossible are dominated by car transport.

When it comes to fertility rates specifically, the evidence is stark. Economists Lisa Dettling and Melissa Schettini Kearney suggest that about 10 percent of the excess births during the mid-twentieth-century baby boom—equivalent to three million additional children—were caused by the Federal Housing Administration and Veterans Administration programs that promoted mortgage lending to new homeowners.[24] The increasingly expensive supply of housing can work in the opposite direction: another paper published by Dettling suggests that a $10,000 increase leads to a 5 percent increase in fertility among homeowners, but a 2.4 percent decrease among nonowners.[25] The fewer young people of childbearing age own homes, the greater the impact on fertility.

One of the most significant effects of the limited housing supply in the West's superstar cities is its impact on inequality. The focus on the haves and have-nots surged back into Western politics during the years that followed the global financial crisis in 2008. French economist Thomas Piketty captured the moment with his book *Capital in the Twenty-First Century*, published in his native French in 2013 and translated into English in 2014. The book sold a million and a half copies in its first two years, bringing Piketty closer to being a household name than any professional economist since Milton Friedman. Inequality in wealth, Piketty argued, was climbing back towards levels last seen during America's Gilded Age, when George's writing was lighting a fire under the political world on both sides of the Atlantic. The cause, Piketty argued, is that the returns on capital (roughly, what the asset owners make from their existing wealth) are once again higher than the rate of economic growth. Since some people have more assets than others, that will mean wealth inequality is magnified over time. In Piketty's argument, combating the climb in inequality would require higher taxes, and particularly taxes on wealth.

But the rise in disparities in wealth that Piketty identified was not a phenomenon largely driven by plutocrats and jet-setting elites. In reality, the vast majority of the rise in wealth inequality since the middle of the twentieth century across the Western world, and increasingly far beyond it, reflects the huge disparities between the haves and have-nots of modern land wealth. In 2015, Matthew Rognlie, then a PhD student at the Massachusetts Institute of Technology, found that the vast majority of the increase in the capital share—the portion of economic output captured by returns to wealth, rather than by workers—was due to changes in the value and distribution of housing wealth all across the Western world.[26] Further research by economist Gianni La Cava determined that the increase in capital income driven by land and housing in America was almost entirely concentrated in supply-inelastic states, ones where the building of new housing is most constrained.[27]

Not only do the rise of housing wealth and the resurgence of land values explain the rise in wealth inequality in the latter decades of the twentieth century and why inequality has remained high today, but they also explain a huge chunk of the differences in wealth inequality between nations. When they explored the relationship between inequality and housing around the rich world, economists Fabian T. Pfeffer and

Nora Waitkus found a limited relationship between income and wealth inequality.[28] In fact, rich nations with very low income disparities, like Sweden and Norway, actually have higher wealth inequality than most comparable countries. The authors discovered that the combination of homeownership rates and variations in home values explains most of the disparity in wealth inequality between nations.

The less flexible the supply of housing is, the more a housing market exhibits all of the unique characteristics of land and magnifies their worst consequences. The value of real estate in the supply-constrained superstar cities is sensitive to moves in interest rates. Since land does not depreciate or decay, its price is based on cash flows and conditions that stretch an extremely long way into the future. When interest rates rise, the price of assets based on very long-term expectations can fall sharply: the expected future earnings from the land haven't changed, but the returns to be made from a safe government bond have, making the land less valuable relative to potential alternatives. When rates fall, the opposite is true—the rich and extremely lengthy stream of cash flows an investor can reap make the land a far more attractive investment.

That means that financial stability is increasingly at risk when the supply of housing does not respond to increases in price. In the places with significant supply restrictions, mostly those that are already very productive and expensive, house prices are most sensitive of all to sudden changes in monetary policy—interest rate cuts and increases alike. Another piece of research by Bruno Albuquerque, with coauthors Martin Iseringhausen and Frederic Opitz, suggests that in the most supply-constrained cities, rising interest rates cause more mortgage delinquencies, more foreclosures and a bigger deterioration in the health of local banks, relative to places where the supply of housing is quite elastic.[29]

A substantial portion of this book has focused on the history of land as an asset in the United States and the British colonies of North America that preceded it. That is not by chance—land speculation and land finance has a deep American history. The country's early financial pioneers blazed a trail for the use of land as a tool for creating credit, which much of the rest of the world followed. The political turmoil over the ownership of land that spread around the world in the late nineteenth century began with an American political entrepreneur. And the monetization of land meant that the United States was home to some of the world's earliest and most spectacular financial blowups. Enthusiasm for widespread homeownership as a cornerstone of a democratic society began as an American preoccupation, and is now one that is shared worldwide.

But today America is in some distinct and important ways better placed than many other nations to weather the problems that land can cause. The country's deep capital markets, its culture of equity investing and its innovative companies have made land far less profitable to own, relative to the aforementioned alternatives, than is the case in much of the rest of the world. In the decade ending in 2024, American stocks offered an annualized return of around 13 percent, handily beating the increase in real estate values over the same period of time. The asset wealth of American households is far more distributed across a variety of financial assets, and much less concentrated in real estate, than any other large industrialized nation. The American financial system is far less dominated by banks than economies in most of the rest of the world, and the ups and downs of lending and borrowing in the United States are far less dependent on the cycles of land prices.

The country also continues to benefit from the favorable economic geography that European colonists discovered four hundred years ago. A century and a half after the closure of the American frontier, the country's land is still comparatively plentiful and relatively unconcentrated into a handful of extremely productive cities, especially in contrast to most developed nations. Only New York and Los Angeles are truly global megalopolises, with urban populations of over ten million people, and collectively the two make up just over a tenth of the American population. Relative to Britain, Japan or China, America retains a far greater number of high-productivity cities and towns of a more modest size all over the country. Productive places like Austin and Dallas in Texas; the Research Triangle of Raleigh, Durham and Chapel Hill in North Carolina; Madison, Wisconsin; and Salt Lake City in Utah have grown in size and wealth, as other hubs—like San Francisco—have refused to expand.

That means land wealth in America is less distorted towards a handful of extremely expensive cities than it is in most other rich nations—its geographical bounty remains a massive advantage. As a result, the share of American private wealth in land is relatively low compared to other more densely populated and less diverse economies. Land accounted for about 15 percent of all private assets in America in 2023. That figure is higher than was true in the recent past—between 1950 and 1975, land never accounted for more than 10 percent of the country's wealth. But the current figure is still below the 21 percent peak for American land wealth, reached during the bubble years before the global financial crisis in 2008.

Many other countries look far less healthy by the same measures, with economic activity significantly more concentrated into a handful of small and highly productive cities. Toronto and Montréal house more than a quarter of the Canadian population. Over 35 percent of Australians live in Sydney and Melbourne. A quarter of the British population lives in London and the surrounding region of South East England. The economic geography of most countries is simply far more concentrated than America's, and the issues related to land and real estate are more desperate. Stock markets in the developed world outside of America have performed far more poorly, returning less than 5 percent on an annualized basis. The fact that other investment options have performed so poorly, lagging returns in both domestic real estate and American equities, is part of what has made land such a growing share of national wealth in so many countries outside of America.

Across the rest of the Anglosphere, the rise in land values has been extreme, outstripping all other forms of wealth accumulation. Even when including all financial assets—pensions, insurance contracts, bank deposits, shares in funds and any other paper investments—land under homes and commercial properties made up 31 percent of all British assets in 2023, up from just 18 percent at the turn of the twenty-first century. In Canada, land accounts for 25 percent of private wealth, up from 17 percent in 1999, and in property-mad Australia, the figure has risen from 29 percent to 38 percent. In all three countries, the share of private-sector wealth accounted for by land is actually higher than it was in 2007, on the eve of the greatest international housing bust that the world has ever seen.

The politics of land in the twenty-first century will be much more complicated than it was at the end of the nineteenth century. The rise of mass homeownership in the twentieth century made landownership far more widespread and egalitarian than it had been at the end of the nineteenth. Any electoral strategy that pits the landless against landowners is unlikely to be a winning one in countries where the latter account for the majority of voters, and an even larger proportion of the older generations who are most engaged with electoral politics.

But the electoral effects of rising land wealth and the disparities it has created are clear in an abundance of new research. The impact of the surge in foreclosures on mortgaged houses after the global financial crisis in 2008 had a meaningful impact on the results of the 2016 election, according to Stanford academics Andrew Hall, Jesse Yoder and Nishant Karandikar.[30] They found that an increase of one foreclosure per one thousand people between 2004 and 2016 cut Hillary Clinton's vote share by between 1 and 1.8 percentage points, offering Donald Trump a boost in a state that Barack Obama won in 2012. Analysis by the Center for American Progress, a liberal think tank, noted a similar correlation: the Midwestern counties that flipped from blue to red between the Obama and Trump administrations had disproportionately high rates of negative equity—homes worth less than the mortgages they had borrowed to purchase them—compared to either solidly red or solidly blue counties.[31] Even in the towns and cities that powered industrial America like Detroit, Flint and Milwaukee, which overwhelmingly voted for Clinton, a narrowed margin provided vital help to push Trump over the line.

The effects outside of America, just like the importance of land wealth itself, are even more pronounced. In Britain, housing wealth had a significant and understated effect on the outcome of the country's referendum on membership in the European Union in 2016. Support for remaining in the bloc was higher—even after controlling for factors like age and income—in places where house prices were particularly high and in places where house prices had risen most considerably for the previous two decades, according to research by Ben Ansell and David Adler.[32] Research along the same lines has found links between the rapid rise in house prices of Scandinavian markets and the populist right in Sweden, Denmark and Finland.[33] In France, the same effect is clear when it comes to support for Marine Le Pen, the presidential candidate of the far-right Front National. Places where house prices have risen more slowly, or even declined, have been far more likely to vote for Le Pen. Even for readers wildly unsympathetic to these populist platforms, it is surely no surprise that left-behind housing markets are a breeding ground for left-behind political movements.

The mass homeownership that began to emerge in the Western world a century ago, and that has since spread around the world, was intended as a bulwark for more democratic, egalitarian and politically harmonious societies. In its early decades, the scaffolding of new subsidies, financial incentives and other forms of government support offered to new homeowners almost certainly did that job. With it came a new way to build widespread middle-class wealth, helping to reduce the extreme inequality of Henry George's era.

But the shift in economic geography across the rich world that gave rise to the superstar cities has lit a fire under the most pernicious effects of land once again. Just as the rising importance of agglomeration in modern economies has yielded far greater productivity and innovation, it has revived the issues that animated the Single Taxers, giving the asset a new and urgent relevance. The rationale of widespread private landownership has been critically undermined, as the winners and losers of the system are determined more and more by accident of birth and the luck of the draw. Land may have disappeared from the political debate, but it has not disappeared from politics. Its relevance bubbles away just below the surface.

Epilogue

t has been eighty years since Wolf Ladejinsky first set foot in Tokyo and began his global campaign for land reform. It has been almost one hundred and fifty years since Henry George rose to stardom, four hundred since John Smith set foot on the east coast of what is now the United States and three and a half thousand since Munnabittu's legal tussle over his land in ancient Babylon. The circumstances of their births and the worlds in which they lived were wildly different from one another, but the economic importance of land is a constant thread that runs through hundreds, even thousands of years of history. The emergence of the modern global financial system has made land more powerful in new and sometimes dangerous ways, even as the world we live in seems to have become more incorporeal.

All around the modern world, countries are trapped when it comes to land. When the asset becomes central to a nation's wealth and financial system, an increase or a slump in its price creates huge risks for households, businesses, governments or all three. When land climbs in value, it inevitably creates gaping disparities between the fortunate owners in newly

expensive hubs and the unfortunate souls who bet on the wrong locations, especially in left-behind places in economic decline. Surging land
prices mean greater and greater borrowing on the part of new buyers and
landowners with growing lines of credit, which in turn raises the risk of
national and international financial crises. The steady upwards climb in
land prices across large parts of the world may even be sapping the productive potential of their economies, driving resources and funding to
companies with land to use as collateral, and depriving those without it.
When prices fall, the disparities in land wealth might well be temporarily
reduced. But the consequences of destabilizing the financial system of a
country that has become completely dependent on ever-rising land prices
can prove a deadly cure for the disease. In the most extreme cases, it can
put a brake on an entire economy for years or even decades.

The stories peppered throughout this book are usually told in very
different ways. The early settlers of America's colonies, the companies that
rode Japan's postwar boom, the British bureaucrats who founded Hong
Kong and Singapore or the Chinese reformers who transformed their
country might otherwise appear to be disparate and disconnected char-
acters. But the way in which land functions as an asset is baked through
all of these events. Tales of the way in which land works follow a familiar
rhythm: during periods of seismic economic change it can seem, even for
decades, that land wealth is relatively well-shared and widespread. A rising
tide seems to be lifting all boats. That is true when it comes to the discovery of a new continent, a shift to new and groundbreaking methods
of transportation, a revolution in agricultural technology or the transformation of a communist economy into a market-driven one. A burst of economic optimism and growth often disguises, for a time, the biggest problems
associated with rapidly rising land prices. Periods of such rapid growth

and transformation go a long way to paper over an inevitable climb in debt and cover up the seeds of political and social strife that are inevitably sown.

By the time the inequities and financial vulnerabilities engendered by a long boom in land prices become clear—through the closure of the American frontier, the collapse in Japan's asset bubble, the global financial crisis in 2008 or the ongoing, slow collapse of China's land-financed debt binge—it is too late to do much about it. By definition, not everyone can be a winner when land prices rise. In this respect, land is a zero-sum asset. When a country's economic geography becomes increasingly fixed in place, when housing cannot be built in its most productive cities and when growth slows to a crawl, the problems with land quickly become obvious. Indeed, when the slowdown, the stagnation or the bust arrives, it is difficult to tell how nobody saw them coming in the first place.

The consequences of an inability to build are taking a greater role in American politics. *Abundance*, a book written by journalists Ezra Klein and Derek Thompson, makes the case that liberal cities have stymied progress with a thicket of political and regulatory restrictions to the expansion of housing and infrastructure. Whether an optimistic, pro-development political coalition can be cobbled together in the places where it is most needed, America's most expensive cities, remains to be seen. But the subject has now entered public debate like never before. If something does not change, national politics will be steadily transformed. As blue states grow more slowly than red states, they will lose electoral college votes and congressional representation.

Saying much with extreme confidence about the future is tough. Over the past four decades or so, during which the superstar cities have really come into their own, there has only been one serious shock to their growing strength: the Covid-19 pandemic. The sudden shift in working patterns caused an immediate change to the economics of cities all over the world: in America, the number of days worked from home (WFH) rose from about 5 percent before the pandemic to over 60 percent in the first half of 2020. Even as the world emerged from lockdowns, travel restrictions ended and physical life resumed, the proportion of days worked from home fell to between 25 to 30 percent and stayed there.[1] Twenty percent of American office space was vacant in 2024, a record high, almost four years after Covid-19 began to spread across the world.[2]

The very core of the superstar cities has suffered from the aftereffects of the WFH revolution. In many city centers, commercial rents have tumbled and vacancies have remained high over the past five years. That has provided a nasty shock to the banks and investors with major exposure to those developments, the impacts of which are still slowly burning: it is a miniature version of the crisis that hit Japan's lenders in the 1990s. Companies that borrowed to buy the pricey real estate in central business districts will be forced to refinance their loans in the coming years, at far higher interest rates and based on asset values that have slumped. For large, national and well-diversified banks, exposure to offices in wounded city centers is manageable. For smaller banks that have specialized in commercial property, the experience will be far more painful.

But even as the centers of big cities have suffered from lower foot traffic and half-empty offices since 2020, the appeal of cities on the whole has been remarkably resilient. For every commuter hub dealing with a sudden decline in the number of workers traveling in, there is a leafy suburb within commuting distance where house prices have boomed in response to new hybrid working patterns. While electronic communication has become exactly as simple and costless as Arthur C. Clarke predicted in 1964, the most productive workers still hold strong preferences for being close to one another, even if they are in the office three days a week instead of five. The shift has created what economists Arjun Ramani, Joel Alcedo and Nicholas Bloom name the "donut effect," in which residents leaving the center of American cities have shifted to the suburbs. In the twelve largest American metropolitan areas, they find that while home values in city centers have dropped since 2020, they have risen by more than 40 percent in the outer suburbs of the same cities.[3]

Other technological and social changes could still shake the existing order when it comes to land, just as industrialization, the growth of the railways and the widespread adoption of personal automobiles did. The booming artificial intelligence industry is still in its infancy, and the changes it will bring to patterns of life and work are unclear. The potential effects of the widespread adoption of self-driving vehicles on patterns of transport and commuting are still unknown. But with so much wealth and financial activity anchored to the current state of affairs, any sudden change—however valuable—will come with major costs too.

Until another transformation arrives, there are no magical solutions for nations facing hangovers from a debt binge, heightened and unmerited wealth inequality or a misallocation of resources across the economy towards land-rich companies. This book does not have a simple fix to offer. The countries where land has become extraordinarily expensive and deeply entwined with the financial system bring to mind an old Irish joke in which a lost traveler asks a farmer for directions back to the city. "Well," the reply comes, "I wouldn't start from here."

Some things could well help to alleviate the worst symptoms of a protracted land boom. With such a massive dearth of building in the priciest cities in the world, evident through rock-bottom vacancy rates and sky-high rents, aggressively expanding the supply of housing and infrastructure would help reduce the share of wealth accounted for by land. Given the enormous value of land across the richest and most productive places in the world today, earned almost entirely by luck rather than merit, a tax on the value of land, even at levels far less confiscatory than those once proposed by Henry George, could do a great deal to mitigate the most damaging modern consequences without penalizing innovation or valuable investment in the way other taxes on wealth would do. In certain parts of the world, like China today or Japan during the peak of its land boom, land is particularly desirable because it gives buyers a way to invest in explosive economic growth when alternatives are suppressed or restricted by the government. Simply allowing the growth of capital markets would help to tamp down the roaring peaks in land markets and reduce the potential for collapses too.

Even making sure that land does not benefit from the huge range of tax reliefs and preferential treatment with which it has been showered could go a long way to keep the greatest problems associated with it in check. Land is still an object of obsession and among the most potent symbols of status and class. But more than anything, it has been an extremely fortuitous investment for millions of people the world over. It is no surprise that the strong and long-running financial returns to homeownership, made at a relatively low level of risk, and with favorable treatment from the government, have proved to be a winning combination for most people.

These potential remedies all face tremendous political hurdles. None of the true global metropolises of the Western world have managed to build anything like the amount of housing that would match the enormous demand to live in them. Individuals who have built up their own modest fiefdoms of land will, quite understandably, not take the idea of a new tax on their primary source of wealth lying down. The solution advocated by the Single Taxers in the closing decades of the nineteenth century placed a target on a narrow elite as the source of society's ills, a coterie of land barons who could be expropriated to make the vast majority far better off. When homeownership rates were far lower and land wealth far more concentrated, the argument had an enormous audience. Today, any effort to tap the enormous wealth in land for the benefit of the broader public would run afoul of the interests of millions of small landowners who have benefited from a windfall that has lasted for decades.

If many nations around the world have a bigger problem with land than America, China is in another category entirely. It has now been five years since the central government pulled the plug on the country's land boom, with no sign of a permanent or lasting resolution. The decision to hamstring the real estate industry without giving Chinese households greater opportunities for their investments, or allowing local governments a better way to raise revenues, has left the country in an economic morass. The state's tight grip on the Chinese financial system may mean the country avoids a 2008-style blowup. But with so much of the economy dependent on rising land prices for so long, and the sudden halt to the construction activity and infrastructure investment that has added so much to its growth, China cannot escape the full consequences of its real estate slump. As in Japan, China's land bust is now dovetailing with a shrinking working population, a dismal demographic problem that will only worsen in the years to come.

Much of the world is still only in the foothills of unlocking the financial power of land as a source of wealth, as collateral for lending or as government finance. While a handful of countries have long records of landownership, the median national land record is just forty-five years old.[4] Dozens of nations still have no formal register of ownership, leaving trillions of dollars of "dead capital" all over the world. They constitute an enormous supply of potential financial firepower: whether they can be used productively is another question. Few places have managed to avoid the pitfalls of the land trap, and none have managed to escape it entirely once the wheels have been set in motion. For nations both rich and poor alike, understanding that the trap exists at all—that land wealth is not like any other wealth, and that it can have pernicious and long-lasting outcomes—is the first step.

Acknowledgments

This book would not have been possible without my wife, Naomi, who has made invaluable contributions to its construction as its earliest reader and editor. Marrying a better writer than yourself is the best piece of advice I could offer to any would-be author.

I also owe my thanks to Noah Schwartzberg, my editor at Portfolio, a fount of support and assistance in the process; to Toby Mundy, my agent; to Chelsea Cohen, my production editor; to Dorothy Janick, who copyedited the book; and to everyone else on the publishing team who made it possible.

For fruitful conversations over more than a decade toying with the subject matter in this book (even when they were not aware), and advice on writing and publishing, my thanks go to Sam Bowman, Ben Southwood, Dan Wang, Gan Li, Anton Howes, Stuart Ritchie, No Sunk Costs, Matthew Campbell, Spencer Jakab and Duncan Weldon.

Notes

Chapter 1: The Lie of the Land

1. Jonathan Woetzel et al., *The Rise and Rise of the Global Balance Sheet* (McKinsey Global Institute, 2021), https://www.mckinsey.com/industries/financial-services/our-insights/the-rise-and-rise-of-the-global-balance-sheet-how-productively-are-we-using-our-wealth.
2. Author's calculations, World Inequality Database, https://wid.world/wid-world/.
3. Bloomberg Billionaires Index, Bloomberg, accessed February 28, 2025, https://www.bloomberg.com/billionaires/.
4. Òscar Jordà, Björn Richter, Moritz Schularick and Alan M. Taylor, "Bank Capital Redux: Solvency, Liquidity, and Crisis," *Review of Economic Studies* 88, no. 1 (2021): 260–286, https://doi.org/10.1093/restud/rdaa040.

Chapter 2: The Making of Nations

1. Captain John Smith, *A Description of New England* (Humfrey Lownes, 1616), 5–13.
2. Smith, *A Description of New England.*
3. *Historical Statistics of the United States, Colonial Times to 1957* (US Bureau of the Census, 1975), 1168.
4. Peter H. Lindert and Jeffrey G. Williamson, "American Colonial Incomes, 1650–1774," Working Paper 19861 (National Bureau of Economic Research, January 2014), https://www.nber.org/system/files/working_papers/w19861/w19861.pdf.
5. John Komlos, "On the Biological Standard of Living of Eighteenth-Century Americans: Taller, Richer, Healthier," Munich Discussion Paper No. 2003-9 (University of Munich, July 2003), https://epub.ub.uni-muenchen.de/53/.
6. Jeffrey G. Williamson and Peter Lindert, "Unequal Gains: American Growth and Inequality since 1700," *VoxEU*, June 16, 2016, https://cepr.org/voxeu/columns/unequal-gains-american-growth-and-inequality-1700.

7. Douglas A. Irwin, *Clashing over Commerce: A History of US Trade Policy* (University of Chicago Press, 2017), 31.

8. William Potter, *The Key of Wealth: Or a New Way for Improving of Trade* (R.A., 1650).

9. Katie A. Moore, "The Blood That Nourishes the Body Politic: The Origins of Paper Money in Early America," *Early American Studies* 17, no. 1 (Winter 2019): 1–36, 15, https://www.jstor.org/stable/e26554723.

10. J. Keith Horsefield, "The Origins of Blackwell's Model of a Bank," *William and Mary Quarterly* 23, no. 1 (January 1966): 121–135, https://doi.org/10.2307/2936159.

11. Claire Priest, "Creating an American Property Law: Alienability and Its Limits in American History," *Harvard Law Review* 120, no. 2 (December 2006): 385–459, https://harvardlawreview.org/print/vol-120/creating-an-american-property-law-alienability-and-its-limits-in-american-history/.

12. K-Sue Park, "Money, Mortgages, and the Conquest of America," *Law & Social Inquiry* 41, no. 4 (Fall 2016): 1006–1035, https://www.jstor.org/stable/26630897.

13. Alvin Rabushka, "Representation Without Representation: The Colonial Roots of American Taxation, 1700–1754," *Hoover Institution*, December 1, 2003, https://www.hoover.org/research/representation-without-representation.

14. Claire Priest, *Credit Nation: Property Laws and Institutions in Early America* (Princeton University Press, 2023), 74–75.

15. Bonnie Martin, "Slavery's Invisible Engine: Mortgaging Human Property," *Journal of Southern History* 76, no. 4 (November 2010): 817–866, https://www.jstor.org/stable/27919281.

16. Benjamin Franklin, *A Modest Enquiry into the Nature and Necessity of a Paper-Currency* (New Printing-Office, 1729).

17. George Athan Billias, "The Massachusetts Land Bankers of 1740," *University of Maine Bulletin* 61, no. 17 (April 1959): 13.

18. William V. Wells, *The Life and Public Services of Samuel Adams*, vol. 1 (Little, Brown and Company, 1865), 27.

19. Claire Priest, *Credit Nation*, 42.

20. Aaron M. Sakolski, *The Great American Land Bubble* (Harper Brothers, 1932), 4.

21. "From George Washington to John Parke Custis, 1 February 1778," *Founders Online*, National Archives, https://founders.archives.gov/documents/Washington/03-13-02-0355.

22. Charles A. Beard, *An Economic Interpretation of the Constitution of The United States* (Macmillan Company, 1913), 151.

23. George R., "The Royal Proclamation of 1763," *The London Gazette*, October 4, 1763.

24. "Mississippi Land Company Articles of Agreement, 3 June 1763," *Founders Online*, National Archives, https://founders.archives.gov/documents/Washington/02-07-02-0134.

25. "From George Washington to William Crawford, 17 September 1767," *Founders Online*, National Archives, https://founders.archives.gov/documents/Washington/02-08-02-0020.

26. Benjamin Franklin, "Observations Concerning the Increase of Mankind, 1751," *Founders Online*, National Archives, https://founders.archives.gov/documents/Franklin /01-04-02-0080.
27. "Signers of the Declaration of Independence," National Archives, https://www.archives .gov/founding-docs/signers-factsheet.
28. Benjamin Franklin, "Scheme for Supplying the Colonies with a Paper Currency, [11–12 February 1765]," *Papers of Benjamin Franklin*, Packard Humanities Institute, https://franklinpapers.org/framedVolumes.jsp?tocvol=12.
29. Aaron Graham, *Bills of Union: Money, Empire and Ambitions in the Mid-Eighteenth Century British Atlantic* (Palgrave Macmillan, 2021), 31–33.
30. John Adams and Jonathan Sewall, *Novanglus and Massachusettensis* (Hews & Goss, 1819), 39.
31. Geoffrey M. Hodgson, "1688 and All That: Property Rights, the Glorious Revolution and the Rise of British Capitalism," *Journal of Institutional Economics* 13, no. 1 (2017): 79–107, https://doi.org/10.1017/S1744137416000266.
32. Kirsten Wandschneider, "Lending to Lemons: Landschafts-Credit in 18th Century Prussia," Working Paper 19159 (National Bureau of Economic Research, June 2013), https://www.nber.org/system/files/working_papers/w19159/w19159.pdf.

Chapter 3: Land Wars

1. Brian Short, *Land and Society in Edwardian Britain* (Cambridge University Press, 1997), 20.
2. Bernard Mallet, *British Budgets: 1887–88 to 1912–13* (Macmillan and Co, 1913), 396.
3. David Lloyd George, "Limehouse Speech," July 30, 1909, Parliamentary Archives.
4. "Letter from David Lloyd George to William George," August 26, 1909, William George Papers, National Library of Wales, item 2282.
5. "Population and Housing Unit Counts. Table 4. Population: 1790 to 1990," US Census Bureau, 1990.
6. Henry George Jr., *The Life of Henry George* (William Heinemann, 1900), 146–150.
7. Henry George, "What the Railroad Will Bring Us," *Overland Monthly* 1, no. 4 (October 1868).
8. Anna George de Mille, *Henry George, Citizen of the World* (University of North Carolina Press, 1950), 83.
9. Henry George, *Progress and Poverty* (Twenty-fifth anniversary edition, Doubleday, Page & Company, 1912), 272–279.
10. Fred Foldvary, "The Business Cycle," The School of Cooperative Individualism, https://www.cooperative-individualism.org/foldvary-fred_business-cycle-1991.htm.
11. John Stuart Mill, ed. Francis E. Mineka and Dwight N. Lindley, *The Later Letters of John Stuart Mill 1849-1873* (University of Toronto Press, 1972), 1653–1655.
12. George, *Progress and Poverty*, 386.

13. "Property in Land, the Duke of Argyll," *Works of Henry George* (University of Michigan Press, 1888), 8–42.

14. Alexis de Tocqueville, "Social Conditions of the Anglo-Americans," in *Democracy in America* (Saunders and Otley, 1835), https://www.gutenberg.org/files/815/815-h/815-h.htm.

15. George, "What the Railroad Will Bring Us."

16. Jeffrey G. Williamson and Peter Lindert, "Unequal Gains: American Growth and Inequality since 1700," *VoxEU*, June 16, 2016, https://cepr.org/voxeu/columns/unequal-gains-american-growth-and-inequality-1700.

17. George Jr., *The Life of Henry George*, 342.

18. "Lord Granville to Mr. Hoppin," September 27, 1882, Office of the Historian, https://history.state.gov/historicaldocuments/frus1882/d199.

19. "Progress and Poverty," *The Times*, September 14, 1882.

20. "Mr Henry George's 'Social Problems,'" *The Times*, January 23, 1884.

21. T. H. Bonaparte, "Henry George's Impact at Home and Abroad," *American Journal of Economics and Sociology* 46, no. 1 (1987): 109–24, 114, https://www.jstor.org/stable/3486714?origin=JSTOR-pdf.

22. Arthur Nichols Young, *The Single Tax Movement in the United States* (Princeton University Press, 1916), 136.

23. George, *Progress and Poverty*, 314.

24. Henry George, *Protection or Free Trade* (Robert Schalkenbach Foundation, 1935), 47.

25. Samuel J. Thomas, "Maligning Poverty's Prophet: Puck, Henry George and the New York Mayoral Campaign of 1886," *Journal of American Culture* 21, no. 4 (December 1998): 21–40, https://doi.org/10.1111/j.1542-734X.1998.00021.x.

26. "Should Catholics Support Henry George?," *Catholic Telegraph* 55, no. 44 (November 1886).

27. John Pullen, "Henry George in Australia: Where the Landowners Are 'More Destructive than the Rabbit or the Kangaroo,'" *American Journal of Economics and Sociology* 64, no. 2 (April 2005): 683–713, https://www.jstor.org/stable/3488107?origin=JSTOR-pdf.

28. Alfred Henry Lewis, "Henry George's Funeral Rites," *The Sun*, October 30, 1897.

29. "The Funeral of Henry George," *New York Times*, November 1, 1897.

30. Henry George Jr., introduction to *Progress & Poverty*, by Henry George, x.

31. J. H. M. Laslett, "Haymarket, Henry George, and the Labor Upsurge in Britain and America During the Late 1880s," *International Labor and Working-Class History* 29 (1986): 68–82, 76, https://doi.org/10.1017/S0147547900000557.

32. Stephen Davis, "Joseph Jay Pastoriza and the Single Tax in Houston, 1911–1917," *Houston Review* 8, no. 2 (1986).

33. Ernest B. Gaston, "True Cooperative Individualism: An Argument on the Plan of the Fairhope Industrial Association," *Liberty Bell*, April 28, 1894.

34. Matthew M. Harris, "Lessons from Attempted Utopia: Fairhope, AL and Arden, DE," Working Paper (Lincoln Institute of Land Policy, 2004), https://www.lincolninst.edu /app/uploads/legacy-files/pubfiles/998_harris_complete_web.pdf.
35. "Fourteenth Census of the United States: Alabama," US Census Bureau, 1920.
36. "IRS Form 990," Fairhope Single Tax Corporation, 2023.
37. Peter d'A. Jones, "Henry George and British Socialism," *American Journal of Economics and Sociology* 47, no. 4 (1988): 473–91, 486, https://www.jstor.org/stable/3486564 ?origin=JSTOR-pdf.
38. Jonathan Rose, "Rereading the English Common Reader: A Preface to a History of Audiences," *Journal of the History of Ideas* 53, no. 1 (1992): 47–70, 56, https://doi.org /10.2307/2709910.
39. Michael Silagi and Susan N. Faulkner, "Land Reform in Kiaochow," *American Journal of Economics and Sociology* 43, no. 2 (1984), 167–77, https://www.jstor.org/stable /3486727.

Chapter 4: Shaky Ground

1. Karl Marx, "Letter to Friedrich Adolph Sorge," Marxists Internet Archive, June 20, 1881, https://www.marxists.org/archive/marx/works/1881/letters/81_06_20.htm.
2. Anna George de Mille, *Henry George, Citizen of the World* (University of North Carolina Press, 1950), 127.
3. Friedrich Engels, "Letter to Friedrich Adolph Sorge," Marxists Internet Archive, June 29, 1888, https://www.marxists.org/archive/marx/works/1888/letters/88_06_29.htm.
4. Arthur P. Dudden and Theodore H. von Laue, "The RSDLP and Joseph Fels: A Study in Intercultural Contact," *American Historical Review* 61, no. 1 (1955): 21-47, https:// doi.org/10.2307/1845326.
5. V. I. Lenin, "Letter from Lenin to Theodore Rothstein," Marxists Internet Archive, January 29, 1908, https://www.marxists.org/archive/lenin/works/1920/jul/15.htm.
6. Jack Schwartzman, "Henry George and George Bernard Shaw," *American Journal of Economics and Sociology* 49, no. 1 (January 1990): 113–127, https://www.jstor.org/stable /3487528.
7. Tjio Kayloe, *The Unfinished Revolution: Sun Yat-sen and the Struggle for Modern China* (Marshall Cavendish, 2017), 287.
8. Sun Yat-sen, "Program I," in *The International Development of China* (Knickerbocker Press, 1922).
9. M. Rothery, "England Changing Hands: Land Sales in England 1918–21, the Country Landowners Association and the Decline of Landed Society: A European Perspective," paper presented at 11th European Social Science History Conference, 2016, https:// pure.northampton.ac.uk/en/publications/england-changing-hands-land-sales-in -england-1918-21-the-country-.
10. Noel Skelton, "Constructive Conservatism," *Spectator*, May 19, 1923.

11. Brian Lund, *Understanding Housing Policy* (Policy Press, 2011), 50.
12. Wendy Wilson and Cassie Barton, *Tackling the Under-Supply of Housing in England* (House of Commons Library, 2023), https://commonslibrary.parliament.uk/research -briefings/cbp-7671/.
13. Alan Holmans, *Historical Statistics of Housing in Britain* (Cambridge Centre for Housing & Planning Research, 2005), 133, https://www.cchpr.landecon.cam.ac.uk/Research /Start-Year/2005/Other-Publications/Historical-Statistics-of-Housing-in-Britain.
14. Sinclair Lewis, *Ann Vickers* (P. F. Collier, 1933).
15. George J. Stigler, "Alfred Marshall's Lectures on Progress and Poverty," *Journal of Law & Economics* 12, no. 1 (1969): 181–83, https://www.jstor.org/stable/724985.
16. Mark Blaug, *Economic Theory in Retrospect* (Cambridge University Press, 1997), 83.
17. Myron T. Herrick, "The Federal Farm Loan Act," *Atlantic*, February 1917.
18. "Historical Census of Housing Tables," United States Census Bureau, updated October 8, 2021, https://www.census.gov/data/tables/time-series/dec/coh-units.html.
19. "The Housing Problem," *American Architect* no. 2343, November 17, 1920.
20. "Joe Day Again Sells Real Estate," *Life*, September 6, 1937.
21. Aaron M. Sakolski, *The Great American Land Bubble* (Harper Brothers, 1932), 341.
22. Herbert Hoover, "Address to the White House Conference on Home Building and Home Ownership," December 2, 1931.
23. Òscar Jordà, Björn Richter, Moritz Schularick and Alan M. Taylor, "Bank Capital Redux: Solvency, Liquidity, and Crisis," *Review of Economic Studies* 88, no. 1 (January 2021): 260–286, https://doi.org/10.1093/restud/rdaa040.
24. G. M. Hodgson, "1688 and All That: Property Rights, the Glorious Revolution and the Rise of British Capitalism," *Journal of Institutional Economics* 13, no. 1 (March 2017): 79–107, https://doi.org/10.1017/S1744137416000266.
25. Stephen Merrett, *State Housing in Britain* (Taylor & Francis, 2021), 52.
26. Tom Nicholas and Anna D. Scherbina, "Real Estate Prices During the Roaring Twenties and the Great Depression," Research Paper No. 18-09 (UC Davis Graduate School of Management, 2011), 23, http://dx.doi.org/10.2139/ssrn.1470448.
27. Federal Home Loan Banks, "Office of Finance Announces Third Quarter 2024 Combined Operating Highlights for the Federal Home Loan Banks," press release, October 30, 2024, https://www.fhlb-of.com/ofweb_userWeb/resources/2024Q3FHLB CombinedOperatingHighlights.pdf.
28. Matthew Chambers, Carlos Garriga and Donald E. Schlagenhauf, "Did Housing Policies Cause the Postwar Boom in Homeownership?," Working Paper No. 18821 (National Bureau of Economic Research, February 2013), 8, https://www.nber.org/papers/w18821.
29. Dennis J. Ventry Jr., "The Accidental Deduction: A History and Critique of the Tax Subsidy for Mortgage Interest," *Law and Contemporary Problems* 73 (Winter 2010): 233–284, https://www.jstor.org/stable/20779054.
30. Christopher J. Tassava, "The American Economy During World War II," Economic History Association, https://eh.net/encyclopedia/the-american-economy-during-world -war-ii/.

Chapter 5: To the Tiller

1. *The Speed of Urbanization Around the World* (United Nations Department of Economic and Social Affairs, Population Division, December 2018), https://population.un.org/wup/assets/WUP2018-PopFacts_2018-1.pdf.

2. Hannah Ritchie, Veronika Samborska and Max Roser, "Urbanization," Our World in Data, February 2024, https://ourworldindata.org/urbanization.

3. Louis J. Wolinsky, ed., *Agrarian Reform as Unfinished Business: The Selected Papers of Wolf Ladejinsky* (Oxford University Press, 2017), 148.

4. Samuel Watling, "The Road from Serfdom," *Works in Progress*, February 16, 2024, https://worksinprogress.co/issue/the-road-from-serfdom/.

5. Albin Krebs, "Rexford Tugwell, Roosevelt Aide, Dies," *New York Times*, July 24, 1979.

6. Wolinsky, *Agrarian Reform as Unfinished Business*, 4.

7. Wolinsky, *Agrarian Reform as Unfinished Business*, 289.

8. Wolinsky, *Agrarian Reform as Unfinished Business*, 131.

9. Michael Lipton, *Land Reform in Developing Countries* (Taylor & Francis, 2009), 190.

10. "Tokyo-Yokohama Metropolitan Area Population from 1920," Demographia, https://demographia.com/db-tok1920.htm.

11. Wolinsky, *Agrarian Reform as Unfinished Business*, 40–41.

12. Wolf Ladejinsky, "Agrarian Unrest in Japan," *Foreign Affairs* 17, no. 2 (January 1939): 426–433, 426, https://www.foreignaffairs.com/japan/agrarian-unrest-japan.

13. Ronald Dore, *Land Reform in Japan* (Bloomsbury Publishing, 2013), 131.

14. Wolinsky, *Agrarian Reform as Unfinished Business*, 149–150.

15. Dore, *Land Reform in Japan*, 132.

16. William Gilmartin and Wolf Ladejinsky, "The Promise of Agrarian Reform in Japan," *Foreign Affairs* 26, no. 1 (January 1948): 313–324, https://www.foreignaffairs.com/articles/japan/1948-01-01/promise-agrarian-reform-japan.

17. Joe Studwell, *How Asia Works: Success and Failure in the World's Most Dynamic Region* (Grove Press, 2013), 197.

18. Andrew J. Grad, "Land Reform in Japan," *Pacific Affairs* 21, no. 2 (1948): 115–135, https://doi.org/10.2307/2752510.

19. Tsutomu Takigawa, "Historical Background of Agricultural Land Reform in Japan," *Developing Economies* 10, no. 3 (1972): 290–310, 291, https://doi.org/10.1111/j.1746-1049.1972.tb00283.x.

20. Wolf Ladejinsky, "Agrarian Revolution in Japan," *Foreign Affairs* 38, no. 1 (October 1959), https://www.foreignaffairs.com/articles/japan/1959-10-01/agrarian-revolution-japan.

21. J. Yoshida, "The Japanese Housing Market," *Oxford Research Encyclopedia of Economics and Finance*, January 22, 2025, https://doi.org/10.1093/acrefore/9780190625979.013.920.

22. Jea Hwan Hong and Duol Kim, "Tenancy, Land Redistribution, and Economic Growth: A Case of Korea, 1920–1960" (working paper, KDI School of Public Policy and Management, 2020), 11, https://archives.kdischool.ac.kr/handle/11125/41658.

23. Jonathan Fenby, *Generalissimo Chiang Kai-shek and the China He Lost* (Free Press, 2003), 462.

24. Studwell, *How Asia Works*, 37.

25. Wolinsky, *Agrarian Reform as Unfinished Business*, 104.

26. Bingyuang Hsiung, "On Resolving the Problems Entailed by the Rent Reduction Act of Taiwan's Land Reform," *Developing Economies* 30, no. 2 (September 1992), 200, https://doi.org/10.1111/j.1746-1049.1992.tb00013.x.

27. Oliver Kim and Jen-Kuan Wang, "Land Reform in Taiwan, 1950–1961: Effects on Agriculture and Structural Change" (working paper, Pennsylvania State University, 2024), http://dx.doi.org/10.2139/ssrn.4951831.

28. John Stuart Mill, *Writings on India*, vol. 30 of *Collected Works of John Stuart Mill*, ed. Martin I. Moir and John M. Robson (University of Toronto Press, 1990).

29. Harsh Deo Malaviya, "Land Reforms in India," Economic & Political Research Department, All India Congress Committee, January 1954, 46, https://ia601407.us.archive.org/7/items/in.ernet.dli.2015.63626/2015.63626.Land-Reforms-In-India_text.pdf.

30. Ajit K. Dasgupta, *Gandhi's Economic Thought* (Taylor & Francis, 1996), 127.

31. Jawaharlal Nehru, *Glimpses of World History* (John Day Company, 1942), 424.

32. Wolinsky, *Agrarian Reform as Unfinished Business*, 377.

33. Pranab Bardhan, Michael Luca, Dilip Mookherjee and Francisco Pino, "Evolution of Land Distribution in West Bengal 1967–2004: Role of Land Reform and Demographic Changes," *Journal of Development Economics* 110 (September 2013), 171–190.

34. "The Administration: Odd Man Out," *Time*, January 3, 1955.

35. James Putzel, *A Captive Land: The Politics of Agrarian Reform in the Philippines* (Ateneo de Manila University Press, 1992), 98.

36. Wolinsky, *Agrarian Reform as Unfinished Business*, 217–220.

37. Wolinsky, *Agrarian Reform as Unfinished Business*, 237.

38. David A. Conrad, "Before It Is Too Late: Land Reform in South Vietnam, 1956–1968," *Journal of American-East Asian Relations* 21, no. 1 (2014): 34–57, 43, https://doi.org/10.1163/18765610-02101002.

39. Chester L. Cooper et al., *The American Experience with Pacification in Vietnam: Elements of Pacification* (Institute for Defense Analyses, 1972), 257.

40. "World: Land For South Viet Nam's Peasants," *Time*, July 11, 1969.

41. Wolinsky, *Agrarian Reform as Unfinished Business*, 297.

42. Wolinsky, *Agrarian Reform as Unfinished Business*, 513.

43. Hung-chao Tai, *Land Reform and Politics* (University of California Press, 2023), 307–308.

44. Ethan B. Kapstein, "Iran: Did Land Reform Backfire?" in *Seeds of Stability: Land Reform and US Foreign Policy* (Cambridge University Press, 2017), 209–211.

45. John Foran, *A Century of Revolution: Social Movements in Iran* (University of Minnesota Press, 1994), 167–169.
46. Caroline Schneider, "Celebrating 100 Years of Dr. Norman Borlaug," *CSA News* 59, no. 3 (March 2014): 4–11, https://doi.org/10.2134/csa2014-59-3-1.
47. Hannah Ritchie, "Yields vs. Land Use: How the Green Revolution Enabled Us to Feed a Growing Population," Our World in Data, August 22, 2017, https://ourworldindata.org/yields-vs-land-use-how-has-the-world-produced-enough-food-for-a-growing-population.
48. Lawrence Busch, *The Eclipse of Morality: Science, State, and Market* (Aldine de Gruyter, 2000), 58.
49. Nick Cullather, *The Hungry World: America's Cold War Battle Against Poverty in Asia* (Harvard University Press, 2011), 201.
50. Wolinsky, *Agrarian Reform as Unfinished Business*, 431.
51. John D. Montgomery, John P. Powelson and G. Edward Schuh, "The Land Tenure Center and U.S. AID Policy," US AID, December 28, 1982.

Chapter 6: Collateral and Damage

1. Ray Kroc, *Grinding It Out* (St. Martin's Paperbacks, 1987), 60–61.
2. "Nonfinancial Noncorporate Business, Z.1 Financial Accounts of the United States," Federal Reserve, https://www.federalreserve.gov/releases/z1.
3. Kroc, *Grinding It Out*, 60–61.
4. John F. Love, *McDonald's: Behind the Arches* (Bantam Books, 1995), 152–162.
5. *Annual Report* (McDonald's Corporation, 2023).
6. Suzanne Kapner, "Macy's Billion-Dollar Question: What's More Valuable, Real Estate or the Business?," *Wall Street Journal*, December 12, 2023, https://www.wsj.com/business/retail/macys-billion-dollar-question-whats-more-valuable-real-estate-or-the-business-e6477c8e.
7. Anthony Burns, *Thailand's 20 Year Program to Title Rural Land* (World Development Report, 2004), http://hdl.handle.net/10986/9213.
8. *Peru: Policies to Stop Hyperinflation and Initiate Economic Recovery* (World Bank Country Study, 1989), 224, http://documents.worldbank.org/curated/en/398651468776408898.
9. Michael Albertus, Mauricio Espinoza and Ricardo Fort, "Land Reform and Human Capital Development: Evidence from Peru," *Journal of Development Economics* 147 (November 2020), https://doi.org/10.1016/j.jdeveco.2020.102540.
10. Jeremy Clift, "Hearing the Dogs Bark," *Finance & Development* 40, no. 4 (December 2003), https://doi.org/10.5089/9781451952018.022.
11. Corinne Deléchat and Leandro Medina, "What Is the Informal Economy?," *Finance & Development*, December 2020, https://www.imf.org/en/Publications/fandd/issues/2020/12/what-is-the-informal-economy-basics.

12. Hernando de Soto, *The Mystery of Capital* (Basic Books, 2000), 36.
13. Rik Frehen, William Goetzmann and K. Rouwenhorst, "Dutch Securities for American Land Speculation in the Late Eighteenth Century," in *Housing and Mortgage Markets in Historical Perspective*, ed. Eugene N. White, Kenneth Snowden and Price Fishback (University of Chicago Press, 2014), 287–304.
14. Michael A. Blaakman, *Speculation Nation: Land Mania in the Revolutionary American Republic* (University of Pennsylvania Press, 2023), 275.
15. "To George Washington from Robert Morris, 7 December 1795," *Founders Online*, National Archives, https://founders.archives.gov/documents/Washington/05-19-02-0172.
16. Nicholas Curott and Tyler Watts, "What Caused the Recession of 1797?," *Studies in Applied Economics* 48 (February 2016), https://sites.krieger.jhu.edu/iae/files/2017/04/Curott_Watts_Recession_of_1797.pdf.
17. Joseph H. Davis, "An Annual Index of U.S. Industrial Production, 1790-1915," *Quarterly Journal of Economics*, 119, no. 4 (November 2004): 1177–1215, https://www.jstor.org/stable/25098716.
18. "Wheat Price Historical Data," US Department of Agriculture, National Agricultural Statistics Service, Washington Field Office, https://www.nass.usda.gov/.
19. Raghuram Rajan and Rodney Ramcharan, "The Anatomy of a Credit Crisis: The Boom and Bust in Farm Land Prices in the United States in the 1920s," *American Economic Review* 105, no. 4 (April 2015): 1439–77, https://www.jstor.org/stable/43495424.
20. Òscar Jordà, Moritz Schularick and Alan M. Taylor, "The Great Mortgaging: Housing Finance, Crises and Business Cycles," *Economic Policy* 31, no. 85 (January 2016): 107–152, https://doi.org/10.1093/epolic/eiv017.
21. Katharina Knoll, Moritz Schularick and Thomas Steger, "No Price Like Home: Global House Prices, 1870–2012," *American Economic Review* 107, no. 2 (February 2017): 331–53, https://www.jstor.org/stable/24911335.
22. Thomas Chaney, David Sraer and David Thesmar, "The Collateral Channel: How Real Estate Shocks Affect Corporate Investment," *American Economic Review* 102, no. 6 (October 2012): 2381–2409, https://www.jstor.org/stable/41724659.
23. Saleem Bahaj, Angus Foulis, Gabor Pinter and Paolo Surico, "Employment and the Collateral Channel of Monetary Policy," Working Paper 827 (Bank of England, 2019), http://dx.doi.org/10.2139/ssrn.3459019.
24. "In Come the Waves," *Economist*, June 16, 2005, https://www.economist.com/special-report/2005/06/16/in-come-the-waves.
25. William Quinn and John D. Turner, "Bubbles in History," Working Paper 2020-07 (Queen's University Centre for Economic History, September 2020).
26. Simon Ray, Denis Fougère and Rémy Lecat, "Real Estate Boom and French Corporate Investment," Banque de France, August 29, 2017, https://www.banque-france.fr/en/publications-and-statistics/publications/real-estate-boom-and-french-corporate-investment.

27. Sebastian Doerr, "Housing Booms, Reallocation and Productivity," Working Paper 904 (Bank for International Settlements, 2020), https://www.bis.org/publ/work904 .pdf.

28. Indraneel Chakraborty, Itay Goldstein and Andrew MacKinlay, "Housing Price Booms and Crowding-Out Effects in Bank Lending," *Review of Financial Studies* 31, no. 7 (March 2018): 2806–2853, https://doi.org/10.1093/rfs/hhy033.

Chapter 7: The Land Standard

1. "Daily Summary of Japanese Press," United States Embassy (Japan), February 1989, 15–16.

2. Lyall Lukey, "Letters," *Press*, August 28, 1989, 16.

3. "Parliamentary Debates (Hansard)," first session, 42nd parliament of New Zealand, volume 500, 1987–1989, 11955.

4. "Australia Turns Profit in Japan—200,000%," *Los Angeles Times*, March 11, 1988, https://www.latimes.com/archives/la-xpm-1988-03-11-mn-1421-story.html.

5. "Japan—Commercial Land Price Index, 6 Large City Areas, per Square Meter," Bank for International Settlements, https://data.bis.org/topics/CPP/BIS,WS_CPP,1.0/Q.JP.4.M .1.4.1.0.

6. Christopher Wood, *The Bubble Economy* (Sidwick & Jackson, 1992), 50.

7. Shigeki Morinobu, "The Rise and Fall of the Land Myth in Japan—Some Implications to the Chinese Land Taxation" (Policy Research Institute, March 2006), 5, https://eaber .org/wp-content/uploads/2011/05/PRI_Morinobu_06.pdf.

8. "Total Value of Exports and Imports (1950–)," Trade Statistics of Japan, Ministry of Finance, https://www.customs.go.jp/toukei/suii/html/nenbet_e.htm.

9. Nicholas D. Kristof, "International Report; World's Stock Exchanges Experience a Difficult Year," *New York Times*, December 31, 1984, https://www.nytimes.com/1984 /12/31/business/international-report-world-s-stock-exchanges-experience-a -difficult-year.html?pagewanted=3&pagewanted=print.

10. Akiyoshi Horiuchi, "An Evaluation of Japanese Financial Liberalization: A Case Study of Corporate Bond Markets," in *Financial Deregulation and Integration in East Asia*, ed. Takatoshi Ito and Anne O. Krueger (University of Chicago Press, 1996), 167–192, 176.

11. "Popcorn, Claret on the Ginza: Nakasone's Import Campaign Hits Hectic Tokyo Intersection," *Los Angeles Times*, April 14, 1985, https://www.latimes.com/archives /la-xpm-1985-04-14-mn-8156-story.html.

12. Theodore H. White, "The Danger from Japan," *New York Times*, July 28, 1985, https:// www.nytimes.com/1985/07/28/magazine/the-danger-from-japan.html.

13. "There's Nothing Wrong with America's Foreign Defense Policy that a Little Backbone Can't Cure," advertisement, *New York Times, Boston Globe, Washington Post*, September 2, 1987.

14. Mariko Fujii and Masahiro Kawai, "Lessons from Japan's Banking Crisis, 1991–2005," Working Paper 222 (Asian Development Bank Institute, 2010), 3, https://papers.ssrn.com/sol3/papers.cfm?abstract_id=1638784.
15. Morinobu, "The Rise and Fall of the Land Myth in Japan," 6.
16. Yukio Noguchi, "Land Problem in Japan," *Hitotsubashi Journal of Economics* 31, no. 2 (December 1990): 73–86, 80, https://www.jstor.org/stable/43295909.
17. Roger Farrell, "Japanese Foreign Direct Investment in Real Estate 1985–1994," Pacific Economic Papers 272, (Australia–Japan Research Centre, 1997), 3.
18. James Sterngold, "Many Japanese Wary on Mitsubishi U.S. Deal," *New York Times*, November 1, 1989.
19. Yukio Noguchi, "Land Prices and House Prices in Japan," in *Housing Markets in the U.S. and Japan*, ed. Yukio Noguchi and James M. Poterba (University of Chicago Press, 1994), 11–28, 21.
20. Noguchi, "Land Problem in Japan," 75.
21. Peter Hill, "Heisei Yakuza: Burst Bubble and 'Bōtaihō,'" *Social Science Japan Journal* 6, no. 1 (April 2003): 1–18, 3, https://www.jstor.org/stable/30209410.
22. David E. Kaplan and Alec Dubro, *Yakuza Japan's Criminal Underworld* (University of California Press, 2012), 181.
23. Morinobu, "The Rise and Fall of the Land Myth in Japan," 6.
24. James Sterngold, "Japan Poised for Postwar Boom," *New York Times*, January 28, 1991, https://www.nytimes.com/1991/01/28/business/japan-poised-for-postwar-boom.html.
25. Clay Chandler, "Yen Master: Japan's Central Banker Begins to Win Praise for Saving Its 'Soul,'" *Wall Street Journal*, April 18, 2012, https://www.wsj.com/articles/SB10001424052702303425504577351441424944650.
26. Steven Brull, "Japan, Like U.S., Finds Rate Cuts Alone Won't Cure the Economy," *International Herald Tribune*, July 28, 1992.
27. Edward J. Lincoln, "Japan's Financial Problems," *Brookings Papers on Economic Activity*, no. 2 (1998): 357, https://www.brookings.edu/articles/japans-financial-problems/.
28. Hideaki Miyajima and Yishay Yafeh, "Japan's Banking Crisis: Who Has the Most to Lose?," Discussion Paper Series 03-E-010 (Research Institute of Economy, 2003), 28.
29. "Foreign Direct Investment: Inward and Outward Flows and Stock," UN Trade & Development, 2024, https://unctadstat.unctad.org/datacentre/reportInfo/US.FdiFlowsStock.
30. Richard Katz, "Restoring Japan's Leadership in Innovation, Part II," *Japan Economy Watch* (blog), March 20, 2023, https://richardkatz.substack.com/p/restoring-japans-leadership-in-innovation-466.

Chapter 8: Learning the Hard Way

1. Mao Tse-tung, "Report on an Investigation of the Peasant Movement in Hunan," in *Selected Works of Mao Tse-tung* (Foreign Languages Press, 1967), https://blogs.law.columbia.edu/uprising1313/files/2017/09/Mao-Readings-Uprising-2-13.pdf.

2. Frank Dikötter, *The Tragedy of Liberation* (Bloomsbury Press, 2013), 83–87.
3. Zhao Ziyang, *Prisoner of the State* (Simon & Schuster, 2010), 108–109.
4. "1842 Map of Initial Land Sales in the Colony," Gwulo, January 16, 2017, https://gwulo.com/media/27278.
5. Frank Welsh, *A History of Hong Kong* (HarperCollins, 1993), 108.
6. Welsh, *A History of Hong Kong*, 141.
7. *Report from the Select Committee on Commercial Relations with China* (Parliament Select Committee on Commercial Relations With China, 1847).
8. Hong Kong Land Commission, *Report from the Hongkong Land Commission of 1886-1887* (Noronha & Co, 1887).
9. "Hong Kong Population History," Demographia, https://www.demographia.com/db-hkhist.htm.
10. Michael Littlewood, *Taxation Without Representation: The History of Hong Kong's Troublingly Successful Tax System* (Hong Kong University Press, 2010), 127.
11. Donald Tsang, "Big Market, Small Government," Chief Executive, The Government of the Hong Kong Special Administrative Region, updated September 18, 2006, https://www.ceo.gov.hk/archive/2012/eng/press/oped.htm.
12. *Free to Choose*, episode 1, "The Power of the Market" (*PBS*, 1980).
13. "Hong Kong," UK Parliament, Hansard, volume 675, April 11, 1963, https://hansard.parliament.uk/Commons/1963-04-11/debates/07e6664e-df6a-4cd9-8a47-f858db4d97d6/HongKong.
14. *Hong Kong Statistics, 1947-1967* (Census & Statistics Department of Hong Kong, 1969), 160–161.
15. Y.C. Jao, *Banking and Currency in Hong Kong* (Palgrave Macmillan, 1974), 263.
16. Roger Nissim, *Land Administration and Practice in Hong Kong* (Hong Kong University Press, 2012), 121–123.
17. Nissim, *Land Administration and Practice in Hong Kong*, 121-123.
18. *Semi-Annual Report* (Sun Hung Kai Properties, 2024); *Semi-Annual Report* (Henderson Land, 2024).
19. David Webb, "Hong Kong Land Lease Reform," Webb-site.com, October–November 2010, https://webb-site.com/articles/leases1.asp.
20. *II IPCCIOS Conference, 1965* (International Council for Scientific Management, 1965).
21. Hong Kong Monetary Authority, "Money and Credit," *Monthly Statistical Bulletin*, https://www.hkma.gov.hk/eng/data-publications-and-research/data-and-statistics/monthly-statistical-bulletin/.
22. Christopher Patten, *East and West* (Crown, 1998), 51.
23. "Real Residential Property Prices for Hong Kong SAR," Bank for International Settlements, https://fred.stlouisfed.org/series/QHKR628BIS.
24. "Property Market Statistics," Rating and Valuation Department, Government of Hong Kong, https://www.rvd.gov.hk/en/publications/property_market_statistics.html.

25. "Land Sale Records," Lands Department, Government of Hong Kong, https://www
.landsd.gov.hk/en/resources/land-info-stat/land-sale/land-sale-records.html.

26. *Global Living 2019* (CBRE, 2019).

27. Thomas Piketty and Li Yang, "Income and Wealth Inequality in Hong Kong, 1981-2020:
The Rise of Pluto-Communism?," Working Paper (World Inequality Lab, June 2021),
https://wid.world/document/income-and-wealth-inequality-in-hong-kong-1981-2020
-the-rise-of-pluto-communism-world-inequality-lab-working-paper-2021-18/.

28. Alice Poon, *Land and the Ruling Class in Hong Kong* (Enrich Professional Publishing,
2005).

29. "Shenzhen's Free-Market Trials Awake Interest in Development," *Australian Financial Review*, August 26, 1988, https://www.afr.com/property/shenzhens-free-market
-trials-awake-interest-in-development-19880826-k2z3w.

Chapter 9: The Biggest Bubble in History

1. Jonathan Chatwin, *The Southern Tour* (Bloomsbury Academic, 2024).

2. "Shenzhen Residential IH/2024," Savills, June 25, 2024, https://www.savills.us/research
_articles/256536/216743-1.

3. Jun Ma and John Norregaard, "China's Fiscal Decentralisation," International Monetary Fund, October 1998, www.imf.org/external/pubs/ft/seminar/2000/idn/china.pdf.

4. S. Lin, "China's Fiscal Policy and Fiscal Sustainability," in *Assessment on the Impact of
Stimulus, Fiscal Transparency and Fiscal Risk*, ed. Takatoshi Ito and Friska Parulian
(Economic Research Institute for ASEAN and East Asia, 2011), 77–116, https://www
.eria.org/uploads/media/Research-Project-Report/RPR-2010-1.pdf.

5. Cui Jun, Yang Qi and Ding Li, "Land Finance of Chinese Local Governments: Forma-
tion and Distortionary Effects on Urbanization," *China Finance and Economic Review* 3, no. 3 (2014): 38–55, https://www.degruyterbrill.com/document/doi/10.1515/cfer
-2014-030304/html.

6. *ILO Review of the Multi-tier Pension System in China* (International Labour Organization, December 2022), https://www.ilo.org/media/7506/download.

7. "Financial Accounts," China Vanke, S&P Capital IQ, accessed January 11, 2025.

8. "Total Liabilities of Enterprises for Real Estate Development," National Bureau of
Statistics of China, accessed April 15, 2025, http://data.stats.gov.cn/english/easy
query.htm?cn=A01.

9. Nicholas Borst, "How Strong is China's Household Balance Sheet?," Seafarer Funds,
March 2022, https://www.seafarerfunds.com/prevailing-winds/chinas-household
-balance-sheet/.

10. Jeff Dawson, "Why Are China's Households in the Doldrums?," *Liberty Street Economics*, September 27, 2023, https://libertystreeteconomics.newyorkfed.org/2023/09
/why-are-chinas-households-in-the-doldrums/.

11. "Evergrande Real Estate Group," Citron Research, June 21, 2012, https://cdn.gmtresearch

.com/public-ckfinder/Short-sellers/Citron%20Research/Evergrande%20Citron %20presentation.pdf.

12. Jamie Powell, "Chinese Real Estate, Charted," *Financial Times*, July 19, 2018, https:// www.ft.com/content/0c425314-9850-315e-9c2f-b5c0de4b3e96.

13. "Top Leadership Vows Steps Against Property Bubbles," *China Daily*, December 22, 2016, https://www.chinadaily.com.cn/bizchina/2016-12/22/content_27742959.htm.

14. Jacky Chan and Karen Huang, "At the Forefront of China Property," AMTD, September 29, 2020, https://www.amtdinc.com/wp-content/uploads/Our-Business/Research /Research-Portfolio/20200929_chinaproperty.pdf.

15. Stella Yifan Xie and Mike Bird, "The $52 Trillion Bubble: China Grapples with Epic Property Boom," *Wall Street Journal*, July 26, 2020, https://www.wsj.com/articles/china -property-real-estate-boom-covid-pandemic-bubble-11594908517.

16. Jing Liu, "Series: China's Real Estate Problem 1. The 'Three Red Lines,'" Cheung Kong Graduate School of Business, July 5, 2022, https://english.ckgsb.edu.cn/knowledge /professor_analysis/series-chinas-real-estate-problem-1-the-three-red-lines/.

17. Harald Hau and Difei Ouyang, "Local Capital Scarcity and Small Firm Growth: Evidence from Real Estate Booms in China," Working Paper No. 7928 (CESifo, 2019), https://www.cesifo.org/en/publications/2019/working-paper/local-capital-scarcity -and-small-firm-growth-evidence-real-estate.

18. Yu Shi, "Sectoral Booms and Misallocation of Managerial Talent: Evidence from the Chinese Real Estate Boom," Working Paper No. 2018/221 (International Monetary Fund, September 28, 2018), https://www.imf.org/en/Publications/WP/Issues/2018 /09/28/Sectoral-Booms-and-Misallocation-of-Managerial-Talent-Evidence-from -the-Chinese-Real-Estate-46277.

Chapter 10: Singapore Fever

1. Chok Tong Goh, "Speech at the Singapore-Guangdong Development Forum," March 24, 2009, https://www.pmo.gov.sg/Newsroom/speech-mr-goh-chok-tong-senior-minister -singapore-guangdong-development-forum-24-march.

2. "Resident Households By Tenancy," Department of Statistics Singapore, 2024, https:// www.singstat.gov.sg/find-data/search-by-theme/households/households/latest-data.

3. Wendell Cox, *International Housing Affordability* (Centre for Demographics and Policy, 2024), https://www.demographia.com/dhi.pdf.

4. Sophia Raffles, *Memoir of the Life and Public Services of Sir Thomas Stamford Raffles* (John Murray, 1830), 380.

5. Lincoln F. Pratson, "Assessing Impacts to Maritime Shipping from Marine Chokepoint Closures," *Communications in Transportation Research* 3 (December 2023), https://doi.org/10.1016/j.commtr.2022.100083.

6. "Head Count: The History of Census-Taking in Singapore," National Library Singapore, January 21, 2020, https://biblioasia.nlb.gov.sg/vol-15/issue-4/jan-mar-2020/head -count-history/.

7. Thomas Stamford Raffles, *The History of Java*, vol. I (John Murray, 1830), 338–342.

8. Raffles, *Memoir of the Life of Sir Thomas Stamford Raffles*, 65.

9. John Bastin, "The Working of the Early Land Rent System in West Java," *Bijdragen Tot de Taal-, Land- En Volkenkunde* 116, no. 3 (1960): 301–12, 312, https://doi.org/10.1163/22134379-90002208.

10. Raffles, *Memoir of the Life of Sir Thomas Stamford Raffles*, 534.

11. Lee Kuan Yew, "Second Reading of the Land Acquisition Act," Singapore Government Press Statement, June 10, 1964.

12. Sock-Yong Phang and Matthias Helbe, "Housing Policies in Singapore," Working Paper Series, no. 559 (ADBI, March 2016), 6, https://www.adb.org/sites/default/files/publication/181599/adbi-wp559.pdf.

13. Anne Haila, *Urban Land Rent: Singapore as a Property State* (Wiley, 2015), 77–78.

14. Lee Kuan Yew, *The Singapore Story*, vol. 1 (Marshall Cavendish, 1998), 104–5.

15. Goh Keng Swee, *The Economics of Modernization and Other Essays* (Asia Pacific Press, 1972), 115.

16. "Own a Flat—for $900 Down," *Straits Times*, February 12, 1964.

17. Sock-Yong Phang and Kyunghwan Kim, "Singapore's Housing Policies: 1960–2013," *Frontiers in Development Policy: Innovative Development Case Studies* (2013): 123–153, 131, https://ink.library.smu.edu.sg/cgi/viewcontent.cgi?article=2543&context=soe_research.

18. Sock-Yong Phang, *Policy Innovations for Affordable Housing in Singapore: From Colony to Global City* (Palgrave Macmillan, 2018), 144–145.

19. "Household Sector Balance Sheet Third Quarter 2024," Department of Statistics Singapore, 2024, https://www.singstat.gov.sg/find-data/search-by-theme/economy/household-sector-balance/latest-data.

20. *Asia Pacific Home Attainability Index* (Urban Land Institute, 2024), https://knowledge.uli.org/-/media/files/research-reports/2024/2024-uli-asia-pacific-home-attainability-index-report.pdf.

21. Si Jia Teo, "Choa Kim Keat's Villa Sold for S$103.8m," *Business Times*, June 8, 2011.

22. Xuyao Zhang, "Innovative Cities: Comparison between Singapore and Hong Kong," Asia Competitiveness Institute, October 6, 2023, https://aciperspectives.com/2023/10/06/chart-of-the-week-october-6-2023-innovative-cities-comparison-between-singapore-and-hong-kong/.

23. Litianqi Fan and Xuyao Zhang, "A Comparative Analysis of Innovation Policies and Performances between Singapore and Hong Kong," Research Paper #04-2023 (Asia Competitiveness Institute, May 2023), http://dx.doi.org/10.2139/ssrn.4461713.

24. "Commercial Banks, Loans and Advances to Residents by Industry," Monetary Authority of Singapore, https://www.mas.gov.sg/statistics/monthly-statistical-bulletin/i-5a-commercial-banks-loans-and-advances-to-residents-by-industry.

25. Hong Kong Monetary Authority, *Monthly Statistical Bulletin*, https://www.hkma.gov.hk/eng/data-publications-and-research/data-and-statistics/monthly-statistical-bulletin/.

26. Hong Liu and Ting-Yan Wang, "China and the 'Singapore Model': Perspectives from Mid-level Cadres and Implications for Transnational Knowledge Transfer," *China Quarterly* 236 (May 2018): 1012–1013, https://www.cambridge.org/core/journals/china-quarterly/article/china-and-the-singapore-model-perspectives-from-midlevel-cadres-and-implications-for-transnational-knowledge-transfer/932FD456103899E6DFCB961F53C88BA8.

Chapter 11: Falling Stars and Superstars

1. Leo Donovan, "Car Output Is Record," *Detroit Free Press*, January 17, 1956.
2. "The Power of Relationships Fuels Historic Ford Motor Company IPO," Goldman Sachs, https://www.goldmansachs.com/our-firm/history/moments/1956-ford-ipo.
3. Peter Collier and David Horowitz, *The Fords: An American Epic* (Encounter Books, 1987), 119.
4. "Housing Characteristics of the Detroit, Michigan Standard Metropolitan Area," 1950 Census of Housing, Bureau of the Census, April 1, 1950; "Wage Chronology, Ford Motor Company June 1941–September 1973," Bureau of Labor Statistics, 1973.
5. "Historic Census of Housing Tables," United States Census Bureau 2000, https://www.census.gov/data/tables/time-series/dec/coh-values.html.
6. "Housing Characteristics of Standard Metropolitan Areas (San Francisco, Chicago, New York City)," 1950 Census of Housing, Bureau of the Census, April 1, 1950.
7. "Automotive Trade Statistics 1965–1980," United States International Trade Commission, December 1981, 2.
8. "Zillow Home Values Index," Zillow, 2024, https://www.zillow.com/home-values/102001/united-states/.
9. "1964: Arthur C Clarke Predicts the Future," BBC, October 25, 2024, https://www.bbc.com/videos/crezjvd55gro.
10. "1964," BBC.
11. Bo Lojek, *History of Semiconductor Engineering* (Springer Berlin Heidelberg, 2007), 68–70.
12. Laura Sydell, "A Rare Mix Created Silicon Valley's Startup Culture," NPR, April 4, 2012, https://www.npr.org/2012/04/04/149870751/a-rare-mix-created-silicon-valleys-startup-culture.
13. Leslie R. Berlin, "Robert Noyce and Fairchild Semiconductor, 1957–1968," *Business History Review* 75, no. 1 (2001): 64, https://doi.org/10.2307/3116557.
14. Joseph Gyourko, Christopher Mayer and Todd Sinai, "Superstar Cities," *American Economic Journal: Economic Policy* 5, no. 4 (November 2013): 167–99, https://www.jstor.org/stable/43189357.
15. Joseph Bishop-Henchman, "Detroit Free Press Explains Why Detroit Went Bankrupt," Tax Foundation, September 16, 2013, https://taxfoundation.org/blog/detroit-free-press-explains-why-detroit-went-bankrupt/.

16. Arun Gupta, Horacio Sapriza and Vladimir Yankov, "The Collateral Channel and Bank Credit," Finance and Economics Discussion Series, Working Paper No. 2022-24 (Federal Reserve, May 2022), https://doi.org/10.17016/FEDS.2022.024.

17. "Summaries of Assessed Values by Property Class," California State Board of Equalization, 2024, https://www.boe.ca.gov/dataportal/dataset.htm?url=PropTaxAssessedValue Summary.

18. *50-State Property Tax Comparison Study For Taxes Paid in 2021* (Lincoln Institute of Land Policy and Minnesota Center for Fiscal Excellence, July 2022), https://www .lincolninst.edu/app/uploads/legacy-files/pubfiles/50-state-property-tax-comparison -for-2021-exec-summary.pdf.

19. *San Francisco Housing Policy and Practice Review* (California Department of Housing and Community Development, October 2023), https://www.hcd.ca.gov/sites/default /files/docs/policy-and-research/plan-report/sf-housing-policy-and-practice-review.pdf.

20. *San Francisco Housing Inventory* (San Francisco Planning Department, April 2024), 5–6, https://sfplanning.org/resource/housing-inventory-2024.

21. "Land Price and Land Share Indicators," American Enterprise Institute, https://www .aei.org/housing/land-price-indicators/.

22. Knut Are Aastveit, Bruno Albuquerque and André Kallak Anundsen, "Changing Supply Elasticities and Regional Housing Booms," Working Paper No. 844 (Bank of England, January 10, 2020), https://papers.ssrn.com/sol3/papers.cfm?abstract_id=3520650.

23. John Myers, Sam Bowman and Ben Southwood, "The Housing Theory of Everything," *Works in Progress*, September 14, 2021, https://worksinprogress.co/issue/the-housing -theory-of-everything/.

24. Lisa J. Dettling and Melissa Schettini Kearney, "Did the Modern Mortgage Set the Stage for the U.S. Baby Boom?," Working Paper No. 33446 (National Bureau of Economic Research, February 2025), https://www.nber.org/papers/w33446.

25. Lisa J. Dettling and Melissa S. Kearney, "House Prices and Birth Rates: The Impact of the Real Estate Market on the Decision to Have a Baby," *Journal of Public Economics* 110 (February 2014): 82–100, https://doi.org/10.1016/j.jpubeco.2013.09.009.

26. Matthew Rognlie, "Deciphering the Fall and Rise in the Net Capital Share," *Brookings Papers on Economic Activity* (Spring 2015), https://www.brookings.edu/articles /deciphering-the-fall-and-rise-in-the-net-capital-share/.

27. Gianni La Cava, "Housing Prices, Mortgage Interest Rates and the Rising Share of Capital Income in the United States," Working Paper No. 572 (Bank for International Settlements, July 2016), https://www.bis.org/publ/work572.pdf.

28. Fabian T. Pfeffer and Nora Waitkus, "The Wealth Inequality of Nations," *American Sociological Review* 86, no. 4 (2021): 567–602, https://doi.org/10.1177/000312242110 27800.

29. Bruno Albuquerque, Martin Iseringhausen and Frederic Opitz, "The Housing Supply Channel of Monetary Policy," Working Paper No. 2024/023 (International Monetary Fund, February 2024), https://www.imf.org/en/Publications/WP/Issues/2024/02/02 /The-Housing-Supply-Channel-of-Monetary-Policy-544046.

30. Andrew B. Hall, Jesse Yoder and Nishant Karandikar, "Economic Distress and Voting: Evidence from the Subprime Mortgage Crisis," *Political Science Research and Methods* 9, no. 2 (April 2021): 327–344, https://doi.org/10.1017/psrm.2021.3.

31. Michela Zonta, Sarah Edelman and Colin McArthur, "The Role of Midwestern Housing Instability in the 2016 Election," Center for American Progress, November 29, 2016, https://www.americanprogress.org/article/the-role-of-midwestern-housing -instability-in-the-2016-election/.

32. David Adler and Ben Ansell, "Housing and Populism," *West European Politics* 43, no. 2 (2019): 344–65, https://doi.org/10.1080/01402382.2019.1615322.

33. Ben Ansell, Frederik Hjorth, Jacob Nyrup and Martin Vinæs Larsen, "Sheltering Populists? House Prices and the Support for Populist Parties," *Journal of Politics* 84, no. 3 (July 2022), https://doi.org/10.1086/718354.

Epilogue

1. Jose Maria Barrero, Nicholas Bloom and Steven J. Davis, "Why Working from Home Will Stick," Working Paper 28731 (National Bureau of Economic Research, 2021), https://www.nber.org/system/files/working_papers/w28731/w28731.pdf.

2. "A New Working Order: Reimagining Offices in a Hybrid World," Moody's, September 10, 2024.

3. Arjun Ramani, Joel Alcedo and Nicholas Bloom, "How Working from Home Reshapes Cities," *Proceedings of the National Academy of Sciences* 121, no. 45 (May 2024), https://doi.org/10.1073/pnas.2408930121.

4. Michelle D'Arcy, Marina Nistotskaya and Ola Olsson, "Land Property Rights, Cadasters and Economic Growth: A Cross-Country Panel 1000-2015 CE," Working Paper Series 2021:3 (Quality of Government Institute, Department of Political Science, University of Gothenburg, March 2021), https://www.gu.se/sites/default/files/2021 -03/2021_3_DArcy_Nistotskaya_Olsson_0.pdf.

Index

real estate developers, 90, 163, 167, 194–96,
198, 200–201, 216–31, 252, 256. *See
also specific company names*
recessions, 15–16, 52
reclamation of land, 7–8, 255
Red Guards, 181–83, 192–93
Red Scare, 119
rents, 112–13, 132, 242, 289–90
repossession of land, 33–34
Representation of the People Act, 82
Republican Party (US), 65, 90
Republic of China, 71–72, 110, 112, 114
Research Triangle, North Carolina, 280
The Retsforbundet, 88
Revenue Act of 1913, 95
Rhee, Syngman, 109–10
Rhode Island, 34
Ricardo, David, 56, 247
Rock, Arthur, 266
Rockefeller Center, 165, 172
Rocky Mountains, 21
Rognlie, Matthew, 277
Roman Empire, 13
Romania, 101
Romanov Empire, 76, 101
Roosevelt, Franklin Delano, 94–95, 103
Roosevelt, Theodore, 65
Royal Irish Constabulary, 60
Royalists (American), 45
Royal Navy, 50
Royal Society, 31, 36
Russia, 39, 71, 76–77, 82, 101–2, 104, 138

Sainsbury's, 134
sales taxes, 201
Salt Lake City, Utah, 280
San Francisco, California, 52–54, 58, 63, 66,
68, 227, 262, 265–66, 269–71,
274–75, 280
San Jose, California, 275
Sanyo Securities, 172
Sapriza, Horacio, 271
scarcity of land, 7–8, 16
Schrameier, Wilhelm, 71, 80
Schularick, Moritz, 142–43
Scientific Revolution, 28
Sears, 134
Seattle, Washington, 269
Second Opium War, 188
Second World War

and demographic trends in Japan, 176
and growth of mortgage lending, 93, 96
and Hong Kong, 188–89
impact on China, 80
and land bubble in Japan, 154–55
and national identity in Singapore, 244
and origins of McDonald's, 129
postwar reconstruction in Japan, 104–10
segregation, 273
semiconductor industry, 266
serfdom, 6–7, 102. *See also* feudalism
Seven Years' War, 39–40
Shanghai, China, 186, 214, 218
Shaw, George Bernard, 78
Shenzhen, China, 204–5, 209, 210, 216, 218,
223, 225
Shenzhen Special Zone Daily, 209
Shenzhen Stock Exchange, 217
Sheung Wan district, 185
Shibuya, Tokyo, 153
Shidehara Kijūrō, 107
Shining Path, 137–38
Shi, Yu, 229
Shockley, William Bradford, 265–66
Shockley Semiconductor, 266, 268
Shuwa Investments Corporation, 172
Sichuan Province, China, 183, 234
Silicon Valley, 267
silver, 26, 29–30
Sinai, Todd, 269, 272
Singapore, 7, 202, 233–38, 238–44, 244–53,
253–58, 286–87
Single Tax movement, 56, 62, 66, 68–71, 75,
77–78, 81, 86–88, 94, 126, 283, 291
Skelton, Noel, 83–86, 89, 250
slavery, 26, 35–36
Smith, Adam, 55, 56, 241, 247
Smith, John, 22, 25, 285
Social Democratic Labour Party, 77
socialism, 11, 17, 63, 74–75, 78, 87, 209
Social Problems (George), 61
social reform movements, 77
Sonneborn, Harry, 131
South Carolina, 34
Southeast Asia, 121–22, 172. *See also specific
countries*
Southern Europe, 16
South Korea, 110, 113, 157, 172, 227, 235
South Sea Bubble, 37
South Vietnam, 119–21